P9-CRR-258

Life and Light

A Guide to the Theology of Karl Rahner

Life and Light

A Guide to the Theology of Karl Rahner

by DONALD L. GELPI, S.J.

SHEED AND WARD / *NEW YORK*

© Sheed and Ward, Inc., 1966

Library of Congress Catalog Card Number 66-12274

Imprimi potest:
    John Edwards, S.J.
    New Orleans Province
Nihil obstat:
    Thomas J. Beary
    Censor Librorum
Imprimatur:
    ✠ Robert F. Joyce
        Bishop of Burlington
December 21, 1965

The Nihil Obstat and Imprimatur are official declarations
that a book or pamphlet is free of doctrinal or moral
error. No implication is contained therein that those who
have granted the Nihil Obstat and Imprimatur agree
with the contents, opinions or statements expressed.

Manufactured in the United States of America

For Mother

Contents

Contents

ABBREVIATIONS

DK: K. Rahner, *Das Dynamische in der Kirche* (Freiburg: Herder, 1958).

EP: K. Rahner and J. Ratzinger, *Episkopat und Primat* (Freiburg: Herder, 1961).

KS: K. Rahner, *Kirche und Sakramente* (Freiburg: Herder, 1961).

MMH: K. Rahner, *Maria, Mutter des Herrn* (Freiburg: Herder, 1956).

PH: K. Rahner and P. Overhager, *Das Problem der Hominization* (Freiburg: Herder, 1961).

S: K. Rahner, *Schriften zur Theologie* (5 vols.; Cologne: Benziger, 1961-2).

SG: K. Rahner, *Sendung und Gnade* (Innsbruck: Tyrolia, 1961).

SI: K. Rahner, *Ueber die Schriftinspiration* (Freiburg: Herder, 1958).

TT: K. Rahner, *Zur Theologie des Todes* (Freiburg: Herder, 1958).

VP: K. Rahner, *Visionen und Prophezeiungen* (Freiburg: Herder, 1960).

Introduction

It is no exaggeration to say that prior to Vatican II most American Catholics were oblivious of the very existence of Karl Rahner. Understanding him and his prodigious theological output was the almost exclusive challenge of a handful of professional theologians in this country whose task it was to decipher the complexities of his style and to grapple with the profound implications of his thought.

But toward the end of the first session, press coverage of the council began to awaken a more popular interest on this side of the Atlantic. The theological renewal among laymen and movements like Sister Formation also helped sharpen the curiosity of many non-seminarians in Rahner's theological speculations.

As translations of some of his articles and books began to appear, the language barrier that previously had rendered the greater part of Rahner's writings inaccessible to most Americans began gradually to fall. Unfortunately, those who attempted Rahner in translation were quick to discover that language is not the only barrier to understanding his thought. Few Americans have either the time or the philosophical and theological background necessary to read through Rahner's myriad articles and books systematically and comprehendingly. A complete bibliography of his writings runs to more than seven hundred titles.

It is for such theological uninitiates that this book is intended. It pretends to be nothing more than a study aid for the average

American undergraduate student in theology—whether layman, sister, or seminarian. It attempts to collect in a single volume and to some extent to correlate a number of the important themes treated by Rahner in the course of some of his major theological books and articles and thus to provide the undergraduate student with some sort of overall frame of reference within which to situate any further reading and study he may do in Rahner himself. As an aid to such study we have appended a list of readings to each chapter selected from those works of Rahner which are currently available in English.

No doubt many people would prefer a more thorough introduction than the one we have attempted in this book. Such people, however, are probably not beginners in theology; and it is precisely for beginners that this book has been written. To be sure, we most certainly need a book in English which attempts in one or more volumes to situate Rahner's theological reflections in their proper historical perspective. It is to be hoped that such a book will be written some day; but if and when it is, the chances are that it will be admired but never read by those for whom the present less pretentious volume is intended.

My own preoccupations in writing this book have, therefore, been primarily pedagogical, although I have attempted to root pedagogy in serious scholarship. This approach has, I feel, been justified by a rather paradoxical situation in the American Church; for the widespread interest in Rahner in this country is at present paralleled only by a widespread unfamiliarity even with his most basic theological writings—and this on the part of the very people who most interested in them. Granted Rahner's prolific output and the difficulties of his style, this is perhaps understandable enough. If the present volume can perform the very practical service of remedying this rather bizarre situation, it will have more than fulfilled the modest hopes of its author.

Those familiar with the writings of Karl Rahner cannot help

noticing that we have given short space in the pages which follow to Rahner's more technical philosophical writings such as *Geist in Welt* and *Hörer des Wortes*. This omission is not intended to be a reflection either upon their importance or the place they occupy in Rahner's thought. Their omission is again primarily for pedagogical reasons. Important as these books are to a complete understanding of Rahner, they seemed to me to be a bit beyond the capacities and interests of those beginners for whom this present volume is primarily intended.

One final word is perhaps in place concerning the arrangement of materials in this book. The approach to Rahner's theology I have adopted in the following pages is, in view of the purpose of the book, more thematic than systematic. Such an approach seemed to me to be justified both by Rahner's own theological methods and by the immediately practical orientation of the book itself. The arrangement of the thematic material is not, however, an arbitrary one. In one of his articles Rahner has suggested that the Christian mysteries can be reduced to three basic ones, the mystery of God as he is in himself and the mystery of God as revealed in the temporal missions of his Son and of his grace-bringing Spirit. Accordingly, I have attempted to group Rahner's theological reflections according to a vaguely trinitarian scheme. Chapters I-IV are concerned with the revelation of the Father to men in Christ (Chapters I and II) and the impact of this revelation upon the goal and meaning of human history (Chapters III and IV). Chapters V-XII are concerned with the mystery of the Church, the sacramental prolongation of Christ in time, which by its kerygmatic word of preaching (Chapter V), by its sacraments (Chapters VI and VII), and by its witness of lived Christianity (Chapters VIII and IX) attempts to mediate the grace and Spirit of Christ to men. I then append a supplementary chapter on Mary. In the final chapter, I attempt to correlate a number of the major theological themes treated in the course of the book. This final chapter is not intended to be a systematic summary of the whole of Rahner's theology. It is intended merely to serve as a practical aid to the reader of this book by pulling together in some sort of coherent pattern some of the principal themes presented in the preceding chapters.

I would like to thank Fr. Rahner for his understanding and tolerance in approving the manuscript. It is my sincere regret that the limitations of time, circumstance, and talent did not permit a book worthier of his immense contribution to Catholic thought. I also owe a debt of gratitude to C. J. McNaspy, S.J., who in addition to innumerable past kindnesses was the first to encourage me in the writing of the book and later was most helpful in the practical matter of seeing it into print. I am most deeply indebted of all to Gerald Van Ackeren, S.J., who guided me through the labor of writing and without whose counsel, help, and encouragement the book would never have reached completion. He, Robert North, S.J., Philip Donnelly, S.J., John Gerken, S.J., Everett Diederich, S.J., and John Powell, S.J., read either the entire manuscript or portions of it and by their suggestions helped to make it a better book than it would have been.

St. Mary's College
August, 1965

Life and Light

A Guide to the Theology of Karl Rahner

I. The Word Was Made Flesh

Karl Rahner was born in Freiburg, Germany, on March 5, 1904. He is a member of the Society of Jesus and at this writing is professor of philosophy of religion and Catholic thought in the philosophical faculty of the University of Munich. After completing advanced studies in philosophy under Martin Heidegger in Freiburg, he went on to receive his *privatdozent* in dogmatic theology in 1937. His teaching career at the University of Innsbruck was interrupted tragically by the Anschluss. During World War II he engaged in pastoral work in Vienna and in a small town in Bavaria. In 1948 he resumed his professorship at Innsbruck, where he remained until he assumed his present post at Munich.

For the beginner in theology one of the things about Karl Rahner which is at once most fascinating and most disconcerting is his tendency to leap into any current theological controversy. It is fascinating because his thought acquires, as a result, an immediacy and a relevance that is refreshing; it is disconcerting because one cannot follow him without some knowledge of all the major movements in contemporary Catholic theology.

One of the striking things about recent Catholic theological speculation, as well as one of the secrets of its progress, is the fact that in the twentieth century theological reflection has become by necessity a cooperative effort. The fragmentation of the speculative theological endeavor into exegesis on the one hand

and dogmatic, biblical, and liturgical theology on the other demands of any creative dogmatic theologian that he keep in vital touch with all of these rapidly moving currents of religious thought.

The genius of Karl Rahner, and the secret of his contemporary relevance, consists in his extraordinary ability to do precisely that. Thus, his dogmatic speculations manifest a real sensitivity to the recent rapid developments in biblical theology. His preoccupation with rendering the gospel message meaningful to modern men and his exploitation in a dogmatic framework of biblical concepts like "the people of God," "the new Israel," "salvation history," and others have lent a genuinely kerygmatic quality to his dogmatic speculations.

Moreover, his responsiveness to developments in dogmatic theology itself has placed him in the mainstream of creative Catholic theological speculation. His reflections on created and uncreated grace, for instance, bear the obvious influence of de la Taille's theory of created actuation and uncreated act. In his theory of the supernatural existential he has not only profited from de Lubac's reflections on the relation of nature and grace, he has also attempted to correct some of the exaggerations of the *théologie nouvelle*. In his sacramental theology he has, along with Schillebeeckx and others, exploited the notion of the Church as the primary sacrament and has capitalized on the historical research of theologians like Poschmann. In his theology of the layman he has built on the solid foundations originally laid by Congar.

The philosophical background for Rahner's theological reflections is contained in his two major philosophical works, *Geist in Welt* and *Hörer des Wortes*. The first of these books is an effort to elaborate a metaphysics of human knowing and willing. The impact of Maréchal upon these philosophical writings is considerable. The vision of man which emerges from them is both that of a knower who can achieve self-possession in consciousness only through his dialectical involvement with the world about him and that of a free and self-determining subject whose openness to and implicit awareness of the Absolute is the *a priori* condition for the possibility of his spiritual self-consciousness and self-transcendence in freedom and love. Moreover, because man is a spirit incarnated in matter, he is forced in the exercise of his free choice and self-determination to assume a position not only with regard to the world about him but also and simultaneously with regard to the Absolute Person who is the transcendental goal of his deepest aspirations.

In *Hörer des Wortes*, in which the metaphysics of person elaborated in *Geist in Welt* is extended into the realm of philosophy of religion, Rahner reflects more explicitly on the social and historical dimensions of human existence. Because he is a spiritual being, man is open to the possibility of a divine revelation; but because man is also a social being immersed in the continuum of human history, he must encounter that revelation, if and when it occurs, in the form of a divine "word," a spatio-temporal event which mediates within human history itself God's message of salvation to men.

It is fitting, therefore, that we begin our journey through Rahner's explicitly theological speculations with some reflections on the meaning of the incarnation. For it is Jesus Christ, the incarnate Word of God, who is the Father's definitive revelation of love and grace to men.

A Dangerous Christological Myth

All of our theologizing is in the last analysis our human effort under faith to mediate through conceptual language the mystery of Christ in all its dimensions. But such is the poverty of conceptual thought that this same theological endeavor is full of pitfalls. In point of fact, Catholic theology has, Rahner suggests, been plagued from its origins by a false mythological notion of the Redeemer. This Christological myth has been at the root of nearly all the major Christological heresies in the history of the Church. It consists in depriving Christ's humanity of any active role in the redemption, with the result that the human nature becomes nothing more than a kind of disguise, an inert façade behind which the divinity is somehow rendered salvifically present among us. In other words, although the human nature is made to symbolize the divine presence externally, it itself reveals to us nothing about God himself.[1]

In Rahner's opinion, the more traditional manual theologians have not always been helpful in exorcising this mythical conception of Christ. Manual theology rarely advances in its Christological speculations beyond the definition of the Council of Chalcedon which, in the year 451, stated that there were two natures, divine and human, united in the single person of the Word. It tends to work toward the Chalcedonian definition as the goal of speculation rather than to use it as the starting point for new, creative thinking.[2]

This speculative sterility is especially evident in two important problem areas of modern Christology. First of all, theologians have in the past all too often neglected to develop a theology of the mysteries of Christ's life. The impression resulting from this significant omission has been that the concrete events of Our Lord's life, and hence the human nature of Christ itself, appear to be of no theological importance in the historical revelation of the Word. Second, the commonly taught theory of St. Augustine, later adopted by St. Thomas, that any person of the Trinity—Father, Son, or Holy Spirit—could have become incarnate has given the further impression that it does not in the concrete make a great deal of difference which of the divine persons actually assumed our human nature. As a result, the nature of man seems to be reduced to an external garment equally fitted to Father, Son, or Holy Spirit.[3]

According to Rahner, this Augustinian-Thomistic theory both

lacks theological proof and is in fact erroneous. There is no trace of it either in apostolic teaching or in the centuries of patristic tradition before St. Augustine. It is, moreover, based on a *non-sequitur* and on a false presupposition. The simple fact that the Word was made flesh does not justify the conclusion that either the Father or the Holy Spirit could have done the same thing had he wished to. Implicit in such reasoning is the erroneous presupposition that the term "person" means exactly the same thing in the case of each member of the Trinity, with the result that the actual incarnation of one divine person automatically grounds the possibility of the others entering into hypostatic union with a created human nature.[4]

In order to avoid the misleading mythological conception of the humanity implicit in this theory, Rahner suggests a return to a pre-Augustinian doctrine of the incarnation taught most especially by the Cappadocian fathers. According to this doctrine, only the Word, only the second person of the blessed Trinity, could have become man. With this doctrine for inspiration, Rahner attempts to elaborate a more dynamic explanation of the union of two natures in the one person of Christ, an explanation in which the humanity ceases to be a superficial disguise symbolizing the divine presence extrinsically and assumes instead a positive function within the divine revelation.[5]

Catholic theologians often attempt to explain the hypostatic union in terms of predication. Thus, they explain, the statement that there are two natures in one person means that the perfections of both the divine and the human nature can be predicated of the single divine person of the Word. Although this solution is valid as far as it goes, its full ontological implications are easily overlooked. The incautious theologian might readily accept such a theory of predication with regard to the hypostatic union and still continue to think of the divine and the human natures uncritically as two juxtaposed but intrinsically unrelated realities within the person of the Son.[6]

A *Theology of Symbol*

In the prologue to his gospel, St. John proclaimed the mystery of the incarnation with the simple statement, "The Word became flesh." To a great extent Rahner's Christological reflections are an effort to elaborate the three terms of this Johannine proposition: "the Word," "flesh," and "became."[7] According to Rahner, the Word, and only the Word, could become flesh because in the divine processions of the Trinity the Word, and not the Holy Spirit, is the real symbolic expression of the Father. This statement needs considerable elaboration. At this point, however, it is only fair to warn the reader that we are about to hit a metaphysical air pocket. But if he will only tighten his seatbelt, we should be able to get through the turbulence of the next few pages without serious mishap.

First of all, in what sense is the Word a real symbol of the Father? We are all too often inclined to think of symbols as purely arbitrary signs of some idea or event. In traditional explanations of Aristotelian logic, for instance, the verbal symbol is usually presented as an arbitrary sign which bears no intrinsic relation to the thing it symbolizes. Thus one and the same reality can be symbolized by different words in different languages. (Note, we do not dispute that symbols are signs; our argument will, however, attempt to show that in addition to the traditional logical concepts of natural and conventional signs there is a properly metaphysical concept of sign which we shall call a real symbol.)

Unfortunately, the notion that verbal symbols are arbitrary signs has often obscured the fact that all being is of itself essentially symbolic. Indeed, one being can be used as a symbol of another only because both of them, symbol and symbolized, agree with one another in some real basic characteristic.[8]

Beings, however, are not only symbolic of one another. They

are in a real sense symbolic (or expressive) of themselves. How can this be? A symbol of its nature seems to imply two things, the symbol itself and the thing it symbolizes. To say, then, that one and the same thing is a symbol of itself would seem to be contradictory. The solution of this apparent contradiction lies in the complex structure of being. For if every being is the unity of several distinct inner elements, then it is possible for one of these inner elements to serve as the symbolic expression of the being as a whole. Now, from revelation we know that it is not only created being which is one-in-many. Within the Godhead itself we find unity in multiplicity, the union of three persons in one divine nature. Hence all being, not just created being, is capable of self-expression through inner multiplicity.[9]

To put the matter a bit more concretely, when one being is composed of several inner moments, these inner moments cannot be simply juxtaposed like bricks in a house if the unity of that being is to be more than an accidental unity. Instead, these different constitutive elements or aspects of the being must be causally interrelated in order to form a single dynamic whole. Note, however, that this causal relation necessarily implies symbolic expression, since every effect resembles and expresses the reality upon which it depends for its being.[10]

If this is true, then not only are all creatures symbols of the creator, but every being as such possesses within itself a plurality of causally related elements which express the meaningful unity of the being itself.[11]

We can go one step further. Every being expresses itself precisely because every being must find its perfection through a plurality-in-unity. We ordinarily associate plurality in unity with limitation. But in God plurality in unity is identical with pure perfection; and even in created being, plurality also implies positive perfection. This is clearest in the case of spiritual beings who achieve full self-possession and personal perfection through acts of knowledge and of love. In the act of knowledge, for instance, the spiritual subject achieves perfection by positing within itself an object distinct from itself. Similarly, in the act of love, a spiritual being achieves perfection and self-possession by the gift of itself to another. In either case the very act by which a spiritual being posits within itself that which is other than itself is the act by which it achieves its perfection and self-possession. Now since a being is also a real symbol precisely by positing within itself a multiplicity of inner moments in causal subordination, we can conclude that there is a direct correlation between self-perfection through multiplicity-in-unity and symbolic self-expression. Conversely, every symbol is the self-perfection of one being in another; and this self-perfection belongs to the essential constitution of the being in question.[12]

The reader will excuse the chill intrusion of these abstract reflections; but the metaphysics of the symbol underlies so much of Rahner's theology that some indication of its basic outlines is necessary for a real appreciation of his thought. We have now to apply what we have just said concerning the ontology of the symbol to the relation of the Father and the Son within the Trinity.[13]

Whatever one may think of St. Augustine's theology of the Trinity, at least this much is quite clear: the Son, the Word, the eternal Logos is the image and expression of the Father. The procession of the Son from the Father is, moreover, a reality connected necessarily with the divine self-knowledge, without which God's absolute act of cognitional self-possession is impossible. In other words, the Father is himself insofar as he generates his own perfect reflection as an image distinct from himself.[14]

By this very fact we are justified in concluding that the Logos is a real symbol of the Father, i.e., the Son is a reality *within* the Godhead *distinct* from the Father and yet *inwardly posited* by the Father through his generative act of self-knowledge. Thus the Son is the perfect expression of the reality of the Father.[15]

This unique symbolic relation of the Word to the Father within the Trinity has important consequences in the history of salvation. It means that if the Father is to reveal himself to men in time, this revelation must take place in and through the Word, who is the perfect symbolic expression of the Father. If, then, the incarnation, the temporal revelation of the Father, is to take place, it must do so by the Word (and only the Word) becoming flesh.[16]

The Mystery of Man

But what is this "flesh" which the Word becomes? What is its relation to the second person of the Trinity? The word "flesh" is a biblical term which designates the whole of man, not just his body, but man considered precisely as weak and fragile.

For Rahner the mystery of God made man is inseparable from the mystery of man himself. Indeed, God and man are great and complementary mysteries. God is a mystery because his infinite perfection places him beyond the limits of immediate human experience. He is the boundless, the unlimited. Man is a mystery because in the very heart of his being he is a hunger for God, as essential openness to the boundless, the unlimited, the mysterious.[17]

When, therefore, the Word takes to himself the nature of man, he does not assume a nature which lacks all relationship with the divine. Rather he assumes a nature which is by its very essence an openness to God. Indeed, for Rahner, it is the incarnation which gives to human nature its whole meaning and purpose. The history of salvation is not a patchwork affair. God did not create the world and then decide to become man as an afterthought in order to repair the damage which Adam's sin happened to cause. Rather the incarnation is the whole reason why God made the world in the first place. The world was truly made for man, but only in the incarnation does man find the complete fulfillment of his yearning for the infinite. The salvific history of the world is, then, a unity; and at its center is Christ. These are key ideas in Rahner's thought, and we shall return to them when we consider the problem of the relation of nature and grace.[18]

The Mystery of Becoming

We have arrived at the point where we can begin to understand what it means to say that God *became* man. We are in fact asserting that the Infinite, the Unconditioned, the Unalterable became the conditioned, the finite, and the alterable, that the Word, the real, uncreated, eternal symbol of the Father, became a temporal, created longing for the divine.[19]

We have already seen that, as the real symbolic expression of the Father, the Word and only he could take on human nature. We have said that the human nature of Christ is not an arbitrary, lifeless disguise behind which the Word is somehow extrinsically symbolized as present among us. The very human nature of Christ reveals the Word to us; for the Word reveals himself to mankind not only by what he says but also and especially by what he is. The human nature of Christ is, then, a real symbolic expression of the Word himself. As the Father posits the Son within the Trinity as the eternal expression of himself, in an analogous fashion the Son posits within himself his human nature as the real-symbolic temporal expression of his own inner reality. The human nature of Christ is, then, the real-symbolic expression of the divine Word in time: it is a reality posited *by* the Word, *within* the Word, yet *distinct from* the Word, and thus as an expression of the inner reality of the Word.[20]

This realization revolutionizes our whole concept of human nature. Man is no longer the rational animal of philosophical speculation. Human nature, this mysterious craving for the divine, is that which comes into being when the self-expression of God, his Word, is lovingly expressed in the emptiness of Godless nothingness.[21]

We must, then, take the words of Christ seriously when he tells us "who sees me sees the Father." The human nature of Christ is a real temporal expression of the reality of the Word just as the Word is the real eternal expression of the Father. The Word made flesh is, then, the absolute symbol of God in the world, the expressive concrete reality of what God in his free and gratuitous grace wanted the world to be.[22]

But note that Christ does not assume the abstract *natura humana* of scholastic philosophy. He expresses himself in a concrete human nature, hence in a given segment of space and time. In the next chapter we shall consider briefly what this means in terms of Christ's human knowledge. Here it suffices to say that the total revelation of the Word in time is and must be a historical process. In himself the Word is eternally immutable, for in himself he is God. But having become flesh, he became also a mutable man. Hence, in positing within himself a given segment of human temporality, the Word gives historical expression to his own eternal reality.[23]

We have arrived at the center of the mystery of God and of man. Man is a mystery because God, who is mysterious, wished to become that which was not God. The mystery of man cannot be separated from the mystery of Christ. All Christology is in a very real sense anthropology; and anthropology in its loftiest expression is Christology.[24]

The misguided effort of some contemporary demythologizers

to desupernaturalize the New Testament springs ultimately from a failure to comprehend in its fullness the dual mystery of God and man.[25]

NOTES

1. S, I, 176–177, note 3; IV, 152.
2. S, I, 169–170; IV, 138.
3. S, I, 203; IV, 117, 159.
4. S, IV, 117–119.
5. *Ibid.*, 119, 223.
6. S, I, 197, 201–203.
7. S, IV, 139.
8. *Ibid.*, 279.
9. *Ibid.*, 279–281.
10. *Ibid.*, 281–284.
11. *Ibid.*, 284.
12. *Ibid.*, 284–290.
13. *Ibid.*, 292.
14. *Ibid.*
15. *Ibid.*
16. *Ibid.*, 292–293.
17. *Ibid.*, 139–142.
18. S, I, 185; III, 43–44; IV, 142–143.
19. S, IV, 148.
20. *Ibid.*, 148–149.
21. *Ibid.*, 122–123, 149–150.
22. *Ibid.*, 293–294.
23. *Ibid.*, 294–295.
24. *Ibid.*, 151.
25. *Ibid.*, 154.

SUGGESTED READINGS

Gerald A. McCool, S.J., "The Philosophy of the Human Person in Karl Rahner's Theology," *Theological Studies* (December, 1961), Vol. 22, No. 4, pp. 537–562.
"Current Problems in Christology," *Theological Investigations*, Cornelius Ernst, O.P. (tr.), (Baltimore: Helicon, 1961), Vol. I, pp. 149–200.

II. Christ's Human Knowledge and Redemptive Death

Rahner has extended his theological reflections into two important problem areas of modern Christology: Christ's human knowledge and his redemptive death and resurrection. He feels that the traditional scholastic presentation of Christ's human knowledge labors under the same theological bias which has for so long troubled speculations concerning the incarnation.[1] This scholastic explanation first appears in Christian tradition in the writings of medieval theologians; but it has found certain resonances in Church documents, notably in the encyclical *Mystici Corporis*, which attributes to Christ explicit knowledge of all men of every age and region of the earth.[2]

Scholastic Theories of Christ's Human Knowledge

Scholastic theology usually attributes to Christ supernatural and preternatural knowledge from the first moment of his conception in Mary's womb. Christ's human mind is pictured as having the beatific vision as well as infused, angelic knowledge of all creatures—past, present, and future—at least insofar as they bear relation to the work of salvation. Later on during his earthly career, Christ acquires a third type of knowledge, experimental knowledge. Thus the schoolmen end by distinguishing three distinct levels of knowledge in Christ's human intellect: the beatific vision, infused knowledge, and experimental knowledge. But at this point serious difficulties begin to arise.

For each of these three different kinds of knowledge involves a knowledge of created beings, with the puzzling result that their objects overlap. For instance, the schoolmen must conclude that Christ's human intellect already knows certain things, say, the events of his own life, with supernatural and preternatural knowledge before he actually learns of these same events with his experimental knowledge. Indeed, the nature and purpose of Christ's truly human, experimental knowledge becomes a difficult thing for the schoolmen to explain.

Rahner suggests that the scholastic explanation of Christ's human knowledge finds its philosophical roots in a basically false Greek conception of human perfection. For a Greek philosopher, man's perfection consisted in the fullness of knowledge. Thinking as they did in the context of Greek philosophical thought, the schoolmen felt obliged to attribute to Christ's human intellect an absolute fullness of knowledge, lest he be subject in any way to imperfection.[3]

But one of the great advances of modern thought over medieval speculation has been to locate human perfection in man's freedom, in his power of self-determination, rather than in his intellect. As a result we have come to realize that the perfection of man can be reconciled with the absence of knowledge, since man achieves a special kind of freedom and hence a special kind of human perfection when he consciously and deliberately commits himself in the face of the unknown. This philosophical advance is bound to have repercussions upon our conception of Christ's human knowledge. A Christ incapable of a free and loving self-commitment to his Father in the face of the unknown does not seem to be either perfectly human or humanly perfect. We shall return to this theme again when we speak of the salvific death.[4]

Rahner also feels that the scholastic idea of a Christ who

from the first moment of his conception knew in detail every event of the life which lay ahead of him fits too closely his definition of a Christological myth. He feels that in the scholastic theory the truly human knowledge of Christ, his experimental knowledge, is deprived of any significant function in the temporal revelation of the Word. It becomes an apparently unimportant and repetitious appendage to the supernatural and infused knowledge. Christ's human knowledge like his human nature seems to be reduced to a mere sensible disguise indicating but not actually revealing the divinity present among us.[5]

But there are more serious objections than this to be leveled against the scholastic theory. Not only is there no actual evidence for it in the Scriptures, but certain texts of the gospels even seem to contradict it. Far from having foreknowledge of all things pertaining to the work of salvation, Christ professes ignorance of the date of the final day of judgment. Moreover, St. Luke says that the boy Jesus "grew in wisdom," the implication being that he made real progress in knowledge. Finally, the very sufferings of Christ reported in the Scriptures indicate that he did not possess the beatific vision prior to his glorification, since the objective vision of God is in fact incompatible with suffering.[6]

Hence, Rahner concludes, what we need is an explanation of Christ's human nature which restores his experimental knowledge to its proper place in the historical revelation of the Word, while at the same time taking into account the information offered in the gospels concerning Christ's human self-awareness.[7]

Some Philosophical Presuppositions

Rahner's own explanation of Christ's human knowledge starts with the Thomistic axiom that being and knowledge are simultaneous moments within one and the same reality.[8] In Thomistic metaphysics a thing exists to the extent that it is able to achieve self-possession in knowledge.[9]

This statement is full of meaning when we apply it to the

hypostatic union. Christ's human nature exists in the reality of the Word. It possesses a way of existing, therefore, which is infinitely superior to that of ordinary men. Since self-possession in knowledge is a direct correlate of the degree of perfection with which one exists, Christ's human intellect must possess an especially elevated self-awareness by reason of its union with the divine being.[10]

But how are we to conceive of this self-awareness? Scholastic theology solved the problem by proposing an immediate *objective* vision of the divine essence. Rahner's explanation attempts to take into better account the psychological makeup of man.[11]

In every human being, he says, there is a center of consciousness from which he looks out upon the world. This center of consciousness is an *a priori*, unobjective knowledge of oneself as a spiritual subject. It includes an awareness of oneself as a person as well as an awareness of one's dynamic orientation to all possible objects of knowledge and of free choice.[12]

The Human Consciousness of Christ

In Christ this subjective center of consciousness is transformed by its immediate union with the Word. With his human intellect Christ is subjectively aware of his own divine person. Deep in the center of his human consciousness he knows himself as the Son of God. As in the case of ordinary men, this basic self-awareness need not be a completely articulated awareness. It is rather a subjective center of awareness from which Christ looks out upon the world. It is this subjective self-consciousness transformed by the hypostatic union rather than an objective knowledge of the divine essence which prior to the glorification of Christ constitutes his *visio immediata*.[13]

Rahner contends that his theory agrees better with the data of the gospels than does the traditional scholastic doctrine. It allows for a genuine progress in Christ's human knowledge rather than scholasticism's relearning of knowledge already possessed by supernatural and preternatural infusion. Indeed the work of Christ's human intellect consisted in the gradual articulation of his inner self-awareness of his own person through vital contact with and reflection upon the religious milieu in which he lived.[14]

In this way the intellectual development of Christ is restored to its proper place in the historical self-revelation of the Word. It is not simply a meaningless appendage to the infused knowledge; it becomes rather an integral part of the self-articulation and self-expression of the Word of God in time.[15]

At the heart of the current discussion concerning the demythologization of the gospels is the doctrine of the resurrection. For some non-Catholic demythologizers, Christ's resurrection from the dead is not really a historical event. It is rather a mythologized elaboration of the subjective religious experience of the primitive Christian community.

By contrast, Catholic theology has always insisted on the reality of the resurrection as a historical fact. But all too often theological manuals have in the past relegated the resurrection to the realms of fundamental theology where it becomes the crowning apologetic proof of the faith. Unfortunately by treating the resurrection almost exclusively as an apologetic argument, manual theology has tended to overlook its deeper salvific meaning as a mystery of faith.[16] This speculative gap in Catholic theology has fortunately been filled in more recent years by the able efforts of thinkers like Durrwell.

The Satisfaction Theory

Moreover, the satisfaction theory of redemption found in many scholastic manuals of Christology has tended to distract theologians from a number of pertinent theological issues. The satisfaction theory forms an important part of our intellectual heritage from the early Middle Ages. It teaches that in a redemptive order in which God demands satisfaction for sin a divine redeemer was necessary to save man because man's offense against the infinite majesty of God required infinite atonement. This atonement man alone was incapable of making; so God himself had to become man and offer satisfaction in the name of the whole human race. Since Christ is God, the theory concludes, any single action which he performed on earth was of infinite merit and by itself capable of redeeming the whole world.[17]

Now in Rahner's opinion, the trouble with this theory is that it blurs the precise meaning of the redemptive death as a salvific event as well as that of all the other particular events of Christ's life. One must conclude from the theory that the free death of Christ does indeed satisfy for sin, but that any other act which he performed could have done the same thing just as well. Once the redemptive death has been thus deprived of any special salvific meaning, the triumph of Easter tends to become the mere personal victory of Christ over his enemies. As such, it becomes an easy target for those who would "desupernaturalize" it.[18]

To forestall such a distortion of the Easter message, two things, according to Rahner, must be done. First of all we must elaborate an adequate theology of death. For if we conceive of death as nothing more than the happy termination of earthly suffering, then the death of Jesus can have no special meaning for us. But if, instead, death is the decisive and culminating point of a man's life which sums up and seals all that has gone before it, then the death of Christ can indeed take on a special and peculiarly salvific meaning. Secondly, we must elaborate a theology of the resurrection as the visible and necessary manifestation of what was already initiated in Christ's salvific death. In his little book, *The Theology of Death,* Rahner lays the groundwork for such a theology.[19] His intellectual debt to Heidegger in this work will be obvious to anyone familiar with the thought of both men.

Rahner distinguishes three sorts of pronouncements of the

Church concerning death. The Church speaks of death as an event, as the effect of sin, and as a participation in Christ's death. Rahner's theology of death is a systematic elaboration of each of these three aspects of death.[20]

Death as an Event

As an event death involves the whole of man. Because man is a unity of person and nature, he is both spiritually free and subject to the necessary laws of material being. Hence, his death must involve both of these aspects of his total human reality.[21]

Human death is traditionally described as the physical separation of the soul from the body. But this formula, though traditional, can only be considered as a description of death, not as a definition of it; for it speaks of death as a physical fact but says nothing of death as a personal and specifically human event. A complete definition of death must, in addition to the mere fact of physical separation of soul and body, express the effects of death upon the human soul itself as well as the reality of death as the ultimate and definitive act of the human person. Let us briefly consider each of these two points.[22]

First of all, what are the effects of death upon the human soul once it leaves the body? As long as the soul is in the body it is integrated into the scheme of material nature. The material universe is neither absolute unity nor absolute diversity, but the unified diversity of subsistent, interrelated parts. Through the body which it informs, then, the soul enjoys a particular kind of openness to the entire material world, an integral insertion into the cosmic pattern of the material universe.[23]

Now, when the soul leaves the body, are we to suppose that it suddenly loses all relation to the material universe, that it becomes simply "other-worldly"? Rahner answers this question in the negative. According to Thomistic philosophy, he argues, the soul even after death retains a transcendental relationship to the body which it possessed in life and which it will one day possess again in the final resurrection. As form of the body the soul contains within itself in some way all the perfections of the body which it forms and informs down to its minutest physical detail. Even the body's openness to the physical universe must therefore be present in the soul as in a formal cause. As a result, the soul can never lose its relationship with the material universe, even in death.[24]

But because through death the soul ceases to inform the body, the character of this relationship must necessarily change. In death the soul is no longer limited to a particular moment of time or to a particular point in space within the space-time continuum of the material universe. Hence, once liberated from the flesh, the soul's relation to the world of matter expands beyond the confines of space and time and assumes the proportions of a universal relationship to the whole of the material world in its radical unity.[25]

There is no question here of a Platonic world-soul: the human soul remains essentially the form of a particular human body. But by being freed from the confines of the flesh, the soul is enabled to participate in some sense in the universal attitude of God to his creation.[26]

The teaching of St. Thomas that angels, who are pure spirits and have never inhabited a body, are still related somehow to the material universe is an additional argument for the possibility of this new relationship in the soul after death.[27] The doctrine of purgatory offers additional confirmation. We know that after death the soul which is in the state of grace at the moment of death must still expiate whatever remnants there are of past sin. Could not this mean that the soul in purgatory must be put in harmony with the whole of God's creation in its radical unity before it is fit to enjoy the direct vision of God? Finally, the Church's teaching concerning the glorified body also fits in with this theory. The glorified body is truly corporeal, but in its freedom from the limitations of matter it seems to express the individual's new universalized relationship to the world of matter.[28]

We said above that death was a personal event as well as the separation of the soul and body. The personal aspect of death is usually expressed by the formula, "Death ends the pilgrim state of man." This expression means that after death man is no longer journeying to God; he has either achieved or forever missed the goal for which he was groping throughout this earthly pilgrimage.[29]

In other words, at the moment of death the personal relation of a man to God becomes fixed for all eternity. All of his previous dealings with God during his lifetime have built up to the definitive instant when his soul passes out of time into eternity. For once the soul leaves the realm of space and time, personal development and hence a change in one's personal attitude to God are no longer possibilities.[30]

This fixation in death of our personal attitude to God constitutes our personal judgment. Hence, the personal judgment is not something arbitrarily associated with death by an extrinsic divine decree. It is an essential moment within the total reality of dying. For if our death is to be truly *ours*, it must be a personal as well as a biological event. It must be the act of the whole man, spirit and flesh, soul and body. Now, in death the body perishes, but the immortal soul cannot perish. It passes instead to a new non-temporal mode of being. Death, therefore, can be nothing else than the culminating personal act of the soul's temporal development, that act by which it brings its life in time to a definitive peak of personal perfection. As an event, then, death is simultaneously a physical end and a spiritual fulfillment.[31]

Death as an Effect of Sin

But death is not only an event. It is also, as we have said, a consequence of sin. It was through the sin of Adam that death

came into the world. This means that before his sin Adam was
by special privilege immortal. If, then, we are to understand in
precisely what sense death is a consequence of Adam's sin, we
must first understand the meaning of Adam's immortality before
the fall. Death is a consequence of sin insofar as it is a privation
of the immortality enjoyed by Adam.[32]

Adam's immortality cannot mean that he would have enjoyed
an indefinitely prolonged temporal existence had he not sinned.
For even Adam had to bring his life to some meaningful and
culminating perfection. He would have had at some point in his
career to pass from temporal existence to a glorified state similar
to that enjoyed by the risen Christ. If, then, Adam's immortality
did not immunize him to the passage from time to eternity, it
must have affected the manner in which this passage took
place.[33]

But at this point the problem becomes more complicated. For
faith teaches us that death is a natural event as well as a consequence of sin. It also teaches us that in the present order of
grace, men can die either the guilty death of Adam the sinner
or a death redeemed by union with the dying Christ. In other
words, in the present order of grace our death must also be the
assumption of a definitive attitude toward the redemptive death
of Christ.[34]

Moreover, in the present salvific order, our death should be a
death of grace in Christ. We should ripen to death as to the fullness of personal perfection in grace. But we also know that not
every death will necessarily be a salvific event. It is possible for
a man to die while spurning the grace of God. Even more,
precisely because death can be an event either of salvation or
of damnation, it is an event shrouded in ambiguity.[35] Not only
does it appear to be the end of the whole man, who departs from
that form of life which is most characteristically human, but
there is no way of verifying empirically whether the apparent
emptiness of a man's death conceals an inner salvific fullness
or not.[36]

We are here at the center of the mystery of death as a consequence of sin. In an order of pure grace without sin, death would possess no such ambiguity. It would be the total transformation of man, body and soul, in grace. If, in the present order of grace, death is in fact ambiguous and obscure, this can only be the consequence of sin. Death, then, is a consequence of sin inasmuch as we must die without being totally transformed in grace. In other words, the salvific ambiguity of death is the manifestation of sin in our very flesh.[37]

Moreover, the present ambiguity of death constitutes one of man's greatest temptations to reject God's saving grace. In the face of death's obscurity man must either surrender himself totally with loving trust into the hands of God, or he must die a death of despair and unreality. Consequently, not only is our way of dying the result of original sin, it can also become for men the definitively deadly sin, the rejection of God in despair or selfishness for all eternity.[38]

We may conclude from all these reflections that only revelation fully explains man's horror of death. For only in revelation do we recognize death as the manifestation in our bodies of the mystery of iniquity. Man's horror of death is a horror before the evil of sin and of the powers of darkness.[39]

Death as a Participation in Christ's Death

Having thus elaborated a basic theology of death both as an event and as a consequence of sin, we are ready to consider the salvific meaning of the death of Christ.

Christ truly died, although we need not suppose that his death was like ours in every respect. To indicate only one difference, Christ's death also includes a "descent into hell." But Christ's death was a death of obscurity like ours.[40]

Still there also remains an essential difference between Christ's death and our own. For us death is the manifestation of the presence of sin in our bodies. But for Christ death could be nothing of the sort. Christ was utterly sinless. Hence, in Christ the very obscurity of death is transformed into a manifestation, indeed the supreme manifestation, of divine grace.[41]

Hence, although the whole of Christ's life is of salvific meaning, his death of obscurity has a special salvific character. It is the very incarnation of his filial love and obedience to his heavenly Father who "delivered him up" to death for the salvation of all men. It is also that definitive personal act by which he sums up, seals, and lovingly offers to his Father the whole of his life and being in propitiation for mankind.[42]

Thus by his death Christ becomes the unique mediator between God and men. By this final definitive act of his earthly life he enters into a new relationship with the world. For having through death transcended the limits of space and time, the soul of Christ like that of other men assumes a new universal relationship with the created universe in its radical unity. But in the case of Christ this relationship is also a salvific one. (Could not Christ's descent into hell mean, among other things, this salvific descent into the inner unifying reality of the world?) In death, Christ's human nature becomes, therefore, the unique bond linking the material universe and all men in it to the Father in a relation of eternal reconciliation.[43]

The world is, therefore, essentially different before and after the death of Christ. His death is the central event of history: it constitutes a definitive salvific situation in which no relation with the Father is possible except through the glorified humanity of Christ. The eternal union of the Word with his human nature thus becomes our definitive guarantee of the everlasting openness of our human limitation to the infinite love of God.[44]

Christ's resurrection is a necessary element within this new salvific situation. The true meaning of the salvific death in darkness and ambiguity does not become clear until Easter Sunday. For Easter is not just the Father's juridical acceptance of Christ's sacrifice, as the satisfaction theory would suggest. It is essentially that unique event in the history of salvation in which God so glorifies his creature by uniting it inseparably to himself that this very glorification becomes the free creature's total and loving participation in the divine reality.[45]

It is essential to any religious offering that it be accepted by God. The more perfect the offering, the more total is God's acceptance. Just as Good Friday is the loving and total self-offering of man to God in the person of the Word made flesh, so Easter Sunday is the total acceptance of man by God in the glorified flesh of the Son of man. The one event is incomprehensible without the other. Indeed, the resurrection is inchoatively present in the salvific death, for in the very act of dying the glorified soul of Christ assumes the salvific relation that will be shared by his glorified body on Easter Sunday. The salvific death of obscurity and the manifestation of salvation in the risen Christ are, then, two moments within one and the same salvific event.[46] We may conclude, therefore, that those demythologizers who seek to terminate Christ's earthly career at Calvary have failed to realize that Calvary without Easter remains essentially meaningless and that the very events of Easter Sunday are already germinally present within the salvific death itself.[47]

But there is more to Rahner's theology of death than a polemic against the dogmatically questionable efforts of some demythologizers. He is much more interested in showing that the salvific death of Christ has transformed the whole of Christian living and dying.[48]

He points out that the sacraments of baptism, the eucharist, and the anointing of the sick in particular have special relationship to the salvific death. By baptism the Christian is baptized into the death of Christ by his own death to sin. By becoming a partaker in the life of grace, he is ordered to a share in the death of Christ through his definitive confirmation in grace at death. Similarly, the eucharist makes the salvific death vitally present to us in our daily living: it is the cultic manifestation of the fact that our death has been conquered in the glorious victory of the cross. And since, finally, sickness is a prelude to death and by that very fact a manifestation of sin in our flesh, the anointing of the sick either restores the sick man to health or grants him the grace of a death in Christ.[49]

The Meaning of Christian Asceticism

Christian asceticism also looks to the cross for its ultimate meaning, for it is essentially a lived participation in the death of Christ.[50] Hence, one should distinguish carefully between Christian asceticism in the strict sense and moral, cultic, or mystical asceticism.[51]

Moral asceticism is the struggle against everything within us that comes from sin and leads to sin. It is self-conquest and the cultivation of the virtues. It is frequently presented as Christian and does in fact form the solid foundation of Christian living. But it is not asceticism in its typically Christian form. Moral asceticism is completely justifiable in terms of human reason alone; as such, it fails to explain the heroic renunciation of the saints. Christian asceticism, on the other hand, is fully intelligible only when seen with the eyes of faith.[52]

Cultic asceticism is aimed at the preparation for worship and is linked with certain taboos which are not directly connected with the moral life. It includes sacrifice in its various ritual forms, ritual purifications, etc. One may well ask whether such practices are truly asceticism or whether they simply bear an external resemblance to asceticism. If the union with God which results from them is considered as a gift of grace, such practices can be truly ascetical. But if the resulting union with God is regarded as the product of human activity, then cultic asceticism is reducible to a form of mystical asceticism.[53]

Mystical asceticism consists of practices which prepare one for religious enthusiasm and the experience of the divine. Mystical gymnastic which pretends to liberate the divine forces within us is, of course, irreconcilable with the Christian conception of grace.[54]

Christian asceticism in the strict sense is none of these things. It is essentially a participation in the passion and death of Christ. In physical suffering we find the same dualism which we found in death considered as an event. Suffering is simultaneously the act of a free, self-determining, personal being as well as a brute event forced upon human freedom. Like death, suffering is possible because of the basic distinction within man of nature and person. Suffering is, then, an anticipation of death and poses the same fundamental problem as death: how can freedom, the essence of man as a spiritual reality, exist side by side with the apparent annihilation of man?[55]

Asceticism is the free acceptance of death in its gradual approach during life in the form of the sufferings which we endure. "Passion" and asceticism are, then, two aspects of the same phenomenon. "Passion" is suffering insofar as it is unavoidable; asceticism is suffering insofar as it is freely and spontaneously accepted. "Passion" implies the necessity of death in man considered as nature; asceticism affirms the freedom of death in man insofar as he is a person.[56]

But just as Christian death has been transformed in Christ's death, so too has Christian suffering been transformed in the passion of Christ. Self-abandonment to God in faith in the midst of suffering, which constitutes the essence of Christian asceticism, is an anticipation of and a preparation for Christian death. Hence, Christian asceticism is essentially the anticipatory acceptance of death in faith through suffering.[57]

But most of all, the death of Christ transforms the Christian act of dying. Though they resemble one another empirically, the death of a Christian is essentially different from the death of a sinner. For the Christian, death is no longer a punishment for sin, but only a consequence of it. We have seen that the decisive

difference in Christ's death was not merely the fact that he died
in the proper frame of mind, but that his death is the manifestation of grace and not of sin. We have also seen that because of
the new and intimate relation of Christ with the world resulting
from his death, this grace is also ours. In death the Christian
experiences the consequences of sin, the darkness and bitterness
of separation from God. But in the midst of it all he believes and
hopes in the divine mercy and lovingly abandons himself wholly
into the hands of his heavenly father. His belief, hope, and love
do not merely accompany death; in the graced act of dying they
achieve their fullest and most perfect expression.[58]

The Meaning of Martyrdom

It is for this reason that martyrdom is the Christian death
par excellence. For the martyr not only dies as a Christian but
in his death renders somehow visible the inner spiritual reality
of a death in faith.[59]

The martyr's death is not merely a heroic death. A hero faces
death courageously, while seeking always to preserve his own
life if this be possible. The martyr seeks out death itself as the
object of his love. As in the case of Christ, no man takes the
martyr's life from him; it is he who freely and willingly chooses
death over life.[60]

Because of his sovereignly free domination over death, the
martyr's death loses some of its ambiguity. Seen with the eyes of
faith, it becomes a manifestation in time of the essential holiness
of the Church. And because his death manifests its inner spiritual
reality more clearly than that of other Christians, it testifies publicly to the triumph of grace which took place in Christ's salvific
death.[61]

Let us try to consider what this means in greater detail. As an
act of public witness to the faith, martyrdom is an essential
characteristic of the holy Church, for it helps to manifest the

inner sanctity which the whole Church lives in hiddenness from day to day. Moreover, because it is an external sign of inner grace, it is truly sacramental. It is a baptism for those who undergo it without having received baptism of water. It is not one of the seven sacraments, because it is not an event in the life of the ordinary Christian. But it is, in a sense, even more than a sacrament. Sacraments can be received invalidly: the sacramental sign can exist without the inner sacramental grace which it symbolizes being present in the improperly disposed subject. But in true martyrdom God's grace is always triumphant to the depths of a man's being.[62]

The Church and the martyr, then, bear mutual witness to one another. The martyr bears witness to the holiness of the Church by freely choosing death not as one who hates the world or seeks an escape from life's misery but as one who understands the supernatural meaning of death in faith. The Church bears witness to the holiness of the martyr in the eucharistic sacrifice, which is the cultic manifestation of what happens in every martyrdom, namely, the saving death of Christ and in him of all his saints.[63]

Though martyrdom manifests the inner reality of Christian death, this does not mean that martyrdom can be understood in purely empirical terms. Martyrdom does in fact differ from other deaths. The martyr's patience, his love of this world, his lack of fanaticism, together with his free choice of death itself—all these things are peculiar to martyrdom, and all point to its inner spiritual reality. As a result, the full significance of the martyr's death can be fully comprehended only in faith, only in and by the Church. Martyrdom is a motive of belief, even though it is not itself an object of faith.[64]

Still, not every unjustly inflicted death is a martyrdom. How, then, does it happen that in martyrdom there is a necessary connection between the objective goodness of the death, the manner in which it is accepted, and the salvific reality to which it bears witness?[65]

We know that all free actions are specified by their objects. The object of a good act must be good; the object of an evil act, evil. When a free act of the will seeks a good object it is not only intentionally but also ontologically good. As personal acts, then, good and bad deaths differ ontologically as well as intentionally, in their physical makeup as well as in their objects.[66]

Now, Rahner argues, a Christian death which is itself the object of a free choice must be both intentionally and ontologically good. Hence, even the external, ontological manner in which it takes place manifests visibly the internal, intentional difference which distinguishes it from an evil death. The martyr loves his death for the only possible reason for which it could be loved: it is a participation in the death of the Lord. Such a death accepted patiently, peacefully, and lovingly must be intentionally good.[67] It is also by its very nature the sublimest witness a man can bear to the salvific character of Christ's death.[68]

We can understand, then, why martyrs have prayed for the grace of martyrdom long before they died as well as why they were saints before they were martyrs. We can also understand why miracles are not necessary for their canonization. The very death of the martyr is itself sufficient proof both of his heroism and of his full and final confirmation in grace.[69]

The Consolation of Time

But, needless to say, not every Christian death is a martyrdom. In fact, the martyr's death is the exception rather than the rule. Still, every Christian can, as the years pass, draw genuine comfort from his own meritorious growth into eternity. Like St. Paul, he presses forward consciously toward his final goal, knowing all the while that Christ, the just judge, will grant him the recompense of all his labors. Even those Christians who at some time in their lives have lost the grace of baptism through serious sins can continue to hope that God will deny them nothing of the full reward which is theirs in Christ Jesus.[70]

But even though Christians have every reason to trust in the generosity of God, they should be careful to keep a balanced attitude toward storing up merit in heaven. Accumulating merit through acts performed in grace is not the same thing as depositing money in a supernatural savings account. Merit is not something quantitative, like money; nor is it some sort of extrinsic legal claim upon God. It is the quality intrinsic to any act performed in grace. That is to say, merit means that, because God has by his grace made us capable of acts of divine love, what we do in time bears an anticipatory likeness to what we shall be in eternity.[71]

To increase in supernatural merit means, therefore, to belong ever more perfectly to God in love. A morbid concern with "accumulating" more and more merit is, then, hardly proper in a Christian. It is a distortion of merit to covet it as though it were a legal title guaranteeing a certain measurable quantity of eternal happiness. Instead, a truly meritorious life is one dedicated to the qualitative improvement in God's eyes of every act that we perform. For God's judgment upon the merits of our actions at the moment of death will not be a legal balancing of supernatural books so much as a concrete revelation to each individual of the sort of person he has become in the course of his life. In other words, the meritorious quality of our present acts means that the kind of person we shall be for all eternity is already in the making here and now as we move forward in time.[72]

But if merit is a qualitative and not a quantitative reality, what does it mean to ask whether God will restore to us the merit of our previous supernatural acts, should we ever lose his grace through serious sin? Theologians have in the past given three different answers to this problem. The first answer proportions the restoration of previous merit to the thoroughness of one's reconversion to grace. The second insists more upon the degree of merit one may have possessed prior to the loss of grace. This second position shows a strong juridical bias and is difficult to establish with any certitude. The third opinion even goes so far as to deny that any merit "accumulated" prior to one's fall from baptismal grace is restored along with sanctifying grace.[73]

To deny the restoration of any merit whatsoever after repentance from serious sin is theologically very questionable. For if merit is proportioned to a person's qualitative worth in grace, the very fact that an individual has in the course of time become a particular kind of person must necessarily be a moment within his restoration to grace after serious sin.[74]

Moreover, what is true of repentance is analogously true of every Christian who dies in grace. For the divine judgment at death regards a man's acts not as individual, isolated realities but as contributing elements which have in the course of time made a particular individual to be the concrete sort of person he is at the moment of his passage into eternity. Now, since, as Sacred Scripture clearly testifies, God is powerful enough to incorporate the very malice of men into his salvific plan, should we not trust that all those who die in the grace of Christ have actually become, despite their sins and imperfections, exactly what God in his saving providence intended them to be?[75]

As consoling as these reflections sound, this last suggestion is apt to cause a certain amount of hesitation. For how can every man who dies in grace actually be at the moment of death what God intended him to be, when even a superficial evaluation of almost any man's life will reveal that he has continually fallen far short of whatever good he was morally capable of accomplishing? Would not such a man have to regret for all eternity the ideal follower of Christ he never became? To this objection one might reply with some pious spiritual writers that, even so, the blessed in heaven are content in their humility to enjoy for all eternity whatever degree of happiness almighty God assigns them; but the matter is perhaps a bit more complicated than such an answer might seem to imply.[76]

What is really at stake here is the concrete way in which we think about our past meritorious acts. Now, if, as we have suggested, eternity is not the continuation of time but the definitive fixation of what we have become in time, then it follows that as long as a man remains in this life, any free act he performs will have an effect upon his eternal destiny. At the same time, we should not exaggerate the significance of the limitations imposed upon free choice by our concrete human condition. For if death involves a man's total "yes" or "no" to the grace of God, then, in a death which is a definitive "yes" to grace, final salvation must necessarily include all that one has become in the course of one's personal evolution in time. Hence, purgatory, as we have already suggested, consists precisely in the gradual personal integration of that residue of a man's life on earth which is incompatible with his final commitment to God in grace. But if this is indeed the case, and if in heaven we will truly love God with our whole heart and not with just a part of it, then it must follow that even though any one individual act of a man's life may lag behind his total supernatural potential, still the whole of his life considered as a vital evolution toward blessedness cannot fall short of what God intended it to be.[77]

We may conclude, then, that even sin can, in the inscrutable wisdom of God, have a positive meaning in a man's spiritual development. Indeed, the enormity of any sin depends upon the degree of human perfection which is actually present within the sinful act but perverted from its final end. To the extent, therefore, that it embodies an element of intrinsic goodness, even sin contains within itself an implicit, frustrated aspiration toward God. But if even sin can thus be integrated into the total salvific meaning of a man's life, how much more can acts which are only naturally good.[78]

Needless to say, Rahner is not counselling sinful acts or suggesting that sinful or purely natural actions are in themselves meritorious of eternal life. But he is counselling an abiding peace of soul in the face of one's shortcomings and a strong confidence in God that whatever we may have done in the past can in the divine plan for our individual salvation contribute something positive to our present growth in holiness and to our ultimate worth as a person redeemed by the passion and death of Jesus Christ.

NOTES

1. S, V, 243.
2. *Ibid.*, 223.
3. *Ibid.*, 230.
4. S, I, 180–181; V, 230, 244; TT, 62.
5. S, V, 243–244.
6. *Ibid.*, 223, 231.
7. *Ibid.*, 226–227.
8. *Ibid.*, 233.
9. *Ibid.*, 234.
10. *Ibid.*, 234–235.
11. *Ibid.*, 236.
12. *Ibid.*, 228–229.
13. *Ibid.*, 236–237.
14. *Ibid.*, 239–241.
15. *Ibid.*, 243.
16. S, IV, 158.
17. TT, 54.
18. *Ibid.*, 55.
19. S, IV, 164.
20. TT, 13–14.
21. *Ibid.*, 15.
22. *Ibid.*, 19–20.
23. *Ibid.*, 19–20.
24. *Ibid.*, 21–23.
25. *Ibid.*, 23.
26. *Ibid.*, 22.
27. *Ibid.*, 23.
28. *Ibid.*, 24–26.

29. *Ibid.*, 26.
30. *Ibid.*, 26–27.
31. *Ibid.*, 29–30.
32. *Ibid.*, 31–33.
33. *Ibid.*, 33.
34. *Ibid.*, 34–35.
35. *Ibid.*, 36, 44.
36. *Ibid.*, 36–38.
37. *Ibid.*, 39–40, 44–45.
38. *Ibid.*, 41–42, 46–47.
39. *Ibid.*, 47–48.
40. *Ibid.*, 53.
41. *Ibid.*, 57–58.
42. TT, 58; S, IV, 165.
43. TT, 58–59.
44. TT, 60–61; S, III, 59.
45. S, IV, 165–166.
46. *Ibid.*, 167–168.
47. *Ibid.*, 168.
48. TT, 66.
49. *Ibid.*, 67–71.
50. S, III, 98.
51. *Ibid.*, 75.
52. S, III, 75–79.
53. *Ibid.*, 80–81.
54. *Ibid.*, 82–84.
55. *Ibid.*, 85–89.
56. *Ibid.*, 90.
57. *Ibid.*, 91–93.

58. TT, 62–65.
59. *Ibid.*, 88.
60. *Ibid.*, 89.
61. *Ibid.*, 90–91.
62. *Ibid.*, 91–92.
63. *Ibid.*, 93–94.
64. *Ibid.*, 94–95.
65. *Ibid.*, 95–96.
66. *Ibid.*, 97–98.
67. *Ibid.*, 98–101.
68. *Ibid.*, 101–102.

69. *Ibid.*, 104.
70. S, III, 169–170.
71. *Ibid.*, 171.
72. *Ibid.*, 172–174.
73. *Ibid.*, 175–176.
74. *Ibid.*, 176.
75. *Ibid.*, 176–179.
76. *Ibid.*, 180.
77. *Ibid.*, 180–184.
78. *Ibid.*, 185–187.

SUGGESTED READINGS

On the Theology of Death, Charles H. Henkey (tr.), (Freiburg: Herder, 1961).

III. Nature, Grace, and the Hypostatic Union

In the preceding chapters we have insisted on the fact that the history of salvation forms a single whole and that the world was created with a view to the incarnation. Perhaps one of the best ways of entering into Rahner's thoughts on this rather difficult problem is through a more detailed consideration of the relation between the incarnation as he conceives it and modern evolutionary theory.[1]

The Evolutionary Outlook

One would suspect that when Rahner speaks of the incarnation as the ultimate goal of the creative act he is echoing not only the Christology of Duns Scotus but the evolutionary theories of his fellow Jesuit Pierre Teilhard de Chardin as well. As a matter of fact, Rahner has taken pains to distinguish his own approach to the problem of evolution from that of Teilhard even though there remains a certain kinship of spirit between them. For Teilhard evolution is a fact to be integrated into the salvific scheme of things. For Rahner evolution is no more than a scientific hypothesis which is of interest to the theologian insofar as it is not in contradiction with revealed truth. There is no question, of course, of attempting to show that the incarnation

is a strict product of natural evolution. To do so would be to fall
victim to a false theological rationalism. But Rahner himself feels
that the theologian must not merely demonstrate the absence of
any contradiction between evolutionary theory and revelation.
He must also explore their similarities and show possible points
of contact between them.[2]

Fundamental to all evolutionary theory is the idea of the unity
of the cosmos. This basic cosmic unity appears most clearly in
man himself. In man spirit and matter are fused into a single
living reality which achieves its perfection in the gradual transformation of the cosmos.[3]

"Spirit" designates the whole of man insofar as he possesses
himself absolutely, and hence insofar as he is directed to the
absoluteness of reality in general, i.e., ultimately to God. Now
the fundamental unity of matter and spirit in man appears precisely in this, that man's spiritual self-possession, his mysterious
openness to the absolute, takes place within his experience of
concrete material things. Hence, matter, as the necessary condition of time and space, is also the necessary condition for the
existence of those sensible objects distinct from man through the
knowledge of which man achieves spiritual self-possession and
openness to the absolute. Moreover, man's physical body is also
the necessary condition for the existence of a multiplicity of
human persons capable of encountering one another in time and
space and of freely evolving in a common history.[4]

The second basic postulate of evolutionary theory is that the
present relationship between matter and spirit is a dynamic one
and is itself the product of historical development. In spite of
the fact that they are united in man, spirit and matter are not the
same thing. But the fact of their essential difference can be reconciled with their present union in man if matter is conceived of
as evolving into spirit.[5]

We know that all created being is in dynamic evolution to

fullness of perfection. In an evolutionary context fullness of perfection comes to mean self-transcendence, even at the level of substance. But once we are willing to ground the self-transcendence of created being in the absolute being of God, there is no fundamental philosophical or theological difficulty in admitting evolution, even the evolution of man.[6]

Once man has been integrated into the evolutionary process, then the history of the physical universe and the history of man constitute a single progressive unity. The goal of natural history becomes the free history of spirit, which includes as part of its inner structure the gradual transformation of nature by spirit through their progress toward a common goal.[7]

In man as a product of evolution, then, nature comes into possession of itself. But since man as spirit is open to the whole of reality, and hence also to the first cause of all created things, in him nature achieves a new and special relationship to God.[8]

But human history is not the history of a single man. Matter, as we have said, necessarily implies the existence of a community of individual men. It is, then, through the progress of this human community to ultimate self-possession that physical nature progresses to its own ultimate perfection and receives its ultimate orientation to the divine. The dissolution of man in death is possible in this context only if each man has contributed something definitive to the ultimate goal of cosmic self-possession. If what we have outlined above correctly represents what may be called the basic evolutionary outlook, then the question still remains: to what extent is this outlook reconcilable with Christian belief?[9]

In a Christian context the ultimate self-transcendence of the world takes place fully and definitively in the order of grace and glory. If cosmic history is fundamentally the history of spirit, then the immediate communication of God to his spiritual creature (and in it to the cosmos) can be conceived of as the meaningful goal of evolution in God's gratuitous salvific providence.

Conversely, it is the experience of grace in the individual consciousness which gives man the strength in faith to assert that the world is actually progressing toward cosmic perfection.[10]

The Incarnation in an Evolving Universe

How, then, would an evolving universe fit into the divine plan for the incarnation? Any attempt to answer this question must rest on two basic presuppositions: first, that the ultimate goal of creation is indeed the gracious and gratuitous self-communication of God to his creature; second, that the evolutionary self-transcendence of the world is intended by God with a view to this divine self-communication.[11]

But how is the self-communication of God to his spiritual creatures to take place? Man is spirit and as spirit is a free agent. Moreover, as we have seen, the progressive self-possession of the cosmos is the product of the cooperative effort of the entire human community. If this is true, then the self-communication of God to man must have as its object a community of free subjects with a common history. The self-communication of God to men requires, therefore, a permanent guarantee in time of the divine self-offering, a guarantee which endures as an irrevocable appeal to all men of all times. This appeal must be one which cannot be ignored, a permanent self-communication of God toward which man in his freedom must take a stand.[12]

This guarantee, this enduring appeal, this permanent self-communication of God is the incarnation. It is a historical moment within the evolution of the world. It is the product not of evolution but of the gratuitous grace of God. It is not even the temporal beginning of grace, which is co-extensive with the development of man. The historical humanity of Christ, is, however, the definitive and culminating point of insertion of God into an evolving human history.[13]

In other words, the incarnation is that unique moment in

history in which grace is definitively imparted to men. It is not only our hope of salvation in spite of its uniqueness. To say with the traditional teaching of theologians that Christ's human nature itself enjoys and imparts the beatific vision to all men is not enough. Nor is it sufficient simply to say that Christ became incarnate in order to save us all. To integrate the incarnation as a salvific event into the historical scheme of things we must show how this specific event which took place at a given point within the temporal evolution of the world can by its very uniqueness transform the rest of history.[14]

First of all, it is clear that such an event must involve a definitive communication of grace by God, a divine self-offering which can be accepted or rejected by men, but one which cannot be withdrawn by God. The incarnation is such an event. It can be defined as man's transcendence of his own human reality into the reality of God through God's absolute and irrevocable communication of himself to man in such a way that this very self-communication by God constitutes an offer of divine self-communication to other men.[15]

As a consequence, God's decision to impart grace to men and his decision to become incarnate are one and the same. The full communication of God to man which takes place in the glorified Christ is the communication of a grace and glory intended for all.[16]

Moreover, the irrevocability of the incarnation as an act of divine grace flows from its very uniqueness. Only in the incarnation does the communication of grace involve the communication of the divine being itself. Every other self-expression of God in history takes place through a limited reality, a word, an event, which belongs to the created order and as such lacks any permanent validity. By contrast, the reality of Jesus is unrepeatable precisely because it is the reality of the only begotten Son of God himself. In addition, since the reality of Christ is also a responsive human reality, this human reality must be constituted abso-

lutely in grace. The grace which Christ in his human nature
possesses as a result of the unique event of the hypostatic union
differs from the grace we are promised only in this, that only
in the hypostatic union is grace also God's definitive offer to share
his life with all men. Only in the human nature of Christ is the
unique and absolute event of the self-communication of God to
man simply, purely, and irrevocably there.[17]

Although Rahner regards evolution merely as a scientific hypothesis, nevertheless certain theological constants emerge from
his handling of evolutionary theory. Evolution is a particular
manner of conceiving history. In Rahner's terms, evolution is
history ordered to self-transcendence. But the central position
he assigns to the incarnation in history remains true whether one
may choose to conceive of natural and human history as evolving
in this strict sense or not. With or without evolution, Christ is
the definitive and irrevocable insertion of grace into the progress
of human events. He is the definitive promise of grace to all men,
the central fact of all history; and as such he is also the ultimate
motive for divine creation.

But here we come face to face with a theological dilemma.
If it is true that God's primary intention in his creative act was
his ultimate self-expression in Christ, then creation took place in
a very real sense in Christ. For the sake of Christ were all things
made and for the sake of an abiding alliance of love between
God and men.

On the other hand, we know that the actual self-communication of God to man is an act of completely gratuitous grace on
the part of God. In saying that all things were created in and
for Christ, are we not dangerously close to the theories of the
théologie nouvelle which were condemned by Pius XII? Are
we not implying that the incarnation is gratuitous in the same
way as is the creative act? Are we not hinting that nature demands the incarnation in order to be complete? Are we not thus
subtly undermining the gratuity of supernatural grace and with

it the whole of Christian belief? The problem of the place of the incarnation in history leads necessarily to the problem of the precise relation of nature and grace.[18]

Historically, however, the problem of nature and grace arose in a different theological context; and we would do well to take a look at its historical background before we proceed any further.

More Recent Reflections on Nature and Grace

The controversy began when certain theologians posed the question of whether or not a supernatural act necessarily lies outside the realm of human consciousness. In Thomistic theology a supernatural act is specified by an object which by definition exceeds the capacities of any purely natural act. The majority of nineteenth-century theologians interpreted this doctrine to mean that supernatural grace is a reality concerning which we have some knowledge by objective revelation even though grace itself can never be experienced subjectively. For these theologians human consciousness remains essentially unchanged whether or not a man is in the state of grace. They supported their position by appealing to the dogma that one can never know with certainty whether or not one is in the state of grace. If we were conscious of supernatural grace, they argued, we would be able to know with certainty the supernatural condition of our soul.[19]

The difficulty with this conception of the relation of nature and grace is that it suffers from a certain "extrinsicism." Grace and nature are conceived of as two separate layers in a man which exist side by side. The only relation between nature and grace becomes the negative one that there is no contradiction between them. Nature remains quite capable of achieving its natural end harmoniously outside of any supernatural order. Nature is, then, completely self-contained. It partakes of the divine nature only by an extrinsic divine decree and knows of its participation only because it has been revealed by God.[20]

Such a conception of grace and nature is both problematic and dangerous. If man experiences himself only as pure nature, then he is always in danger of understanding himself exclusively in terms of pure nature. Moreover, grace, if it resulted from an external decree of God, would then come to nature as a disturbance for which nature was never really intended. Finally, in such a conception of the supernatural, man must live a spiritual life on two separate and unrelated levels, all the while believing with purest faith in (but never subjectively experiencing) the existence of the supernatural superstructure which has been imposed on his natural conscious life.[21]

This nineteenth-century teaching concerning faith came under attack from numerous quarters. In philosophy Maréchal's conception of man as a conditioned natural desire for the beatific vision stirred up a storm of controversy. By qualifying this natural desire as "conditioned," Maréchal hoped to preserve the divine freedom in actually fulfilling man's natural desire. Still, for many theologians, Maréchal seemed to be calling into question the gratuity of grace. But out of all the squabbling came an increasingly general acceptance of the desire for God as an implicit and transcendent *a priori* of man's spiritual life.[22]

Theologians themselves also began to become aware of a certain evolution of the idea of the supernatural. They began to reflect more seriously on certain aspects of Christian teaching which had been partially lost sight of in the course of the years. They rediscovered St. Thomas's *desiderium naturale visionis beatificae*. They reflected more seriously on the meaning of actual grace which precedes justification, on the relation between sacraments and personal acts, on the meaning of uncreated grace. The ecumenical dialogue shifted attention to a Christ-centered conception of grace, then to an elaboration of a notion of grace which is more than a supernatural superstructure imposed on man's natural powers.[23]

Finally, the impact of existentialism has led to a rethinking of grace in terms of concrete human living. This in turn has led to a re-evaluation of the ecclesial aspects of grace and to a consideration of the problem of the justification of non-Christians.[24]

We shall proceed in our own reflections in three steps. First we shall reflect on certain traditional scholastic conceptions of grace. On the basis of this reflection we shall proceed to the problem of nature and grace. Finally we shall attempt to connect grace with the doctrine of the incarnation.

Scholastic Teaching on Created and Uncreated Grace

Traditional scholastic theology distinguishes carefully between created and uncreated grace. Uncreated grace is the presence of God in the soul of the just man, God's self-communication of his own reality to each individual soul. Since this participation in the divine life is utterly supernatural and beyond the merely human capacities of man, the scholastic theologians insisted on the necessity of a created grace in each individual soul. They conceived of this created grace as an ontological alteration of man which constituted both the *consortium formale* and the *consortium terminativum* of the divine nature. By the *consortium formale* the schoolmen meant the formal ontological ground of a human participation in the divine spirituality and holiness. By *consortium terminativum* they meant the basis of a new relationship of indwelling between God and men. The schoolmen, however, tended to ground man's justification primarily in his possession of created grace. And in doing so their approach to the problem differed notably from that of the Fathers of the Church.[25]

The Fathers in general place greater emphasis on uncreated grace and tend to look on created grace rather as a consequence of divine presence within us. Is it possible for us to reconcile the scholastic and the patristic approaches to the problem?[26]

Before we can ourselves approach the subject of grace properly, we should first explain certain presuppositions. First of all, grace leads to the direct vision of God. It is in a real sense the imperfect initiation of that vision here on earth, or, in scholastic terms, the *incohatio visionis beatificae.* Since this is true, any principle which is ontologically valid for the beatific vision can be applied in an analogous manner to grace.[27]

Second, in the beatific vision, God is present immediately to the intellect since no created image of God is capable of giving us knowledge of the divine essence in itself. Hence, in the beatific vision the very being of God may in some sense be said to inform the human intellect. Natural human knowledge attains analogous knowledge of God as the uncreated efficient cause of created being. To know God by way of formal causality, i.e. through the immediate presence of God himself in the human intellect, exceeds all the needs and exigencies of human nature and is an utterly supernatural act.[28]

But to try to conceive of the beatific vision in terms of formal causality poses serious speculative difficulties both from the part of God and from the part of man. In strict scholastic terminology, God cannot really be said to inform the human intellect. Strictly speaking, every formal cause is limited by that which it informs. The soul, for example, informs the body and is simultaneously individualized by it. How then can the infinite God be said to inform the human intellect without somehow being limited by the intellect which he informs?[29]

Here we must beware of a false rationalism. The reality of grace escapes the confines of strict Aristotelian categories. We must adapt the categories to the reality, not the reality to the categories. Since we know that God can never be limited by any created thing, we must construct a new category to express the peculiar relationship of God to his creature whereby he "informs" the intellect without being thereby limited. This category has the name, "quasi-formal causality." The addition of the prefix "quasi" is intended to exclude the idea that God is in any way limited in his being by this new relationship with creatures.[30]

But there are serious problems on the side of the human intellect also. The beatific vision exceeds the natural capacities of the human soul. In order to expand those capacities to receive the intelligible being of God, Catholic theology concludes to the presence in the glorified intellect of a supernatural disposition which prepares it to receive the quasi-formal causality of the intelligible being of God. This supernatural disposition is called the light of glory. It exercises formal causality on the intellect while at the same time demanding the quasi-formal presence of God in the intellect. The intellect, therefore, disposed by the light of glory, serves as a quasi-material cause of the immediate presence of God. But there is also a certain reciprocity here inasmuch as the light of glory itself depends on the divine presence for its being.[31]

We are now in a position to reflect a bit more closely on the relation of created and uncreated grace. We have said that grace is the germinal presence in the soul of the beatific vision. Precisely what this statement means should be much clearer now. Uncreated grace corresponds to the immediate presence of God in the glorified intellect. It is not produced efficiently by created grace any more than the beatific vision is the product of the efficient causality of the light of glory. There is rather a proportionality between the relation of the beatific vision with the light of glory and that of uncreated with created grace. Uncreated grace is that initial, quasi-formal imparting of God to the soul which is the ontological presupposition of face-to-face vision. Created grace, like the light of glory, is the ultimate disposition of the soul to receive this initial presence of God. Like the light of glory it is a formal determination of the soul which in turn demands the quasi-formal presence of God in that soul. The soul disposed by created grace is related to this presence as a quasi-material cause, while the created grace in turn owes its whole being to the actual presence of uncreated grace in the soul. Only in this sense can the presence of created grace imply the justification of man.[32]

The reader has perhaps been wondering precisely where this excursion into scholastic thought has been leading us. For one thing it has led us to a realization of the limitations of scholastic terminology when used to express the transcendent reality of grace.[33] But it has also led us to uncreated grace, the quasi-formal presence of God in the soul, as the heart and center of the mystery of grace. For if God is present in the soul as a quasi-formal cause, then the soul enters into a special personal relationship with each of the divine persons. The immediate quasi-formal presence of the triune God in the soul means that God communicates himself to each human soul in a trinitarian manner. Just as in the beatific vision the three divine persons are grasped in their own proper reality and hence exercise a quasi-formal causality upon the soul, each person according to his own personal reality, so in an analogous fashion the soul which possesses uncreated grace enters into an intimate personal relation with each of the divine persons according to the peculiar personal reality of each of them.[34]

The Father gives himself to the soul as the Father. That is, while remaining in himself he imparts himself to the soul in the gift of his Son. And Son and Father together, in their mutual and loving affirmation of one another, give themselves to the soul in the Holy Spirit of love.[35]

The Gratuity of Grace

It should be clear by now that Rahner is far from denying the supernatural nature of grace. But is he not in some sense denying its gratuity? If God creates man with a view to the supernatural order, is not God in some sense bound to raise man to that order?[36]

In the whole problem of nature and grace, much depends upon the meaning of the term "nature." The theologians of the nineteenth century assumed that human experience is always of pure nature. It did not occur to them that there might be a distinction between the experience of grace and the experience of grace *as grace*. When on the basis of human experience we define man as a rational animal, we have no way of judging whether man would be exactly as he is were he not destined for a supernatural goal. Is it not reasonable to suppose that if God in point of fact created man with the ultimate intention of elevating him to the supernatural order, he would have gone about his creative activity somewhat differently than if he had no such intention? Even when we attempt to define "pure nature," are we not implicitly presupposing that the supernatural order actually exists?[37]

The error of the *"théologie nouvelle"* was to suppose that the gratuity of grace is greater than the gratuity of creation but is essentially the *same kind* of gratuity. This is false.[38]

On the other hand, the utter gratuity of grace is not so easily the correlative of "pure nature" as nineteenth-century theology presupposed. Brute beasts are utterly incapable of grace. They have been so constituted in their nature by God as to be utterly incapable of elevation to the supernatural order. When God made them he could have had no intention of giving them a supernatural end. But created persons, because they must give and receive gratuitous love, are in some sense capable of elevation to the supernatural order.[39]

Here, however, we must be very cautious in our conclusions. From the mere fact that God has created a nature capable of such an elevation we can deduce very little concerning the concrete relation of nature and grace. For if God wills a supernatural and unmerited end for a given nature, and if God so wills this end that the created nature in question shall have a positive and unconditioned disposition to this supernatural end, then it follows only that God also actually gives the nature in question this disposition. We cannot conclude from the mere fact of creation with an ultimate view to grace that this disposition belongs to the nature as such.[40]

How, then, are we to conceive of the relation of nature and grace? Rahner's solution is basically a simple one. God desired to communicate himself to his creature in love. This is why he created man. And because God wished to communicate himself to man he created man in such a way that man could ultimately partake of this divine love. But he also created man in such a way that man could participate in the divine self-communication only as the reality it is, an eternally astonishing and gratuitous gift, gratuitous not only because man is sinful, but gratuitous still, even when man through love abandons his sinfulness.[41]

Let us consider in greater detail what this means. Since self-communication in love is the motive of divine creation, man must be truly able to receive this love. He must, therefore, possess a real, permanent "potency" for it. Even the damned have this "potency"; it belongs to the central and enduring existential makeup of man as he actually exists.[42]

But because this self-gift of God to man is one of purest love, man must be able to receive it as a gift that is truly free, that is, as a gift which utterly surpasses the needs and capacities of human nature. Otherwise, man as a free person could always reject the divine gift and thus violate his own nature, but he could never regard divine grace as the gratuitous manifestation of divine love.[43]

We must conclude, then, that there is a real difference between human nature and the capacity to receive supernatural love. But we must be careful to define human nature correctly and within the particular context in which we are speaking. In theology, "human nature" is a negative concept. It is that which is left in man as we know him once the supernatural is taken away. In other words, for the theologian "nature" means "man minus the supernatural," what is left of him when his supernatural makeup is thought of as lacking.[44]

The theologian, then, finishes with a concept of nature which cannot be defined with philosophical precision. We experience nature as it is, but we have no way of determining what it would have been if the order of grace had never existed. One should be very wary of identifying the negative concept of nature found in theology with the philosophical concept of human nature as a rational animal. Strictly speaking the two concepts are not the same. Natural and supernatural are distinct in man, but they are not chemically separable by human analysis.[45]

The Supernatural Existential

Scholastic theology speaks of the capacity of human nature to be raised to the supernatural as an obediential potency. This teaching should be interpreted correctly. There is no need to read into it the extrinsicism of nineteenth-century theology, which interpreted obediential potency as meaning the absence of contradiction between nature and grace. The obediential potency means rather that nature is open to a supernatural existential. This openness is more than an absence of contradiction. It is the transcendental condition of the possibility of a truly supernatural life, which, however, is meaningful in its turn only if it is given as a gratuitous grace.[46]

The theologian must ultimately reconcile himself to the fact that grace can never be fully explained in terms of our philosophical and ontological categories. Since this is so, it is imperative that he rethink divine revelation concerning grace in the more meaningful terms of love, nearness, and intimacy rather than in terms of strict Aristotelian causality.[47]

Finally, if in fact we live in a concrete order of grace and therefore in a supernatural existential, can we say in any true sense that man experiences himself as directed to the immediate possession of God? This statement as it stands need not be false. It becomes so only when we regard it as expressing the essential desire of pure nature as such for the beatific vision or when we wish thereby to deny that pure nature could exist even though it does not. Much of what we experience and call nature may in fact be the result of grace.

This is one reason why medieval speculation was not too much concerned with elaborating the idea of a purely natural beatitude. Not only is man, in the present order of grace, not destined for purely natural beatitude, but any conceptualization of purely natural beatitude can only be the formalized abstract expression of what theological teleology recognizes as the supernatural end of man.[48]

Grace transforms our conscious existence just as it transforms our being. The extrinsicism of the nineteenth century was, as we have said, derived from the Thomistic doctrine that the formal object of a supernatural act cannot be attained as such by any purely natural act. This teaching of St. Thomas is true if it is understood properly. The key lies in understanding the meaning of a formal object. The formal object of any conscious act is not a particular object of knowledge, nor is it the abstract composite of a group of individual objects of knowledge. It is rather an *a priori* limit or horizon which accompanies knowledge and within which individual objects of knowledge are grasped. It is, in scholastic imagery, the light under which and in which all particular objects of knowledge are grasped.[49]

Once we have understood this, we can recognize as illegitimate the conclusions of nineteenth-century theology that grace has no repercussions upon human experience. For the formal object of the spiritual powers of man is being as such. By his intellect and will man is open to the infinite, divine reality. By grace he is gratuitously ordered to the face-to-face vision of the same reality. In either case, "formal object" means, not a particular object of knowledge nor a composite of particular objects, but the transcendent limit by and within which particular objects are grasped. It is scarcely possible that man by posterior reflection could clearly distinguish in his experience between the natural and supernatural manners in which he is open to the divine reality, even though they should be both present in consciousness. Consciousness is transformed by the supernatural even though the supernatural cannot be grasped formally and as such.[50]

The Thomistic teaching is in fact an effort to express in metaphysical terms the scriptural doctrine that grace is a transformation of the human spirit in the Spirit of God. This gift of the divine Spirit is not only the entitative elevation of man whose existence is known by extrinsic revelation. It is also an inner life, an inner anointing, an inner consolation, an inner light which bears testimony to the inner transforming presence of God. As an interpreter of Scripture, St. Thomas must be read in the light of Scripture. How else, indeed, can we make any sense out of the Church's teaching that supernatural actual grace is an illumination and inspiration of the mind?[51]

Creation and Incarnation

With this understanding of the relation of nature and grace, there is no difficulty in saying that the creation of nature took place in Christ and with a view to the incarnation. We have seen that Christ is the self-expression of the Word of God in time, that he is the unique mediator and the definitive promise of grace to all men. In him the eternal alliance of love between God and men which ultimately motivated the creative act is definitively consummated. Still, the gratuitous communication of divine life in Christ remains different from the gratuitous constitution of nature in the creative act, precisely because it was necessary to constitute man in his nature in such a way that he could recognize the incarnation as God's supreme and gratuitous act of love. And this was possible only because the incarnation utterly transcends the exigencies of pure nature as such. But since nature is not simply the opposite of grace but the necessary presupposition for the gracious and gratuitous imparting of divine love, we can in the concrete salvific order speak of the state, prolongation, and perfection of nature as grace, but only insofar as all is contained in the divine, gratuitous, absolute, and unchangeable will to become incarnate.[52]

NOTES

1. S, V, 183 ff.
2. *Ibid.*, 183–184.
3. *Ibid.*, 187–188.
4. *Ibid.*, 189–190.
5. *Ibid.*, 190–191.
6. *Ibid.*, 191.
7. *Ibid.*, 194–195.
8. *Ibid.*, 196.
9. S, V, 197–198; TT, 26–28.
10. S, V, 199–200.
11. S, I, 186; S, V, 201.
12. S, V, 201.
13. *Ibid.*, 202–206.
14. *Ibid.*, 208–209.
15. *Ibid.*, 209.
16. *Ibid.*, 210–211.
17. *Ibid.*, 210–212.
18. S, I, 204–205, 323.
19. S, IV, 210–212.
20. S, I, 324–326; IV, 212–213.
21. S, IV, 210–212; I, 326.
22. S, IV, 214–215.
23. *Ibid.*, 216–219.
24. *Ibid.*, 219.
25. S, I, 352–353.
26. *Ibid.*, 251, 253.
27. *Ibid.*, 254.
28. *Ibid.*, 354–356.
29. *Ibid.*, 356–358.
30. *Ibid.*, 358–359.
31. *Ibid.*, 360–361.
32. *Ibid.*, 361–363.
33. *Ibid.*, 343.
34. *Ibid.*, 348.
35. S, IV, 124–127, 221.
36. S, I, 329.
37. S, I, 324–328; IV, 140–141.
38. S, I, 330–331, 333.
39. S, I, 331; IV, 213.
40. S, I, 331–332, 334–335.
41. *Ibid.*, 336–337.
42. *Ibid.*, 338–339.
43. *Ibid.*, 339–340.
44. *Ibid.*, 340.
45. *Ibid.*, 341.
46. S, I, 342–343; IV, 142–143.
47. S, I, 343.
48. S, IV, 232–234.
49. *Ibid.*, 224–226.
50. *Ibid.*, 227–228.
51. *Ibid.*, 227.
52. S, III, 266–271; IV, 142–143.

SUGGESTED READINGS

"Concerning the Relationship between Nature and Grace," *Theological Investigations*, Cornelius Ernst, O.P. (tr.), (Baltimore: Helicon Press, 1961), Vol. I, pp. 297–318.

"Some Implications of the Scholastic Concept of Uncreated Grace," *Theological Investigations*, Cornelius Ernst, O.P. (tr.), (Baltimore: Helicon Press, 1961), Vol. I, pp. 319–346.

"Nature and Grace," *Nature and Grace*, Dinah Wharton (tr.), (New York: Sheed and Ward, 1964), pp. 114–143.

IV. Salvation History

We have said that the incarnation is the central, culminating event of human history. In the incarnate Christ, the divine offer of grace and salvation is irrevocably present as a loving appeal to the hearts of all men of all times. But if our salvation has been accomplished in and through a series of historical events— Christ's life, death, and resurrection—and if these events are themselves the culmination of a long period of preparation, then the question necessarily arises: how concretely do these salvific events transform the rest of world history? What relation do they have, for instance, to the millions of non-Christians who have lived and are still living without knowledge of Christ? Or again, what is the relation between a Christian view of history and the technological utopias promised by contemporary materialistic ideologies? These questions are all related to one another, and in the present chapter we shall attempt to summarize Rahner's answers to them. In so doing, we shall prolong and in some sense complete the reflections of the three previous chapters.

The Meaning of Salvation History

Salvation history takes place within world history. This is so even though perfect salvation transcends the confines of this world. For history is by definition the ever unfulfilled progress of the human race toward its final perfection. Hence, complete salvation, or mankind's achievement of perfect fulfillment in grace and glory, must necessarily lie outside the historical process itself.[1]

Still, the salvation of mankind is being accomplished here and now within the events of modern history. It takes place in the progressive, secret, and loving self-communication of God to men in grace. The events which make up salvation history are, then, in their fullness interior events—the secret, ever renewed faith, hope, and love of God's people. Their inner aspirations are not just the acts of so many isolated individuals but constitute an historical and salvific pattern. Moreover, since salvation claims the whole of man, and with him all of the different possible objects of human freedom, the acceptance and rejection of salvation is taking place at every level of human endeavor.[2]

But the hiddenness of salvation history within human history does not mean that salvation history is not an objective reality or that it exists only subjectively for individual human consciousness. What it does mean is that profane history, like man himself, remains ambiguous in the face of salvation. Profane history is always capable of being interpreted as the history either of salvation or of perdition.[3]

How, then, are we to understand the salvific meaning of history? We know that the ultimate and complete revelation of history's salvific meaning will not take place until what we call the final judgment. And significantly enough, this revelation will put an end to all history. Until that definitive revelation, our only insight into the salvific process must come from God's prophets who interpret the divine intention in history and from the miracles and signs which summon and support belief in the salvific life, death, and resurrection of Jesus Christ.[4]

Certain conclusions are already clear from these reflections. We can conclude, for instance, that the events of salvation history differ in several notable respects from profane history. Unlike profane history, salvation history is never open to ambiguous interpretation. In and through Christ, salvation has been definitively accomplished. On the other hand, because salvation is also being accomplished within the souls of men, neither is it subject to strict historical verification. We know from experience that we can never verify reflexively all the motives of our own actions, not to mention the religious motives of other men. The clear and certain manifestation of one's personal acceptance of grace will come for each individual in the face-to-face vision of God, which like the final judgment is trans-historical. We do not, then, grasp the history of salvation itself by purely empirical verification, but only in faith and hope.[5]

Moreover, though different from world history, salvation history is nevertheless materially coextensive with it. God's salvific will embraces all men of all times: all men have the duty, and hence also the possibility, of saving their souls. No man is excluded from God's offer of grace. This is an important point, and we shall return to it later on.[6]

Now, grace, as we have seen, alters the structure of human consciousness in the sense that the formal object of man's spiritual powers, like the spiritual limit or horizon in which he experiences individual objects, is illuminated by the supernatural light of faith. This alteration of human consciousness in the free acceptance of grace is fundamentally what we mean by revelation. Revelation is, then, much more than the enunciation of this or that religious truth. In a fuller sense, it is the enlightenment of the soul by grace. If this be true, then salvation history, or God's self-revelation to men in time, is much more than the history of the Old and New Testaments. Indeed, a comparative study of the Old Testament and other pre-Christian religions might well reveal that the Old Testament is simply the model case of pre-Christian belief.[7]

How, then, are we to locate the Old and the New Testaments in the total pattern of salvation history? Although salvation history in the broad sense is coextensive with world history, salva-

tion history in the strict sense means the salvific events recorded
in the Bible. By his own word, God has condescended to interpret and clarify for man the salvific meaning of a specific portion
of history and by this act has converted it specifically and officially into the recorded history of salvation.[8]

But biblical salvation history is more than the revealed word
of God translated into human words. The events of the Bible
are constituted salvation history as such only through the mediation of the recorded word. These words become as a result an
inner moment of salvation history itself, so that the verbal expression of the history of salvation, the Bible, itself has a history.[9]

Salvation history in the strict sense of the salvific events related
and interpreted in Sacred Scripture clarifies profane history. It
reveals the salvific meaning at the heart of human events. It
demythologizes the natural world by showing it to be the mere
creature of God and not the divine corporeity of pagan animism.
It shows that world history is different from salvation history
and that man in his ambiguity can place himself outside the
inner dynamism of salvation history. Moreover, by that very fact,
it reveals the salvific mission of God's people who by their activity are destined to transform profane history and to become the
instruments of universal salvation.[10]

The written history of salvation also reveals profane history as
antagonistic and obscure. Salvation history is sceptical of world
history because salvation is not simply the fruit of human endeavor. Salvation is from God alone, and man must achieve it
in the dark light of faith, which reveals the historic threads of
good and evil as inextricably tangled until the final revelation of
God at the last judgment. Until then the progress of human history is bound up inextricably with the ever increasing conflict
between the powers of light and of darkness.[11]

For the Christian, the meaning of world history is feeble indeed
when viewed in the light of salvation history. For he knows that
human history has already been conquered in Christ. He sees the

world as created by and in the divine word of the Father, who because he is eternal love and wished to express and communicate himself to others, established creation refashioned in grace.[12]

Thus it is ultimately the distinction of nature and grace which grounds the distinction between world history and salvation history. Just as material nature is the condition for the existence of finite spirit which seeks transcendence in its dynamic quest for Absolute Spirit, in the same way world history is the condition for the history of salvation which finds its center in the history of Christ, in the history of God himself.[13]

Christianity and Non-Christian Religions

This Christ-centeredness of salvation history necessarily throws new light on the problem of the historical relation of Christianity to the non-Christian religions. It shows that the religious evolution of mankind in general has been centered upon this definitive act of divine self-revelation. Let us reflect a bit on exactly what this last statement means.

Because it possesses God's definitive self-revelation in Christ, the Christian religion alone is capable of judging clearly and definitively the meaning and significance of other beliefs and philosophical systems. Non-Christian religions cannot, of course, be forced into facile formulas. Still, one can detect within them some kind of belief in a transcendent person who is lord of nature and history. (Note, we do *not* speak here of the doctrinal divisions within Christianity itself.) Outside Christian revelation there is the constant tendency to reduce the infinity of God to an infinite plurality of immanent natural forces which are personified in the pantheons of pagan cults. As a result, the divine mastery of history becomes obscured, and the cult of a multiplicity of natural forces supplants the cult of the living God.[14]

Within the total pattern of salvation history, the religion of Israel holds the unique position of being the immediate prep-

aration for the revelation of God in Christ. But we should be
wary of reading into Jewish belief elements it did not actually
contain.[15]

Jewish monotheism was not a static, metaphysical concept. Its
God was not the ultimate unifying principle of the world, like
the god of the Greek philosophers. He is rather a God who is
personally involved in human history. He freely chooses for himself a people to whom he binds himself by a covenant and who
are bound to him. Through his alliance with them he becomes
their God, they his people. From that decisive historical moment
on, there can be no other God for Israel. In comparison with
Yahweh all other gods are as nothing. To him and him alone
the people of God owe their allegiance. For the Jews, then,
monotheism meant above all the single-minded commitment of
Israel to its God.[16]

The one God reveals himself to his people through his dealings with them in history. What distinguishes the old alliance
from the new is that in the old alliance the divine commitment
and self-revelation to men is not yet definitive. It can at any point
be broken off because of the infidelity and sinfulness of God's
people.[17]

In Christ, however, God has performed the unique and definitive act of grace. In the sacred humanity of the incarnate Word,
God has forever united mankind to himself in a mutual bond of
faithful love. In Christ he has inaugurated the definitive era of
salvation, the last age of man.[18]

But if this is so, how are we to integrate non-Christian beliefs
into the total pattern of the history of salvation?

Christianity has always been conscious of being the only true
religion for all men. It cannot allow the claims of any other
religion to rival its own. Far from being a symptom of pride, this
conviction stems from the realization that religion is made by
God and not by men and that God has spoken his definitive
revelation in his own incarnate Word. The Church of Christ is,

then, the only true Church; and by that fact it calls into question the objective legitimacy of all non-Christian beliefs.[19]

On the other hand, we should not be too quick to deny all relation whatever between Christianity and non-Christian religions. For if Christianity can have a pre-history, as Scripture clearly shows, then in its pre-history Christianity has already in some sense begun. Moreover, Christ's mandate to preach the good news to all nations means that not all men enter into contact with the salvific events of Christ's death and resurrection at the same moment of time. Must not the religious development of a people prior to its contact with Christianity be in God's providence the pre-history of Christianity for that particular nation and culture? Moreover, the precise moment in time when a given culture may be said to encounter Christianity may be left open to dispute.[20]

The encounter with Christianity may not even be a serious possibility for the majority of individuals in a pagan culture until the Christian religion becomes an important factor within that culture. It is even difficult to determine at what point in the historical evolution of a given culture the absolute duty to become a Christian passes into the order of a concrete objective obligation.[21]

Of course, until this encounter takes place pagan religions remain in constant need of genuine purification, for the natural knowledge of God contained in them has necessarily degenerated under the ravages of original sin and human depravity. But we are not to suppose that prior to the advent of Christianity pagan religions are totally illegitimate and utterly lacking in grace.[22]

We can conclude to the presence of moments of grace even among the corruptions and errors in pagan religion for three reasons: (1) the universal salvific will of God, (2) the efficaciousness of the redemption wrought in Christ, and (3) the need for religion to exist in a community. Let us consider a little what this means.[23]

First of all, if, as we have already seen, God actually wills the salvation of every individual man, this means that all men, even non-Christians, must actually be in a position to accept or refuse the redemptive grace of God. Second, we should be slow to suppose that God's grace is ineffective in the case of the majority of men, in spite of apparent human resistance to revelation. To do so would be to assert that the salvific death of Christ has in fact had little effect on the history of the world, that Christ has brought only the possibility of salvation and not, as Scripture testifies, salvation itself.[24]

Now, if individual men must have the opportunity to participate in a genuine salvific relation with God during their lives and in all the possible situations of human history, it seems unthinkable that they should do so independently of the religious milieu in which they live. Religion implies of its very nature a community of believers in which and through which man must work out his salvation. If man must seek God, then he must in the concrete seek him in the religious environment in which he finds himself. This does not mean that the pagan has no obligation to seek a genuine reform and purification of his faith; but it does mean that in a society in which Christianity has not yet become a significant factor, the prevalent religion may serve as the legitimate and concrete form of God's law for an individual pagan.[25]

We can perhaps clarify the function of non-Christian religion by a brief comparison with the religion of the Old Testament. For not even the Old Testament could make the claim of being utterly free from errors and abuses. Even more, these errors and abuses, especially on the part of the priests and leaders of the people, were such as to threaten the very essence and survival of the Jewish religion itself. Although the function of the prophets in such a situation was to denounce abuse and error and to recall Israel to the true worship of Yahweh, there was at the time no sure way to distinguish true and false prophets. There was not even a fixed canon to determine which religious books were divinely inspired. Nor did Israel ever fully free its religious belief from nationalistic aspirations.

Yet despite the existence of error in the time of the Old Testament, and in spite of the lack of a sure norm at that time for the individual to decide the difference between true and false religion, grace was certainly present within the religion of Israel.[26]

If we apply these reflections to the situation of other, even contemporary, non-Christians, we can better understand the temporary legitimacy of these religions. It is true that whenever error belongs to the very essence of a religion, it is to that extent a false religion. But even so, the matter is not as simple as that; for we must still ask to what extent the individual adherents of any given religion themselves admit such errors or make them the focal point of their belief. In any case, an institutional, non-Christian religion can in a concrete circumstance serve as a positive means for the correct relationship of a man to God and can as such be integrated into the history of salvation.[27]

Such religions, to the extent that they serve in God's salvific providence as genuine vehicles of grace, are not simply non-Christian but in a very positive sense pre-Christian. The gospel should not come as something completely new to the devout members of such religions. The good news is in reality nothing more than the fulfillment and explicitation of their actual religious experience. For since Christ's salvation is in fact the only salvation, everyone who believes in him with even implicit faith is in a real sense an anonymous Christian. His conversion is his achievement of a reflexive awareness with and in the Church of the full meaning of his religious belief.[28]

This in no way implies that the gospel need no longer be preached to non-Christians. Both the incarnational character of the redemption and the communitarian structure of grace make the spread of the gospel a serious obligation for all Christians. Moreover, salvation for an anonymous Christian remains much more hazardous than salvation in the Church. Nor do we wish to imply that the gospel cannot or should not be announced to non-believers in the full sense of the term.[29]

We are merely suggesting that it is possible to rethink the historical and salvific relation of the Church to non-Christian believers. The Church is not a closed community of the saved but the vanguard, the historical and communal manifestation, of what the anonymous Christian already possesses implicitly.[30]

We have good reason to believe that religious pluralism will always be with us. Scripture teaches that the opposition to Christ will continue till the end of time. But if God is active even where the Church is not, then the Church has already overcome its opposition. This should give us cause, not for a slackened zeal in the spreading of the gospel, but for tolerance, modesty, and persistence in our dealings with non-Christian religions.[31]

Christianity and Modern Utopias

But the history of salvation is not only the past and the present. It is also the future, and this in a very special sense. As the definitive presence of eschatological grace in the world, Christianity looks to the future as that to which the present is decisively orientated. Indeed, in Christ the future has already begun.[32]

For this reason the Church can never be indifferent to human plans and utopian dreams for the future. We live in an age in which human history has expanded from national to planetary dimensions. No nation can go its way without involving the fate of the rest of the world. Moreover, technology has given man unheard-of powers to shape his own material destiny and environment. Man has even begun to make himself into an object

of technical manipulation. The result of this technological development has been the growing tendency of modern men to
look upon themselves as a new reality. As the eschatological
presence of grace in the world, the Church cannot be indifferent
to these new tendencies and prospects for the future opening
before us today.[33]

One would, however, be wrong to suppose that the Church as
such offers concrete programs or concise formulas for this-
worldly development of man. The Church is not a political
party. On the other hand, each Christian has received from the
Church general principles of action, derived from the natural
law and from revelation, which he must convert into concrete
moral imperatives both in his present living and in his plans
for the future. All our programs for the future must, then, be
positively and concretely reconciled both with Christian principles and with the essence of man implied in those principles.
All too often Catholics fail in this regard and retreat into negative
and defensive criticism of modern technological utopias instead
of sharing in every man's legitimate pride in our ability to shape
our own futures.[34]

Christianity also corrects the errors implicit in modern utopias.
It instills in man a healthy realism with regard to the future.
The present structure of reality limits any possibility of future
development. These structures possess an inner dynamism of
their own and are not just static forms of space and time; and
because all human activity must take place in space and time,
it automatically falls under their limitations.[35]

Christianity reminds man that the ultimate limit of human
activity is death and that even though man can prolong his life,
he cannot do so indefinitely. Far from benefiting man, such a
prolongation would actually condemn him to an endless state
of imperfection, to a frustrated existence among things which
can never fully satisfy him. Human progress is aways subject
to stagnation. Our plans for the future never fully satisfy our

expectations. Our disillusionment is inevitable; and if it is not now, yet it will come ultimately in death. For the Christian, then, man's longing for perfect satisfaction in this life is nothing less than an expression of his gratuitous orientation by God to ultimate glory.[36]

Christianity also possesses a time-concept unknown in human utopias. For the Christian, the future has in a very real sense already begun to exist in the present. We shall have more to say on this subject when we treat of Christian eschatology.[37]

Moreover, unlike those who profess their belief in modern utopias, the Christian can never overlook the value of each human person; nor can he in the manner of the communists countenance the ruthless violation of human dignity now for the achievement of some distant earthly paradise. He knows and must insist that a better future for the generations to come can only be built on the present respect for man's spiritual reality and for his ultimate supernatural destiny.[38]

Finally, only Christianity truly offers man a new future. Modern utopias promise a new future to the "new man" of the modern era. But the future they promise is not essentially different from that of the old man of past eras. All they really offer is material prosperity shared on a broader basis.[39]

Christianity goes much further. It recognizes the fact of human transcendence, of man's inner, insatiable need for the absolute. It asserts triumphantly that the divine absolute is already present within us through the grace that is ours in the incarnation of the eternal Word of God. Modern utopias can only replace one limited thing with another. In Christianity the Infinite has itself erupted into space and time by taking to himself a given segment of human history. In the risen Christ every believer sees the actual beginning of a new heaven and a new earth.[40]

Yet, for that very reason Christians should avoid any trace of false conservatism and negativity in their attitude toward modern technological progress. Christianity is more than the proclamation of eternal principles. The individual Christian must look upon his share in the construction of a Christian society as a pale anticipation of the new heaven and earth promised by God's grace. For he knows that the human aspiration for earthly utopias will find its true fulfillment in the ultimate triumph of the one and universal Church.[41]

The Meaning of Eschatological Statements

But it is not enough to say that the Church looks forward to a new heaven and a new earth. Religious statements about the end of the world are in fact shrouded in obscurity and complicated symbolism, as any reader of the Book of the Apocalypse knows. The New Testament is filled with such symbolic imagery: the last trumpet; the appearance of the Son of Man like lightning, riding upon the clouds of heaven; the joyful throng of the saints chanting around the throne of the Lamb; etc. Sensitive as he is to the problems of demythologization, Rahner feels that we must be careful to interpret the statements of the Church and of Scripture concerning the end of time with special carefulness. Much time has elapsed since the biblical descriptions of the "day of the Lord" were written, and for a twentieth-century reader there is considerable danger of confusion and misinterpretation.[42]

But before we proceed any further, there are perhaps a few points in need of clarification. Since Christianity of its very nature looks forward to the end of time, prophecy is an integral part of the Christian message. The divine omniscience is not just a metaphysical statement. It is also a matter of Christian belief. We believe, then, that God foresees future events. So there is nothing that could prevent God from imparting to man a knowledge of future events which as future exceed the limits of human discernment. What follows, then, is in no way intended to call into question the fact that the prediction of free future events is a divine prerogative and can be used as a proof of divine intervention in human affairs.[43]

On the other hand, we would be mistaken to interpret the eschatological statements in Scripture about the end of time as the eyewitness description of an event in all of its details before it actually takes place. Such an interpretation of these eschatological statements would in fact deprive them of their real meaning, for it would transform eschatological events into purely future events without any actual reference to, or meaning for, the present.[44]

God has not revealed in Scripture exactly what the day of the Last Judgment will be like in all of its details. We do not know when it will take place. We do not even have a clear idea of what man's ultimate perfection will be. Far from being the simple disclosure of a group of facts concerning a future event, the revelation of the last judgment is the proclamation of a mystery.[45]

Moreover, any eschatological statement we find in Scripture is necessarily conditioned by the historical character and situation of the man who wrote it. This means that the future is present differently in a man's eschatological thoughts according to his concrete place in history. On the other hand, since salvation is not just a matter of our present relation to God, but includes the ultimate total fulfillment of man, the content of eschatological statements cannot be deprived of all reference to the future. The effort of some demythologizers to reduce the content of eschatological statements exclusively to some present actuality is in fact the mythologization of such statements, since it deprives man's dealings with God of their essentially historical character.[46]

Every eschatological statement looks forward to a salvific event which is already germinally but really present. This anticipatory presence of the future in the present moment is, then, necessary for a proper understanding of the present itself. Although the future reality which is within the present moment need not be fully comprehended by one who speaks eschatologically, it must express the definitive advent of salvation clearly enough to leave man free to react one way or another to it.[47]

In interpreting eschatological statements, then, one should presume at the start that the author knows only as much about the future as can be gathered from its actual germinal presence within his own present moment. If this is so, then the progress of eschatological revelation is historically identical with the gradual revelation of salvation itself. Only such an interpretation of eschatological statements can explain in what sense these statements actually reveal the future or why they draw their imagery from past events rather than anticipate future modes of thought.[48]

If this interpretation of the eschatological statements we find in Scripture is true, then we can draw some further conclusions concerning them. First of all, we can conclude that eschatological statements are not concerned with the salvation or damnation of individual men as such. It is of the essence of an eschatological statement that it leave human liberty intact before the mystery of salvation in Christ.[49]

Second, because eschatological statements project into the future the ultimate perfection of the whole man, body and soul, they must express both his spiritual and corporeal perfection without either confounding the two or unduly separating them.[50]

Third, it is meaningless to attempt to construct an opposition between a close and a distant parousia. This might be meaningful were eschatological statements the mere revelation of future facts before they actually take place. But an eschatological reality is of its nature both near and far: it is near because it is present within the present moment, it is far because it looks into a future which is necessarily obscure.[51]

Finally, every eschatological event is of its nature Christological. Only in Christ is grace definitively and eschatologically

present. It is from his awareness of his own salvific reality that
we have derived certain basic principles concerning the salvific
meaning of history, its orientation to a definitive end, its opposition to grace, its enduring ambiguity, the ultimate triumph
of grace, etc.[52]

But in seeking the meaning of concrete eschatological statements, we must proceed with caution. We should not be over-
hasty to separate the reality expressed from the image in which
it is expressed. By a careful comparison of several eschatological
statements, we can at best arrive at an analogous content which
can then be translated into Christological or anthropological
terms. But this new formulation will always remain dependent
for its full interpretation upon the imagery from which it is
derived.[53]

In this context Rahner suggests that all human knowledge is
bi-polar. At one pole is the abstract, the conceptual, the metaphysical; at the other is the concrete, the graphic, the imaginative. The boundary between the thing signified and its graphic
representation is not always easy to determine. This is particularly true when we speak (as we must) of things concerning
which we have no direct knowledge, such as human pre-history
and eschatology. The imaginative biblical descriptions of the
origins of man and of the end of the world place us in contact
with realities of which we would otherwise have no knowledge
whatever. It is for us under the guidance of the Church's *magisterium* to attempt to elaborate conceptually precisely what these
images mean.[54]

The Problem of Monogenism

A case in point is the problem whether all men are actually
descended from a single human ancestor, as the account in
Genesis would lead us to believe. The doctrine of monogenism
claims that Adam was a single individual, while the theory of

polygenism maintains that Adam was in fact a group of individuals and not a single man. Although the *magisterium* does not forbid further scientific investigation into the matter, Catholics are not free to hold a polygenistic hypothesis on the basis of the evidence to date available, since in our present state of knowledge polygenism can be reconciled with the sources of revelation only with considerable difficulty. In his defense of monogenism, Rahner argues that the universality of redemption in some sense presupposes a physical unity of descent from a single ancestor so that all men can become involved in one and the same history of salvation. He also argues that since sexual union is the only concrete means of bringing an individual into being within the human species, by creating a being with such a power, God manifests his concrete intention to bring all other men into existence only by this means. Hence he regards the creation of several distinct Adams as contrary to the clear intention of God as manifested in human nature itself. This is not the place to elaborate these arguments. What is important here is that whether he is arguing from a *de facto* soteriological or anthropological basis, Rahner is in fact projecting back into history a concept of human origins based on man's concrete salvific situation. Such a mode of argumentation is justified by the basic unity of salvation history, and something analogous to it takes place in the scriptural projection of man's ulitimate salvation on the basis of the redemption already his in Christ.[55]

The Meaning of Bodily Resurrection

We can understand, then, why statements of faith concerning the resurrection of the body necessarily contain a certain amount of obscurity. In treating the doctrine of the resurrection of the body, Rahner is particularly concerned with some contemporary reinterpretations of the scriptural accounts of the Last Judgment. It is one thing, he insists, to recognize the scriptural images surrounding the resurrection of the body—the fire, the falling stars, the angelic trumpet—as meaningful images, and quite another simply to attempt to eliminate the realities of which they speak from Christian belief.[56]

What, then, do we mean when we say in the Creed that we look forward to the resurrection of the body? We have already seen in a previous chapter that in death man, by passing from time to eternity, achieves a definitive relationship with God. The eternity upon which he enters at death is not just an extension of time. It is a new way of existing and living.[57]

The teaching of revelation concerning the afterlife seeks to explicitate and perfect the spontaneous and universal belief of men in a life after the grave. At the moment of death, man achieves total self-possession in a moral decision which transcends time and space; but only revelation teaches us the full dimensions of this transcendence.[58]

The afterlife means neither the flight from the material universe nor a half-life of darkness and shadows. For the Christian, the afterlife means ultimately the perfection of the whole of man, soul and body.[59]

As we have already seen in our discussion of the redemptive death, since man is a complex being and subject to original sin, this perfection does not come to be all at once at the moment of death. In death only the human spirit achieves the vision of God which constitutes the essential happiness of man. But the glorified soul retains an essential relation to the world, in such a way that even while enjoying the vision of God, it is ultimately bound up with the fate of the material world.[60]

That world is wholly temporal. It does not last, as the Greeks thought, for an infinity of time. Instead it has a beginning, a middle, and—an end. This end is nothing else than the full participation in the perfection of glorified spirit. The beginning of human history in Adam is, then, the beginning of the development of the world in freedom toward its complete realization in a state of definitive and total perfection.[61]

Because spirit is part of the world and because the world is destined to share in the ultimate perfection of spirit, the history of spiritual persons constitutes a real unity. This unified history, as we have seen, found its culmination in the history of God made man. The goal of human history is, then, the salvation realized in the risen Christ. His final coming transcends the limitations of the world as we know it. It is an event of a world transformed, perfected, and fulfilled by its share in the perfection which he already possesses. His glorification is nothing less than the revelation of the inner mystery and meaning of all history.[62]

This, then, is what Christians mean by the resurrection of the body. It is a doctrine essential to the Christian message. It consists in the belief that not only will world history reach an end when the number of those who have achieved salvation is complete, but at that moment the whole of the physical universe will be made to share in the salvation and perfection of the blessed. How this cosmic perfection will take place we do not know. We only know by faith that it will take place and that it will be the transformation and fulfillment of the world as we know it.[63]

Still, in the risen Christ we already have a concrete intimation of the glory that is to come. Through his resurrection we know that we can look forward to possessing a "spiritual body," that is, one which is endowed with true corporeity but which is at the same time the purest expression of a human spirit perfectly united with the Spirit of God. It is a body freed definitively from the limitations of time and space and from death.[64]

Hence, inasmuch as corporeity is an essential part of our ultimate glory, we also know that heaven is not just a state. It is, then, also a "place." This "place" already exists as a result of the glorification of the bodies of both Jesus and Mary. But it is not a place in the sense of place as we know it. It is a place transformed and spiritualized in the glory that is to come. To attempt to locate heaven with respect to our present order of time and space is, therefore, meaningless. The Christian can in this matter take a lesson from the modern physicist and learn to think of glorified matter in non-visual terms.[65]

Christian belief, then, offers the human longing for transcendence perfect fulfillment in the promise of total redemption. As all things, both matter and spirit, find their source in the creative Word of God, so too do they find in him their ultimate perfection. The resurrection of the body cannot be eliminated from Christian belief. Instead, conscious at once of the illumination and of the darkness of that belief, we can only look forward with hope to the day when darkness will give way to the fullness of light. We pray with St. John at the close of the Apocalypse, "Indeed I am coming soon, be it so then, come, Lord Jesus."[66]

NOTES

1. S, V, 115.
2. *Ibid.*, 116–117.
3. *Ibid.*, 117–118.
4. *Ibid.*, 117–118.
5. S, I, 100; V, 119.
6. S, V, 121–122.
7. *Ibid.*, 119–124.
8. *Ibid.*, 125.
9. *Ibid.*, 126–127.
10. *Ibid.*, 129–130.
11. *Ibid.*, 131–132.
12. *Ibid.*, 133–134.
13. *Ibid.*, 135.
14. S, I, 97–98.
15. S, V, 105–106.
16. S, I, 106–107.
17. *Ibid.*, 99.
18. *Ibid.*, 100.
19. S, V, 139.
20. *Ibid.*, 140–142.
21. *Ibid.*, 142–143.
22. *Ibid.*, 143.
23. *Ibid.*, 143–144.
24. *Ibid.*, 143–144.
25. *Ibid.*, 147–148.
26. *Ibid.*, 148–149.
27. *Ibid.*, 148, 150–152.
28. *Ibid.*, 154–155.
29. *Ibid.*, 156–157.
30. *Ibid.*, 156–157.
31. *Ibid.*, 157–158.
32. *Ibid.*, 159.
33. *Ibid.*, 159–162.
34. *Ibid.*, 163–165.
35. *Ibid.*, 165–166.
36. *Ibid.*, 166–168.
37. *Ibid.*, 168.
38. *Ibid.*, 169–171.
39. *Ibid.*, 171.
40. *Ibid.*, 171–173.

41. *Ibid.*, 175–178.
42. S, IV, 402–403; V, 174; II, 218–219.
43. S, IV, 404–407.
44. *Ibid.*, 407–408.
45. *Ibid.*, 408–410.
46. *Ibid.*, 410–411.
47. S, IV, 411–413; V, 168, 173.
48. S, IV, 414–416.
49. *Ibid.*, 420–422.
50. *Ibid.*, 423.
51. *Ibid.*
52. *Ibid.*, 425–426.
53. S, II, 218–219; IV, 426–427.
54. S, II, 216–217.
55. S, I, 311–321; II, 216; PH, 35–36.
56. S, II, 211–213, 215–216; IV, 411, 417; V, 174.
57. S, II, 219; IV, 429–430; TT, 26 ff.
58. S, IV, 430–434.
59. *Ibid.*, 435.
60. S, II, 219–220.
61. *Ibid.*, 220–222.
62. *Ibid.*, 222.
63. *Ibid.*, 222–223.
64. *Ibid.*, 223.
65. *Ibid.*, 223–224.
66. *Ibid.*, 224.

SUGGESTED READINGS

"Theos in the New Testament," *Theological Investigations*, Cornelius Ernst, O.P. (tr.), (Baltimore: Helicon, 1961), Vol. I, pp. 79–148.

"Theological Reflexions on Monogenism," *Theological Investigations*, Cornelius Ernst, O.P. (tr.), (Baltimore: Helicon, 1961), Vol. I, pp. 229–297.

"The Resurrection of the Body," *Theological Investigations*, Karl Kruger (tr.), (Baltimore: Helicon, 1963), Vol. II, pp. 203–216.

V. Scripture and Tradition

In the previous chapter, we distinguished salvation history in the broad sense from that portion of salvation history which God himself interpreted for us in the books of the Old and New Testaments. This official account of salvation history in the narrower sense differs from any other historical document in that it claims God as its author. Hence it possesses a privileged place among the historical sources of revelation. Because of this privileged place, the Bible is in a real sense the Church's book, inasmuch as the Church, which is the visible eschatological manifestation of the grace of Christ in the world, stands before men as the official interpreter of divine revelation.

Some Questions Concerning Inspiration

Implied in the preceding series of statements is a host of complex theological problems. What, for instance, does it mean to say that God is the author of the books of the Bible? The Scriptures are human documents written down and preserved by men. How, then, can we call God their author? Also, what is the relationship between the teachings of the Church and Sacred Scripture? The message of salvation proclaimed by the *magisterium* has developed with time. Is it possible to reconcile the new dogmas defined by the Church with the faith of the primitive community expressed in the Scriptures? What are the laws and limits which govern the evolution of Catholic dogma? What is the relation between Catholic dogmatic theology and Scripture?

In the present chapter we shall attempt briefly and schematically to present Rahner's answers to these difficult questions.

The basic problem in any theology of Sacred Scripture is to explain how God and man can both really be the author of one and the same document. For if, as faith teaches, God is in a very real sense the author of Scripture, even a cursory examination of the sacred texts will most certainly reveal that they are the work of men as well. Moreover, the human writers of the sacred books appear to be anything but divine secretaries, or the passive recorders of truths dictated to them word for word from on high. They themselves often testify that they have worked hard in the production of their book in the manner of any other human author; and the books themselves clearly witness to the individual personality, interests, and cultural background of the men who wrote them.[1]

In attempting to explain how both God and man can be author of one and the same book, one must beware of facile solutions. One might be tempted to suggest, for instance, that God and man collaborate in somewhat the same fashion as human authors, God being responsible for one part of the book and man for another. But this will never do. The whole of Scripture is inspired, not just a part of it. If God were author only of a portion of Scripture, only that section could lay claim to divine inspiration.[2]

In its solution to the divine and human authorship of Scripture, Catholic theology has traditionally appealed to the notion of instrumental causality. The argument goes something like this. When I write a letter with a pencil, it is not I alone nor the pencil alone that produces the effect, but both I and the pencil together are the total cause of the letter I write. Cannot something analogous take place in the inspiration of Scripture? Cannot the human author be an instrument in God's hands in such a way that both God and the human author together constitute the total cause of the sacred book?[3]

This explanation is valid as far as it goes. Unfortunately, it does not seem to go far enough. The concept of instrumentality is abstract and can be filled with a variety of concrete meanings. There is, for instance, a great difference between a lifeless, passive instrument like a pencil, and a free, self-determining, personal instrument. Can a free person become the instrument of the divine authorship without in some sense losing his freedom and personality? The mere appeal to instrumentality does not explain why this need not be the case.[4]

Moreover, there is in fact considerable disagreement among Catholic theologians as to the precise sense in which a man is an instrument of the divine inspiration. They tend to divide into two camps. Some have likened inspiration to a conscious, quasi-"prophetical" enlightenment; others to an unconscious illumination of the mind of the sacred writer. The first opinion seems to fly in the face of the testimony of the scriptural writers themselves, who for the most part seem quite unconscious of any special celestial illumination, while the second opinion is considerably hard put to explain how an unconscious illumination is an illumination in any recognizable sense of the term.[5]

In Rahner's opinion one need not necessarily appeal to a miraculous illumination in order to verify the notion of instrumental causality in inspiration. Sufficient would be some sort of special providential influence of God upon a human writer which would not only permit but actually foster and form his human authorship of the sacred books. Later on we shall suggest more precisely how this could come about; but before we do, we would do well to reflect on the theological complexity of this problem.[6] How, for instance, can the Church possibly know whether God is actually the author of a book or not? The books of Scripture themselves make no clear claim to being written by God. Even had they done so, what possible norm could one use to determine whether such a claim was justified or not? Not all the writings of the apostles were inspired; we know, for instance, that St. Paul actually wrote letters other than those contained in the Bible, and that these other letters can make no claim to divine authorship. It is also extremely unlikely that any of the apostles left behind a list indicating those documents of the primitive Church which had God for their author and those which did not. The sacred writers themselves seem unconscious of divine inspiration, and the Church itself in its early centuries of development manifested considerable uncertainty as to the inspired nature of some of the books now included in the sacred canon.[7]

We may conclude from all of this that any explanation of the nature of inspiration must also explain how the post-apostolic Church could verify the inspired quality of any given book of Scripture without this being explicitly revealed in apostolic times. A special revelation to the post-apostolic Church after the deposit of faith had been closed with the death of the last apostle is, of course, out of the question.[8]

But the problem is still more complex. The fixation of a canon of divinely inspired books by the *magisterium* raises the further problem of the relation between the inspired books as inspired and the infallible teaching authority of the Church. For if the infallible *magisterium* can itself decide which books are truly expressions of the divine revelation and which are not, then what need has the Church for an infallible canon of Scripture? Why is not the infallible *magisterium* alone a sufficient rule of faith? Or are we to suppose that there are two infallible yet completely independent sources of divine revelation, the inspired Scriptures and the *magisterium*? An adequate theory of inspiration must have something to say to all these questions.[9]

One final difficulty is perhaps worth mentioning before we go on to Rahner's doctrine of inspiration. Among the writings of the New Testament is St. Paul's letter to Philemon. Because this letter is included in the canon of Scripture, we know that it is divinely inspired and has God as its author. But if it is true to say that God is the author of this letter, then why is it in fact false to say that God himself wrote a letter to Philemon? An adequate theory of inspiration must be so constructed as to reconcile these apparently contradictory statements.[10]

The Meaning of Inspiration

Rahner introduces his theory of inspiration with a few clarifications. First of all he calls attention to the fact that it is God who founds the Church. He wills the Church absolutely and in such a way that its historical formation follows a formal divine predefinition. Since the Church is man's free response under grace to the divine offer of salvation in Christ, this divine predefinition includes the free acts of men under grace.[11]

Moreover, since Christ is himself the ultimate and irrevocable offer of grace in time, the Church in distinction to the synagogue is an eschatological reality, a manifestation of the definitive presence of grace in the world. Since, then, the Church is caused and formed by an absolute, definitive, and altogether gratuitous intervention of God into human affairs, then God must be said to be author of the Church in a very special sense quite distinct from that in which he is said to be the author of nature.[12]

Secondly, in the historical development of the Church according to divine predefinition, the primitive Church possesses a special constitutive function which is peculiar to it and distinguishes it from the Church of post-apostolic times. The belief of the primitive community serves as a rule of faith for all subsequent generations of Christians. Since, then, in founding the primitive Church, God is in fact establishing a binding norm of

belief for all times, the act by which he positively establishes
such a norm differs qualitatively from his negative conservation
of the post-apostolic Church in fidelity to that norm.[13]

We may conclude, then, not only that God is the author of
the Church as a whole, but that he is the special author of the
primitive Church as well.[14]

Now, the formation of the primitive Christian community was
not completed on Pentecost. It lasted, in the traditional phrase,
"until the death of the last apostle." Hence the problem becomes
a bit more complex.[15]

Not everything about the primitive Church is normative for
future generations. Many practices of the first Christians (like
the agape) have fallen into disuse. If, then, the primitive community was to be the definitive tradition for all future generations of Christians, it had to be able to offer those future
Christians a concrete norm by which they could distinguish the
essential from the non-essential elements in primitive Christian
belief. In other words, because it is the normative tradition, the
primitive Church must possess the power of self-definition, that
is, of forming a definitive canon of belief which is both apparent
to and binding on future generations. Such a canon the teaching
authority of the post-apostolic Church must be able to apply but
never to replace.[16]

An essential part of the canon of belief established by the
apostolic Church is the book of Sacred Scripture. The Bible,
especially the New Testament, is the verbal crystallization of
the religious faith of the first Christian community; and as such
it is normative for the belief of all future Christians.[17]

We are now in a position to understand what Rahner means
when he says that Scripture is inspired. God wills the Church
with a will that is absolute, formally predefined, historical, and
eschatological. He wills the primitive community and all its
essentially constitutive elements as normative for all subsequent

belief in the Church. He is by that fact author both of the Church as a whole and in a special manner of the primitive apostolic community. Therefore, inasmuch as the canon of Sacred Scripture constitutes one of the essential, normative elements of the apostolic Church, God is also truly the author of the sacred books. And because these books truly have God as their author, they are therefore truly inspired. The inspiration of Scripture, then, is nothing more than the divine authorship of the Church itself insofar as the belief of that Church is formally constituted and nourished by the canon of the sacred books.[18]

Inspiration and the Old Testament

Rahner's theory is not without difficulties, as he himself is quick to acknowledge. One might question, for instance, whether inspiration as he defines it is applicable to the books of the Old Testament as well. How can the divine authorship of the Church explain the inspiration of a book which was written before the Church ever existed? In his answer to this objection, Rahner appeals to the concept of canonicity and its relationship to inspiration. He argues that although the two concepts are not identical, they are not completely unrelated either. A book is inspired when it has God as its author; it is canonical when its inspiration has been officially acknowledged by the Church. On the other hand, until the Church infallibly established the canon of inspired books, there was no absolutely sure way of telling which were the books that could actually lay claim to the divine authorship. The synagogue, because it was not the definitive manifestation of eschatological grace, simply lacked the necessary infallibility to establish such a canon. The canon of Old Testament books could not and did not receive its definitive form until it was confirmed by the Church of the New Testament. Hence, Rahner concludes, it is in the definitive enlightenment of the New Testament that the Old Testament writings receive in God's ultimate intention their final validity and function.[19]

The books of the Old Testament are, therefore, inspired insofar as they form an integral part of God's providential predefinition of the primitive Christian community, that is, insofar as they are the definitive record of the pre-history of the Church and came to express the Church's own experience of God's salvific dealings with men and of his special relationship to his Church.[20]

Some Important Corollaries

Rahner claims a number of advantages for his theory of inspiration. He tries to show that it helps to explain the numerous problems which we raised earlier in this chapter.

First of all, he says, it helps us to understand how both God and man can be truly authors of one and the same book. God is the author of the book because his predefining will that the Church should exist causes the Scriptures both to exist and to say what they say. Man is truly author of the book because he and his authorship are an essential part of the divine predefinition. Paradoxically, then, God becomes himself an author only by willing the production of the book at the hands of a human author. The latter is truly God's instrument, but with an instrumentality peculiar to divine inspiration, which preserves his freedom and personal initiative intact.[21]

Secondly, we can conclude that inspiration can never be a completely unconscious process. The human author need not recognize that he is divinely inspired, but he does need to realize that he is giving authentic expression to the self-revelation of Christ contained in the primitive community of belief to which he belongs and which is the foundation of all future Christian belief. Should the sacred author also recognize explicitly that his work is normative for future generations of Christians (though he need not do so), then the whole process of inspiration becomes a conscious one.[22]

Third, with this theory one can understand a bit more easily how the Church comes to recognize the inspired quality of certain books. The basic problem here is to advance an explanation which is more historically plausible than the hypothesis that the apostles themselves made up an official canon of Scripture before their deaths.[23]

Rahner distinguishes between the actual revelation of the fact of the divine authorship of the sacred books and the Church's reflexive grasp and expression of this revelation in the canon of Sacred Scripture. Since we know that revelation closes "with the death of the last apostle," the revelation of inspiration must have taken place some time within the apostolic age, even though the reflexive grasp of revelation could be and was postponed until post-apostolic times. In Rahner's theory such a revelation would in fact take place during apostolic times if the books now listed in the sacred canon were actually constitutive of the faith of the apostolic community. The post-apostolic Church, by reflecting on the constitutive nature of these books in the development of Christian belief, would need no further information in order to declare them divinely inspired.[24]

Fourth, in Rahner's view of inspiration, the relationship between Scripture and the *magisterium* becomes clearer. First of all, we can understand better why no document written in post-apostolic times, not even the official documents of the Church, can make a claim to being inspired, since only those writings can be inspired which are constitutive of the primitive apostolic tradition.[25]

Moreover, Rahner's theory reconciles the infallibility of Scripture with the infallibility of the *magisterium* without rendering either superfluous. Either one is in danger of becoming superfluous only if we assume that they constitute two completely distinct infallibilities. There is, in fact, only one continuous infallibility, that of the eschatological Church. In apostolic times, this infallibility constitutes a binding norm of belief. In postapostolic times, this same infallibility assures the subsequent fidelity of the Church to the norm established in apostolic times. Both manifestations of the Church's infallibility are completely necessary, though modally different, since the Church not only needs to be constituted in belief but as the eschatological manifestation of grace must remain faithful in that belief until the end of time.[26]

Finally, Rahner suggests that his theory helps clarify how God can be the author of Scripture without being personally responsible for the literary forms the biblical writings assume: how, for instance, God can be author of the letter to Philemon without personally writing Philemon a letter. This paradox ceases to be a problem once we reflect that God's authorship of Scripture is strictly analogous to that of the sacred writer and need not contain all the modalities of human authorship.[27]

There are many other problems with inspiration which Rahner's theory helps to explain: why, for instance, the inspired author need not be an apostle; or why some letters of St. Paul were inspired and others were not; or why some of St. Paul's letters could be lost. But there is no need to go into these problems here.[28]

The Inspired Scriptures and Tradition

Far more important is the difficult question of the relationship between the consitutive tradition of the Church as embodied in the Scriptures and later doctrinal developments of Catholic belief.

The church now teaches as infallible dogma many truths which are not contained explicitly in Sacred Scripture. The dogma of the Assumption is perhaps the best example of such a teaching, although there are others. The theological theory of the "two sources" of revelation to a large extent represents an effort to explain the post-apostolic Church's right to define dogmas which are not easily found in the written sources of revelation. According to the two-source theory, these new dogmas must have actually been handed down from apostolic times by word of mouth in such a way that this unwritten tradition constitutes a source of dogmatic belief independent of the Scriptures but equal to them in stature and binding force.[29]

Rahner feels that this approach to the evolution of dogma rests in fact on a gratuitous postulate. Is it not, he contends, just as advantageous and considerably more probable to assume that the later developments of Christian belief are all contained in the books of Scripture, though some of them only implicitly? Is it really either historically or theologically necessary to assert that all belief must be explicit from the very beginning of Christianity? Why not concede frankly that the evolution of dogma is a genuine evolution? Scripture is the beginning of belief, but need be only the beginning.[30]

For even if we know through the definition of the infallible *magisterium* that a particular truth actually does belong to the deposit of faith, we still have the duty to prove historically that it has been handed down by a continuous tradition from apostolic times. But since, apart from the Scriptures, we have very few written documents from the first three centuries after Christ, to postulate an oral tradition for whose content we have no direct historical evidence does not make our historical proof any easier or more convincing.[31]

Moreover, if Scripture is inspired by God as the normative expression of the belief of the apostolic Church binding on all generations of Christians, then it must have some relation to all subsequent developments of belief. Otherwise, why would God have gone to the trouble of constituting a definitive canon of belief in the first place?[32]

Finally, the Catholic faith is not a belief in a group of separate and unrelated sentences revealed by God. It is belief in a salvific reality which gives unity and homogeneity to all authentic expressions of belief. The reality of which the Scriptures speak is the same reality expressed in later dogmas. As a result, any infallible statement of faith somehow implies every other. Is it really reasonable to suggest that a dogmatic definition is so unrelated to the totality of truth expressed in Scripture as to be nowhere implicit in the inspired books?[33]

But to concede the existence of the actual evolution of dogma is not to explain it; and the question remains an extremely tricky one. For one thing, it is a relatively new theological problem: only since 1900 have we begun to distinguish the history of religious truths from history in general. For another, it is all too easy to try and find a facile solution in some sort of historical relativism. Finally, the problem is to a great extent polemical in origin. Catholics need to be able to defend the Church from the charge of inventing dogmas not found in the deposit of faith.[34]

Rahner feels that the evolution of dogma in post-apostolic times will become more intelligible to non-Catholics when it is recognized to be the continuation of a doctrinal development begun and carried on within the apostolic Church itself. If there is dogmatic development within the very books of the New Testament, one could legitimately expect such a development to continue in the post-apostolic age as well. Instead of being a body of immutable statements inexpressible in any other terms, the New Testament would become our guaranteed model for all subsequent dogmatic evolution.[35]

We can as a matter of fact detect a clear doctrinal evolution in the books of the New Testament. The sacred writers do not only report the truths of faith, they reflect upon them and elaborate them. In this sense they are truly theologians. What distinguishes their theological effort from that of other theologians is that the sacred writers were also divinely inspired, that is, their reflections became the officially approved and constitutive expression of the faith of the apostolic Church.[36]

Moreover, unless one is willing to recognize the existence of doctrinal development in the New Testament, one is in danger of misinterpreting the meaning of the scriptural texts themselves. For the ultimate meaning of any statement of Scripture depends largely on how the author has come to know what he states. Could not, for instance, many points of St. Paul's soteriology and his doctrine of original sin be clarified by a study of his sources of information? Would not a similar study of the scriptural sources of the eschatological statements of Jesus help considerably in our interpretation of their meaning?[37]

Five Basic Elements in Dogmatic Development

But even if all this is true, we are still far from an adequate explanation of the development of dogma; for the simple fact remains that the revelation in Christ was both definitive and unrepeatable, and that it was closed with the death of the last apostle. How can a revelation which is both definitive and closed still give rise to new dogmas?[38]

Too often, Rahner feels, theological attempts to explain the evolution of dogma fail because of oversimplification. He himself distinguishes five major elements active in the development of dogma and essential to any explanation of how it comes about. Let us consider briefly each of these five elements.[39]

The first element is the formative presence of the grace of the Holy Spirit within the Church. We know that every divine revelation must be made to someone and that this someone must be a spiritual person created by God and capable of hearing the divine word spoken to him. We know that since revelation is supernatural, no one can hear the word of God without the enlightenment of the divine presence within his soul. Moreover, since human words, like man himself, are obedientially capable of being transformed by faith, it is through the very mediation of words themselves that God graces the soul with his presence and reveals to it the meaning of his message. The modernist error tended to overlook the importance of words in the process of revelation. Modernists liked to speak of revelation as a wordless experience of God which somehow generated a multiplicity of verbal expressions and conceptualizations about him. Theological nominalists, on the other hand, attribute far too much importance to the revealing words themselves. As a result, they tend to speak of a purely verbal revelation in which the divine reality never really becomes an enlightening presence within the soul.[40]

The truth lies between these two extremes. The presence of God in the soul through grace is a genuine enlightenment, as we have seen in a previous chapter. But the words of revelation are a necessary inner moment within this supernatural enlightenment and like human nature itself are transformed and illumined by the divine presence. The spirit of God within the Church is, therefore, a dynamic force within the consciousness of the Church which forms and molds the words with which the Church at any given moment of history proclaims the good news of Christ.[41]

The second element in the development of dogma is the official *magisterium*. Since the Church has the important duty of proclaiming the truths of revelation to all men of all times, this duty rests in a special way on those who speak officially in the name of the Church. The *magisterium* of the Church is, then, an important element in the development of dogma. But we should avoid distorting its importance. The *magisterium* is far from being the only enlightened voice in the Church. On the contrary, the development of belief presupposes a constant dialogue between the Church's official and unofficial voices, between the charismatic *magisterium* and charismatic individuals and movements within the Church; for the Spirit of God has been given to the whole Church and not to the hierarchy alone.[42]

Moreover the *magisterium* is not an arbitrary power to teach anything at all, as non-Catholics sometimes erroneously suppose. Any declaration of the *magisterium*, especially one which is infallible, must have a solid, conscious basis in both Scripture and tradition. To suppose anything else would be to deny that revelation is closed and that tradition is continuous.[43]

The third dynamic element in the development of dogma is the very concepts and words which the Church uses to express God's revelation of himself to men. Because dogma is expressed in words, dogmatic evolution must have a rational dimension and must depend on the development of theology. But here again we must be careful not to exaggerate. Not every new dogma need be *ipso facto* explicable in terms of a clear rational deduction from the deposit of faith. Decision and insight are complementary moments in human knowledge and certitude, and theology is no exception to this law of the mind. Its explanations frequently involve something more than syllogistic or analytic certitude.[44]

Rahner suggests as a good example of non-syllogistic certitude the theological argument from suitability. Such an argument seeks to demonstrate that for God to act in a particular manner would be reasonable, but the conclusion of the argument that God did in fact so act actually receives its final degree of certitude from the fiducial understanding of the Church.[45]

The human need to hand down a tradition from generation to generation is the fourth basic element in the development of dogma. Its direction is controlled by the previously mentioned elements, particularly by the transforming presence of the Spirit within the Church and by the official teaching of the *magisterium*. Here the danger is to think of tradition as tending necessarily to an ever expanding multiplicity of statements about God. Because the revelation of God is not the revelation of abstract truths but of the concrete presence of God in the Church, the development of theology in fact tends ideally to simplicity in the darkness of faith.[46]

The fifth and crucial element in the evolution of dogma is the Church's reflexive awareness of a dogma as revealed by God. We are here at the heart of the problem of dogmatic development. This reflexive awareness need not always be present in the consciousness of the Church from the historical beginnings of belief. We know that because revelation is closed, that is, because all the truths necessary for salvation have been revealed to us in Christ, there can be no question of another new revelation to the post-apostolic Church. How then does this new awareness come about?[47]

One explanation sometimes offered attributes this new awareness to the action of the *magisterium*. But the explanation really sidesteps the basic question. For why is it that the *magisterium* must wait several centuries in order to act? One might reply that the action of the *magisterium* results from a rational deduction which had never before been made. But can deduction alone provide sufficient grounds for a new dogmatic definition? If, prior to a solemn definition by the *magisterium*, theological investigation of a doctrine reveals that it has never before been presented reflexively in the sources of revelation as belonging to the deposit of faith, then on what purely rational grounds could either the pope or an ecumenical council know for certain whether this doctrine is in fact part of the deposit of faith or not? We cannot explain this new reflexive awareness until we introduce a new dimension, the dimension of faith itself.[48]

Rahner suggests that the transition of a dogma from implicit affirmation to reflexive awareness as divinely revealed is analogous to the transition of an individual person from non-belief to belief. In an individual conversion the rational arguments which lead to the act of faith demonstrate the reasonableness of religious commitment, but they do not produce the final acceptance of revelation or the commitment itself.[49]

Rahner feels that we often tend to underestimate the role of freedom in the beginning of faith as well as in its development. Wherever there is free choice, there must be some antecedent insight into the meaning of the choice and our duty to make it. But this need not mean that our decisions are nothing but the execution of a prior insight. A free choice can also generate its own light and thus become its own ultimate justification.[50]

There are, moreover, two fundamental reasons which lead us to assert that the definition of a new dogma cannot be explained in rational terms alone. First of all, the progress in faith of which there is here question is not that of an individual but of the entire universal Church. We know *a posteriori* that no dogma has ever been defined which was not the actual belief of the entire Church. Also, in many cases at least, the dogma reaches reflexive articulation in the mind of the Church even before it is defined. In such a case, this fiducial awareness of the Church institutes the concrete norm by which the *magisterium* can decide whether a belief belongs to the deposit of faith or not. Second, the development of dogma, as we have seen, is a genuine progress of faith. It moves from belief to belief.[51]

The Laws of Dogmatic Development

Before we go on to a more detailed analysis of how this movement comes about, we would do well to pause a bit and take stock of where we are in our reflections. We have seen that the

Scriptures are the official expression of the faith of the apostolic Church and are a binding norm of belief for all subsequent generations of Christians. We have also seen that no human words, even when they are inspired, can give complete expression to the mystery of God revealed to us in Jesus Christ and that as a consequence the development of Christian belief is not only possible but even necessary if the faith is to remain a dynamic force in human history until the end of time. We have distinguished five basic elements in the development of dogma, and we have insisted on the fact that neither the *magisterium* alone nor rational reflection alone can explain the progress of dogmatic evolution. We must now attempt to indicate more concretely how dogmatic development actually takes place.

Any attempt to describe the laws which govern the development of dogma is extremely difficult. The evolution of belief is a unique process in human history and one which lasts as long as the Church exists. Although it must have inner laws controlling its development, still, the very uniqueness of the phenomenon prevents us from having a complete knowledge of these laws until the total development has been accomplished. We cannot, as in the case of natural development, seek analogies in the world of experience. As a result, anyone attempting to explain the precise nature of dogmatic development is forced to adopt an empirical approach. He must first observe the concrete forms this develement has assumed in the course of the Church's history and then, on the basis of these actual developments, reach some understanding of the laws at work within them. But if he is completely realistic, he must admit that there is inevitably much obscurity here. His only comfort lies perhaps in the reflection that each new development of dogma increases his knowledge of the basic laws of development while at the same time limiting the possibility of future development through the further exclusion of error from actual belief. Indeed, our very ignorance of all the laws of dogmatic development is itself one of the striking proofs of the Church's need of the guidance and enlightenment of the Spirit.[52]

We have said that the development of dogma is the development of belief itself. We know that God's self-revelation in Jesus Christ is made, not to any one individual, but to the entire Church, and that the Church is rendered capable of receiving this revelation through the enlightening presence of the divine Spirit within it, which transforms the consciousness of the Church and illumines the words of divine revelation.[53]

Both Scripture and defined dogma express infallibly but inadequately the Church's reflexive awareness of this divine reality with which it is in constant vital contact. To explain the connection between any new reflexive awareness which finds expression in a new dogma and the original formulation of this new awareness contained in the sources of revelation, theologians have traditionally appealed to the notion of the explicitation of what is implicit. That is to say, any new dogma is presented as the explicit expression of what is said only implicitly in the sources of revelation.[54]

Unfortunately these terms "implicit" and "explicit" do not explain a great deal, and theologians quarrel over their specific definitions. For our purposes here we can distinguish two basic kinds of implicit statements which would be capable of giving rise to later explicit dogmatic definitions: the formal implicit and the virtual implicit. The latter, we shall see, is open to certain complexities.

There is no great difficulty about the development of dogma through the explicitation of a formally implicit statement. The formally explicit dogma merely re-expresses the original formulation of an idea in different words. For instance, formally implicit in the statement that no one lives more than two hundred years are the statements that man is mortal, that his life-span falls within fixed limits, that no one can extend his life-span indefinitely, etc. Because the change is only verbal, there can be no real doubt that a formal implicit can be a true dogma.[55]

But not every new dogma is a formal implicit; and unfortunately the virtual implicit is more difficult to handle. The virtual implicit does a good deal more than re-express the same idea in different words. For instance, the statement that "Socrates is dead" is also implicit in the statement that "No one lives more than two hundred years." Still, "Socrates is dead" does not simply translate the idea that no one lives more than two hundred years into different terms. No amount of analysis of a statement about the life-span of man in general will yield me information about the actual state of health of Socrates. The statement about Socrates is, then, only virtually implicit in the statement about the life-span of man.[56]

When we try to apply the concept of the "virtual implicit" to the development of dogma, the problem becomes this: Can a statement that is only virtually implicit in the sources of revelation actually be "revealed by God," believed with "divine faith" and on "God's authority"? Or must it be considered as human knowledge believed with ecclesiastical faith on the authority of the Church? Of the two possibilities Rahner feels that the former is the more theologically exact.[57]

He points out that although in the concrete it is often difficult to distinguish the virtual from the formal implicit, nevertheless there are a number of dogmatic pronouncements which are something more than the verbal re-expression of the sources of revelation. To attempt to reduce such statements to formal implicits is simply flying in the face of facts.[58]

In addition, there is no real difficulty in saying that God revealed something which is only virtually implicit in Scripture. When a man makes a statement, he is seldom if ever conscious of all its implications. But this is not the case with God. When God inspired the Scriptures, he was fully conscious of everything they implied. The Church's task is progressively to realize and articulate this revealed reality in its entirety. Every new realization must of course be objectively connected with the sources of revelation. Moreover, only those salvific truths can be said to be revealed by God in Scripture which God in his omniscience foresees will actually be explicitated in the course of time.[59]

To the objection that God cannot reveal any more in Scripture than the inspired author is himself conscious of, Rahner replies by distinguishing revelation and inspiration. Although it is true that inspiration extends only to what the sacred author actually wrote, the full reality revealed in Scripture can well exceed the explicit consciousness of the inspired writer himself.[60]

We may conclude, then, that dogma develops through the Church's explicitation of truths which are either formally or virtually implicit in the sources of revelation. Because it is a development of belief, this explicitation takes place in and through the illumination of faith, even though it remains an open question whether the rational ground supporting the explicitation need always be logically coercive or not. But unfortunately the matter is even more complex.[61]

Too often we tend to think of all statements as if they were mathematical formulas having a perfectly fixed and defined content which exhausts the reality it expresses. But the normal human statement is not a mathematical formula. Most statements are partial introductions to realities far more complex than the statement which introduces them. Instead of being like a mathematical formula, most statements are more like windows through which we look out upon a total reality. As a result many implicits are not so much the logical conclusion from an original statement as they are realities which are inarticulately affirmed along with the original statement. For instance, implied in the statement that Christ died for us is the whole human experience of death and all that it implies.[62]

We have here a process of explicitation considerably more

complex than either the formal or the virtual implicit. It may be
reduced to three basic steps. First of all, a complex of statements
in the sources of revelation reveals along with their basic content
a reality which is greater than the explicit content of the statements themselves. This reality is then expressed explicitly and
reflexively. Finally, from this new reflexive expression there
emerges still another virtual or formal implicit.[63]

In concluding these reflections on the implicit, we might do
well to reflect a bit on the place of love in the development of
belief. An example might be useful: When a young man falls
in love, his own awareness of his love is itself an inner moment
of the love he feels. When he tries to express his love, he becomes more reflexively conscious of it; and as a result, the love
itself becomes more intense. This increased intensity leads to
further expressions of love, and something like a chain reaction
is set up. In the process, his initial inchoate awareness of his
love is increasingly enriched by becoming more and more reflexive.[64]

The apostles experienced something analogous to this process
in their dealings with Christ. Their initial love of Jesus sought
spontaneous expression and enrichment in words and discourse.
Moreover, in the evolution of dogma, the Church continues this
process begun with the apostles. This is possible because not
only has she received from them the documents which express
their loving experience of the divine reality, she has received
from them the reality itself which they experienced, the very
object of their love.[65]

The Historical Evolution of Divine Law

There is another aspect of the development of belief which
deserves our explicit attention, even though it will be impossible
to explore its many complexities. Ordinarily, we think of the

development of belief as a purely theoretical process, but it has a practical aspect as well. It has resonances, for instance, in our understanding of the meaning of divine and ecclesiastical law in the Church.

There are in the Church certain institutions which are unchangeable because they are of divine origin, like the papacy, the episcopate, the seven sacraments. The problem of explaining the development of such institutions, especially to Protestants, is to show that once these institutions have reached a certain fullness of historical development, they are still identified with the original "seed" of authority in the primitive Church from which they evolved. Are we to suppose, for example, that the papacy in its *de facto* evolution was present in the Church *de jure* from the very beginning?[66]

We can get some insight into the difficulty of this problem if we reflect that not everything that exists in the Church today is of divine law. Moreover, even a Church institution which does exist by divine law can, while remaining essentially unchanged, vary from age to age in the concrete forms it assumes. How then do we come to know exactly what is of divine law in the Church? And even once we know that a particular institution is of divine law, how can we actually distinguish what is really essential to it as established by God from what is only its accidental historical trappings? The problem is analogous to that of the dogmatic implicit. Just how much of an institution's later development is implicit in its original divine foundation?[67]

We cannot at this point go into all the complexities of the development of divine law in the Church. Instead we must content ourselves with a brief presentation of Rahner's reflections on the meaning of the term "divine law."

These considerations are of interest to us inasmuch as they are closely related to some aspects of the problem of inspiration discussed earlier in this chapter.

Rahner insists first of all that the historical evolution of any institution, and hence of a Church institution as well, can in the course of time achieve moments of development which possess a permanent legal validity with regard to its subsequent evolution. It is, then, false to assume that an institution which did not exist in apostolic times explicitly and in the same manner as it does today cannot for that reason be of divine law.[68]

Moreover, these moments of permanent, legally binding validity often result from the completely free decisions of those in authority, and not directly from the essence of the developing institution as such. Of course, if these new developments are to establish a legitimate and irrevocable right, they must of necessity be proportioned to the essence of the developing institution. But that essence alone may be incapable of explaining their existence, as, for instance, in the case of an institution which is open to development in a number of legitimate directions, but actually develops in only one of them to the exclusion of the others as a result of the free decision of its own legitimate authority.[69]

When we apply these abstract reflections to the primitive Church, we can arrive at a somewhat clearer understanding of what it means to say that certain of its institutions exist by divine law. The only way that we can know that any institution exists by divine law is if the fact is revealed. Since, however, revelation closes with the death of the last apostle, the revelation of a divine law must have taken place during the apostolic age. The precise problem which interests us here is the manner in which this revelation comes about.[70]

Rahner suggests that the divine law which establishes a given Church institution need not be revealed verbally. Events as well as words are an integral part of the process of revelation. Moreover, an event, like a statement, can give rise to subsequent events implicit within it. As we have seen, it was through an event rather than through words that the fact of inspiration was revealed. Could not the special divine origin of a Church institution have been revealed by a similar event?[71]

Moreover, as we have seen, this event could have involved a completely free choice on the part of the legitimate authorities in the primitive Church. For example, the free decision of Peter to make Rome his permanent see would have been sufficient revelation of the primacy of the Bishop of Rome over the other bishops. A similar decision was the rejection of circumcision as a necessary preliminary to baptism.[72]

But when would such decisions constitute special revelations of a law of God? We have already seen that the constitution of the primitive Church was no haphazard affair. The entire Christian community, and not only the Scriptures, was constituted in its essential structure by a special divine predefinition. Hence, the power of the Church to define itself as a constitutive norm for all future believers included the power to establish definitive and permanent rights and institutions within the Church. These rights and institutions, to the extent that they belong to the constitutive apostolic tradition and hence fall under the constitutive divine predefinition of the Church, can, in a sense analogous with the sacred books, be truly said to have God as their author.[73]

The fact that a given Church institution is of divine law could, then, have been revealed in the early Church in the form of an authoritative decision proportioned in God's predefinition of the primitive community to the essential nature of the Church, even though this decision was in every sense a free choice on the part of the apostles and not deducible *a priori* from the essence of the Church as such. Indeed, prior to the definitive decision there could even have been a conflict of social forces within the community itself.[74]

We cannot go into the problem of the evolution of divine law in the post-apostolic Church. In these brief and somewhat parenthetical reflections we have been interested in simply showing the possibility of grounding the revelation of divine law in the concrete development of the constitutive apostolic tradition. For the moment we only caution the reader against excluding too quickly the possibility of genuine development of divine law in post-apostolic times. In subsequent chapters we shall have occasion to return to this problem in somewhat different contexts.[75]

Exegesis and Dogma

One final problem remains before we close this long and necessarily somewhat rambling chapter. It is the problem of the place of Scripture in modern dogmatic theology. The problem is a contemporary one and has been occasioned by the recent spectacular developments in modern biblical research. One sometimes has the impression that contemporary dogmatic theology has failed to keep pace with these developments, with the result that a growing intellectual estrangement has come to exist between the dogmatic and the biblical theologian. Symptomatic of this estrangement are, on the one hand, the attitude of detachment which some exegetes maintain with regard to what they consider purely dogmatic questions and, on the other, the tendency of some dogmatic theologians to place unreasonable *a priori* limits on the work of exegesis. One should be wary of exaggerating either the importance or the extent of this estrangement, but there is no point in closing one's eyes to it. Rather, by attempting to meet the problem head on, we can perhaps help Catholic theology through its present period of growing pains to the great benefit of theology itself and ultimately to the development of Catholic belief.[76]

We shall proceed in two basic steps in these closing considerations. First, we shall reflect explicitly on the meaning of dogmatic theology. Secondly, we shall make some modest suggestions to both dogmatists and exegetes which may help to overcome their present estrangement.

Given the importance of dogmatic theology in Catholic thought, the frequent failure of theologians to reflect on the precise nature of a dogmatic statement is perplexing to say the least. Rahner attempts to supply in some measure for this failure.[77]

To begin with, he suggests that a dogmatic statement, inasmuch as it is a statement made by men, necessarily shares the modalities of any profane human statement with regard to its logic, its relation to its object, the historicity of its conceptual elements, its place in a concrete historical context, its use of literary genres, etc. In other words, although a dogmatic statement is more than purely natural, it does also contain distinctly human elements. As in the case of Scripture, this is an important point; for when it is a question of official Church documents, Catholics tend to overlook those aspects of a dogmatic statement which are conditioned by human sinfulness and limitations.[78]

Still, even though conditioned by these human elements, dogmatic statements can rightfully claim to be true. They express an objective reality and not the pure subjectivity of the speaker. But unlike other human statements, dogmatic statements express realities which are essentially mysterious. From this fact follows another important conclusion, namely, the verification of dogmatic statements takes place in a manner which is only analogous to purely human statements.[79]

For besides being both true and human, dogmatic statements are also expressions of faith. We are not referring here simply to the dogmatic content of the statement. A dogmatic statement is not simply a profane statement about a sacred mystery. It is itself an exercise of faith, a more perfect subjective assimilation and articulation of what we believe. As we have seen, it is the enlightenment of human consciousness through faith and the divine indwelling which transforms human statements about God into acts of faith. The dogmatic statement, then, is something more than a factual statement about reality. It is the attempt to bring a man into vital existential contact with salvific truth.[80]

Nevertheless, the dogmatic statement is not just the expression of a purely personal faith. It is also in a special sense an ecclesial statement. Dogmatic theology results from the confrontation of faith and historical experience. But this confrontation is not just a personal matter. The theological reflections of individuals are only moments within the total historical experience of the Church.[81]

What we say here about individual theologians is analogously true of the official theology of the Church as well. This official theology suffers all the necessary limitations to which theology as a whole is subject both in its dependence on the sources of revelation and in the poverty of its conceptual material to express the complexity and mystery of salvific realities. For example, even in official documents shifts in terminology are possible, as in the case of St. Augustine's formulation of the doctrine of original sin, which dominated the Councils of Carthage and Orange but has, for all practical purposes, been abandoned in more recent Church documents. Even defined dogmas can do no more than express certain aspects of revelation.[82]

In addition, official statements of the Church often express much less than theologians are eager to read into them. Often they consciously leave the door open to further discussion and seek only to fix the terminological limits of debate.[83]

Finally, because they are statements about the mystery of God, dogmatic statements, whether official or not, always point beyond their immediate content. They are conceptual statements leading to the grasp of a nonconceptual reality in supernatural faith.[84]

We are now in a better position to understand the relation

between a dogmatic statement and a scriptural one. In Scripture we have the Church's original proclamation of the events of salvation. But announced revelation is not something distinct from believed revelation; to the extent that each word is the reflexive expression of revelation, it belongs already, as we have seen, to the realm of theology. The kerygmatic message of Scripture, therefore, is not the pure and unchanging word of God, and theology is not just the words of men. Were this the case, theology could evolve, but not belief itself.[85]

Still, as we have seen, there remains an essential difference between a scriptural statement and a dogmatic one. The statements of the New Testament, even when they have a theological character, are part of the constitutive tradition of the Church and are divinely inspired. Dogmatic statements continue the theological development begun in Scripture but must always return to Scripture as to a normative source.[86]

In view of these facts, the growing estrangement between dogmatic theology and exegesis is somewhat alarming.

An exegete cannot afford to forget that he is a professional theologian. What he says concerning the interpretation of Scripture has a positive relation to the faith of the Church.[87]

Hence, though the exegete must be faithful to the methods of his science, still, he cannot be simply indifferent to the dogmatic implication of his conclusions. There are occasional complaints in scriptural circles about the second-rate exegesis of some dogmatic theologians. But if professional exegetes are themselves unwilling to come to grips with the dogmatic implications of modern scripture studies, they hardly have the right to despise the efforts of dogmatists to do so, however fumbling those efforts may appear.[88]

Moreover, there are many points of contact between exegesis and dogmatic theology which need the professional attention of the exegetes. Why, for instance, do not exegetes manifest more

interest in demonstrating that the new methods of biblical research are actually in conformity with Church teaching and the
decrees of the Biblical Commission? Why could they not from
time to time attempt to show scriptural foundations of important
scholastic teachings? Would it really be too much to ask them to
interest themselves in explaining the decrees of the Biblical
Commission, even if such decrees are not definitive? Might they
not make more of an effort to calm the apprehensions of the
faithful sometimes aroused by the new exegesis? Finally, all of
us have need of their reflections on such problems as the historicity of the gospels, the meaning of miracles, and the theological meaning of the resurrection, etc.[89]

On the other hand, dogmatic theologians should also be willing
to make their peace with the exegetes. When a dogmatic theologian launches into the exegesis of a text, he must be prepared
to give an explanation that is convincing even to a professional
exegete. He must acquire greater familiarity and patience with
the method of modern exegesis. This method with its insistence
on the importance of historical milieu in the concrete development and meaning of scriptural texts is complex in the extreme
and has a right to patient treatment. Moreover, through increasing familiarity with the methods and problems of the exegete,
the dogmatic theologian may gradually come to realize that the
new exegesis actually facilitates his own handling of many difficult biblical texts.[90]

The dogmatic theologian must also beware of placing unreasonable *a priori* restrictions on the work of the exegete. The
metaphysical principles at work in dogmatic theology should
never be allowed to hamper the scientific investigation of the
actual historical meaning of a given text. Why, for instance, need
a dogmatic theologian be offended by the exegete's suggestion
that the evangelists interpret the life of Christ in terms of the
Easter experience? Why should a dogmatic theologian feel bound

to follow St. Augustine's interpretation of the *"in quo"* of Romans 5:12? Is it really necessary to interpret the words of Christ found in Scripture as direct quotations? Why need the dogmatist's concern for the historicity of Scripture lead him to ignore the existence of literary forms in the Bible? On these and other points, many dogmatic theologians could show much more openness and understanding than they do.[91]

This does not mean that the dogmatic theologian and the exegete are not bound to criticize one another on a professional scientific basis. But for mutual criticism to be fruitful, it must be based on mutual understanding and respect.[92]

Only in this way can both the exegete and the dogmatist become the useful servants of the Church they are intended to be. For it is through them and through their work that the Church must bring the message of salvation to modern men. Only through their brotherly cooperation can that message proclaimed definitively in Christ be assimilated ever more effectively to the needs of Christians everywhere.[93]

NOTES

1. S, I, 18–24, 26.
2. *Ibid.*, 24.
3. *Ibid.*, 26.
4. *Ibid.*
5. *Ibid.*, 27.
6. *Ibid.*, 29–31.
7. *Ibid.*, 32–36.
8. *Ibid.*, 37.
9. *Ibid.*, 37–41.
10. *Ibid.*, 46.
11. *Ibid.*, 47.
12. *Ibid.*, 47–48.
13. *Ibid.*, 50–53.
14. *Ibid.*, 52.
15. *Ibid.*, 53.
16. *Ibid.*, 53–54.
17. *Ibid.*, 55–57.
18. *Ibid.*, 58.
19. *Ibid.*, 58–61.
20. *Ibid.*, 61.
21. *Ibid.*, 64–68.
22. *Ibid.*, 70–72.
23. *Ibid.*, 72–73.
24. *Ibid.*, 74–75.
25. *Ibid.*, 68.
26. *Ibid.*, 78–80.
27. *Ibid.*, 64–65, 85–86.
28. *Ibid.*, 86–88.
29. *Ibid.*, 84.
30. *Ibid.*, 81–84.

31. "Schrift und Tradition," *Wort und Wahrheit*, XVIII (April, 1963), pp. 277–278.
32. *Ibid.*, 278.
33. *Ibid.*, 278–279.
34. S, IV, 12–13.
35. *Ibid.*, 14–15.
36. S, V, 38–43.
37. *Ibid.*, 43–45.
38. S, I, 58–60; IV, 18.
39. S, IV, 21.
40. *Ibid.*, 21–24.
41. *Ibid.*, 24.
42. *Ibid.*, 25–27.
43. *Ibid.*, 27–29.
44. *Ibid.*, 29–34.
45. *Ibid.*, 34–36.
46. *Ibid.*, 36–39.
47. *Ibid.*, 40–41.
48. *Ibid.*, 41–44.
49. *Ibid.*, 44–45.
50. *Ibid.*, 45.
51. *Ibid.*, 45–49.
52. S, I, 51–53.
53. *Ibid.*, 63–64.
54. *Ibid.*, 68–69.
55. *Ibid.*, 69–70.
56. *Ibid.*, 70.
57. *Ibid.*, 70–71.
58. *Ibid.*, 71–72.
59. *Ibid.*, 73–74.
60. *Ibid.*, 74–75.
61. *Ibid.*, 75.
62. *Ibid.*, 81–85.
63. *Ibid.*, 85–86.
64. *Ibid.*, 75–77.
65. S, I, 77–80; V, 50–53.
66. S, V, 249–251.
67. *Ibid.*, 252–255.
68. *Ibid.*, 257–259.
69. *Ibid.*, 259–262.
70. *Ibid.*, 262–263.
71. *Ibid.*, 264–269.
72. *Ibid.*, 269–270.
73. S, I, 58; S, V, 271–272.
74. S, V, 271–273.
75. *Ibid.*, 274–277.
76. *Ibid.*, 82–84.
77. *Ibid.*, 54–55.
78. *Ibid.*, 56–57.
79. *Ibid.*, 59–60.
80. *Ibid.*, 61–64.
81. *Ibid.*, 65–67.
82. *Ibid.*, 67–70.
83. *Ibid.*, 70–72.
84. *Ibid.*, 72–73.
85. *Ibid.*, 75–76.
86. *Ibid.*, 77.
87. *Ibid.*, 85.
88. *Ibid.*, 86–87.
89. *Ibid.*, 87–92.
90. *Ibid.*, 93–98, 101–102.
91. *Ibid.*, 98–101.
92. *Ibid.*, 101–103.
93. *Ibid.*, 103–110.

SUGGESTED READINGS

Inspiration in the Bible, Charles Henkey (tr.), (Freiburg: Herder, 1961). "The Development of Dogma," *Theological Investigations*, Cornelius Ernst, O.P. (tr.), (Baltimore: Helicon, 1961), Vol. I, pp. 39–78.

VI. The Sacramental Word

As we have seen in the previous chapter, the Church as the definitive manifestation of eschatological grace in the world is the definitive custodian of the word of God. She has the privilege and unique responsibility of proclaiming the truths of salvation to all men until the end of time and for that reason enjoys the special promise of God that she shall never lose the light of truth that is hers in Christ.

But this proclamation of salvific truth is not the Church's only responsibility. Christ did not come merely to enlighten us; he came to make us holy and acceptable in the sight of God. As the visible manifestation of the grace of Christ in time, the Church is also the source of our sanctification. This double role implies in turn the Church's double power of preaching and of administering the sacraments.[1]

The Kerygmatic and the Sacramental Word

Now, as we also saw in the previous chapter, the word of God comes to us in the form of human words, such as the words of Scripture or the teachings of the Church. But unfortunately until relatively recently, Catholic theology has been little inclined to investigate the important relationship which exists between the Church's words of divine teaching and her words of divine sanctification. One reason for this omission was a tendency among theologians to think of revelation as a body of teachable sentences rather than as a salvific event. But under the impact of biblical theology, patrology, and the ecumenical dialogue, Catholic theology has begun to recognize the salvific relation which exists between the preaching of the Church and her sacramental words. In this chapter we shall reflect briefly on some of the implications of this important problem.[2]

The words of sanctification and of instruction which the Church speaks to men are still the word of God even though they are spoken by men. They are an inner moment within God's salvific dealings with men, although salvation is, of course, much more than the simple words themselves.[3]

Still, human words are truly necessary if man is to assimilate the reality of salvation. They are an inner constitutive element within his growing reflexive awareness of the transforming presence of grace.[4]

Now, this growing awareness is not simply a personal affair. Man is essentially a social being and achieves full consciousness of his own experience of grace only through membership in a community. The Church's public proclamation of the word of God in time must, then, be an essential inner moment in God's dealings with mankind.[5]

For while, on the one hand, the historical word spoken by the Church in the name of God actually brings to reflexive awareness the inner word of enlightenment spoken by God to the soul, it is, on the other hand, God's inner illumination (or word) which enables man to understand the external words of the Church in the light of faith and to accept them precisely as coming from God.[6]

This complex salvific word of God spoken to man through the Church is, then, the external manifestation of an inner salvific reality. In other words, the kerygmatic words of the Church, by sensibly manifesting God's grace, actually cause that grace to exist.[7]

Anyone acquainted with Catholic sacramental theology might be a bit startled with this claim of Rahner's that even the Church's extra-sacramental proclamation of the word of God is actually effective of grace. But the point he is trying to make is perfectly valid and orthodox. For although it is true that it is only in the sacraments that the word of God spoken by the Church effects grace *ex opere operato,* still no one can seriously contest that even extra-sacramental words can on occasion be genuine events of grace. If this is so, then why are not theologians justified in speaking of extra-sacramental words in their most perfect and efficacious form instead of contrasting them in their most deficient manifestation with the *opus operatum* of the sacraments?[8]

Moreover, the thesis that extra-sacramental words are actually capable of effecting the grace they signify is also in complete conformity both with the biblical notion of the efficacious word of God and with the traditional theology of belief. In the Bible the word of God always effects what it signifies. In the theology of faith, the proclamation of the word of God is a summons to belief. Now, in belief, God, who is the object of faith, communicates himself to the soul. Hence, in every believing acceptance of the word of God, the word actually renders present the reality it signifies.[9]

But lest there be any misunderstanding on this particular point, Rahner is quick to insist that the eventful, grace-bringing word of God is found in the Church in essentially different forms and in varying degrees of intensity. We know, for example, that not all the teachings of the Church demand of us our absolute assent. This assent is always proportioned to the degree of commitment with which the Church teaches any particular doctrine.[10] Now, because only in the sacramental word does the Church commit itself definitively to an individual Christian in a decisive salvific situation of his life, it follows that only in the sacramental word does the word of God achieve its highest realization as a salvific event.[11]

The Church as Primal Sacrament

To understand precisely what this last statement means is in a certain sense to understand the nature of the Church itself. In contrast to the state, the Church is not just a religious institution founded to fulfill the needs of its members. It is the people of God constituted by the gratuitous intervention of God in history through his own incarnate Word. Moreover, since, as we have seen in a previous chapter, God wills the salvation of all men, and since, too, the effects of the incarnation actually stretch far beyond the visible Church itself, the historical mission of the Church is actually to be the visible manifestation of the grace of Christ present among men. The Church is, therefore, in a very real sense the visible prolongation in time of God's initial sacramental word spoken to men in Christ.[12]

Now, because in Christ our humanity has been united definitively to the Word, who in the name of all mankind has said in the darkness of the cross a permanent yes to God's offer of salvation, Christ is himself the enduring promise of grace to every man, the sacramental word *par excellence*.[13]

Moreover, because the Church is the visible manifestation of the abiding presence of the definitive and victorious grace of Christ in the world, it is the real sacramental symbol of Christ himself, the visible sign of the eternal, salvific union of God and man effected in the incarnate Word.[14]

As the sacrament of Christ, the Church, then, has been so constituted in grace that it can never relinquish the end for which it was constituted, the salvation and sanctification of all men. By the same token, whoever enters the Church receives thereby God's promise of personal salvation. Moreover, because it prolongs in time the redemptive presence of the incarnate Word, the Church through Christ is the unique source of grace for all mankind. To imagine anything else would be to imply either that grace is not incarnational or that Christ is not our only source of salvation.[15]

The Meaning of Opus Operatum

The seven traditional sacraments are, then, nothing more than concrete realizations of the essence of the Church as the primal sacrament of Christ. At the same time, the *opus operatum* of the sacraments means that each sacrament, like the Church itself, is a visible sign of the definitive eschatological presence of God's grace in the world. Let us reflect briefly on what this last statement means.[16]

In the traditional theology manuals, *opus operatum* is usually explained by saying that the grace of the sacrament is effected by the very fact that the sacramental action has been performed, so that the effectiveness of the sacrament seems to be independent of any consideration of the worthiness either of the minister or of the recipient.[17]

Grace received *ex opere operato* is thus contrasted with grace received *ex opere operantis*. In the latter case the reception of grace is not necessarily guaranteed by the nature of the act performed, but depends on the subjective dispositions of the person who himself performs the action.

Upon reflection, however, this traditional explanation of the distinction between *opus operatum* and *opus operantis* is less satisfying than it might at first appear. Let us imagine, for instance, two men both in the state of mortal sin. One of them makes an act of perfect contrition and is restored to grace *ex opere operantis;* the other goes to confession in order to be restored to grace *ex opere operato.* Is it true to say that the man who went to confession is automatically sure of having received God's grace by the very fact of having performed the external sacramental action? We know as a matter of fact that this need not be the case; for it is quite possible for a man to make a bad confession, to perform the sacramental action without having the proper inner dispositions. We also know that a confession of this sort does not confer grace on the so-called penitent at all but only deepens his guilt. But if this is so, if the actual reception of sacramental grace is not automatic but also depends in some sense upon the dispositions of the one who receives the sacrament, then what precisely is the difference between grace received *ex opere operato* and *ex opere operantis?*[18]

According to Rahner, the distinction, though a real one, is perhaps not as radical as we sometimes suppose. As we have seen, sacramental words are not the only grace-bringing events in a man's life. They are rather a special kind of grace-bringing event.[19]

What distinguishes the sacramental word from other graced events is that it possesses an irrevocable eschatological value. It is a manifestation of the new and eternal covenant between God and man. We can get some insight into the eschatological meaning of the sacraments if we consider briefly the radical difference which exists between the old and the new covenants.[20]

The old covenant was of its very nature a temporary one. Not only was its continued existence constantly threatened by the infidelity of men, but it was in fact finally replaced by the new covenant in Christ. Still, most theologians agree that the "sacraments" of the old covenant, such as circumcision, possessed a special salvific value which distinguished them from pagan worship.[21]

Now, since the new covenant in Christ is the triumph of definitive grace over the instability of the old covenant, the sacraments of the New Testament constitute a definitive and permanent offer of salvation which distinguishes them essentially both from acts of personal piety and from Old Testament rites. Outside of the Christian sacraments, one can only affirm that if God accepts the mediation of this external sign it will become an event of grace. Only in the case of the Christian sacraments can one say with certainty that this sacramental action is indeed a manifestation of the grace-bringing will of God. In this external sign, I know that God truly offers me his grace without this offer being merited either by the sacramental minister or by the recipient. In other words, *opus operatum* in no way implies that the sacraments confer grace automatically or magically. It implies, rather, that in the sacramental sign God on his own initiative freely and gratuitously offers man the saving grace definitively promised him in Christ and that man's response under the influence of that grace is wholly dependent upon that free, divine initiative.[22]

Sacrament and Symbol

To put the matter a bit differently, the effectiveness of the sacramental sign can be regarded as the effectiveness of a real symbol. In traditional theological explanations of the *opus operatum*, one often gets the impression that the sacramental sign is somehow separate from the grace conferred and that the causal effectiveness of the sacrament is consequently due either to God alone or to grace alone rather than to the sacramental symbol itself. But, as the reader may recall from the first chapter, a real symbol is an inner moment within the reality it symbolizes. In the natural order, it exists wherever a being manifests itself by positing within itself a reality which is distinct from itself but which renders the being graspable in the spatio-temporal order. Moreover, in contrast to arbitrary symbols, in a real symbol the symbolized reality achieves a new fullness of being in the very positing of the symbol. The real symbol is, therefore, the cause of the thing it symbolizes insofar as it is the manner in which the thing symbolized actually achieves fuller self-realization. Thus, the real symbol can result either from the very nature of the reality which expresses itself symbolically (as the body is the real symbol of the soul) or from a free act (as a bodily gesture is the real symbol of a man's personal attitude).[23]

In the supernatural order, the Church is the real symbol of Christ in time, the historical manifestation of the presence of his victorious grace in the world. Now just as the Word of God, who is the real-symbolic expression of the Father within the Trinity, posits within himself the sacred humanity as the real-symbolic expression of his own divine person, so analogously the glorified Christ, in sending forth the Holy Spirit to the Church, posits the Church within himself as the real-symbolic expression of his own sacramental reality. Similarly the Church, in an analogous fashion, posits the sacraments within itself as real-symbolic expressions of its own sacramental essence. There is, then, in the sacraments of the Church, a certain reciprocal causality between the sacramental sign and sacramental grace. It is in manifesting the grace of Christ that the sacramental sign actually effects that grace, just as it is the grace itself which transforms the external sign into a salvific event.[24]

The sacramental word is, therefore, the highest example of God's effective word and differs from any extra-sacramental word which may be able to effect grace on occasion. When we say that the sacramental word works *ex opere operato,* we mean that it is the fullest actualization of the Church as the primal sacrament of Christ, because in the sacraments the Church's real-symbolic expression of her sacramental essence takes place through her absolute commitment to an individual Christian in the decisive salvific situations of his life. Unlike the "sacraments" of the old law, the truly sacramental word is God's eschatologically unconditioned word of grace to man, a word which can never be replaced or endangered, as were the "sacraments" of the old law, by any other word in salvation history.[25]

The Divine Institution of the Sacraments

There is one other problem we should reflect upon before moving on to a consideration of each individual sacrament and its relationship to the Church. It is the question of the divine institution of the seven sacraments. The Council of Trent tells us that there are only seven sacraments and that they were all

instituted by Christ. This statement poses some difficult theological and historical problems. The basic difficulty lies in attempting to explain the divine institution of all seven sacraments
in a manner that is historically plausible. The solution is not as
easy as the reader may perhaps suppose.[26]

For instance, the supposition that Christ himself instituted
each of the seven sacraments by a separate verbal formula is
hard to reconcile with the historical evidence we possess. For
one thing, we can discover no reference in Scripture or in the
first four centuries of the Church's tradition to the sacramental
nature of matrimony. A similar problem exists in the case of holy
orders. If we assume, then, that Jesus went to the trouble of
explicitly instituting these two sacraments, then we must also
explain how they came to be overlooked during the formative
centuries of Christian belief.[27]

Confirmation and extreme unction pose a slightly different
problem. As far as we can tell, the rite of confirmation was initially part of the baptismal rite. With time and the growing practice of infant baptism, it became separated from the baptismal
rite itself and took on a separate sacramental status. The evidence
here points rather clearly to the development of one sacrament
from another. From a theological standpoint there is no great
difficulty with such a development, since we know that the
graces conferred by the different sacraments imply one another,
as in the case of the eucharist and extreme unction, which can,
like penance, forgive sins. In the face of such an historical
development, is it really meaningful to insist that Christ himself
instituted the sacrament of confirmation by an explicit formula
which clearly distinguished it from the other six sacraments?[28]

Extreme unction also offers us historical problems. Our only
scriptural grounds for asserting the existence of extreme unction
in the primitive Church is a single text in the Epistle of St. James
which refers to an anointing of the sick by the presbyters of the
Church. Prior to Trent, many theologians felt that this text alone

was too vague to prove the specifically sacramental character of this anointing. How, then, did the Church come to an explicit awareness at the time of Trent that the anointing of the sick referred to by James was truly a sacramental rite?[29]

Rahner feels that the problem of the divine institution of the seven sacraments is best explained in terms of the historical evolution of divine law. The Tridentine definition of the divine institution of the seven sacraments was made in a dogmatic rather than in a purely historical context. There is no evidence in Trent that the Council Fathers wished to assert that Jesus himself explicitly instituted each of the seven sacraments with a special verbal formula. Rather, in the face of Protestant attempts to eliminate some of the sacraments as being not of divine institution, the Council merely asserts the actual existence of seven, and only seven, sacraments and insists on the fact that all of them exist by the institution of Christ.[30]

But once we recognize the fact that the Church is itself the primal sacrament, most of the difficulties concerning the divine institution of all seven sacraments disappear. For necessarily implicit in the institution of this primal sacrament are those sacramental self-realizations of the Church which now constitute the seven individual sacraments. Moreover, granted the nature of the evolution of divine law, the seven sacramental rites defined in Trent could still claim to be of divine institution even should they have received their definitive historical explicitation through a free decision on the part of legitimate ecclesiastical authority rather than by a necessary deduction from the essence of the Church as such (provided, of course, that each of them was proportioned to the Church's essential nature and constituted a genuine self-realization of the Church as the primal sacrament). Rahner is even inclined to leave it an open question whether in the course of time other sacraments might be explicitated within the present system of seven sacraments. The generic nature of the sacrament of holy orders, which now includes the episcopacy, the priesthood, and the diaconate, would seem to indicate that such a development is possible. For although the number seven is not an arbitrary one, we need not necessarily think that an *a priori* deduction of the sacraments is automatically possible. Rather, we must attempt to determine *a posteriori* which actions of the Church constitute definitive sacramental commitments to the individual Christian, and hence which actions of the Church are in fact genuine sacramental signs. In the rest of this chapter we shall attempt just such a consideration by examining briefly the relation between the sacramental actions of the Church and the nature of the Church as the definitive sign of grace.[31]

The Ecclesial Dimension of the Sacraments

The eucharistic word is the sacramental sign *par excellence*. The words of consecration pronounced by the priest are the very words with which Christ established God's new and eternal covenant with men at the Last Supper. Not only is Christ himself sacramentally present through the formula of consecration as a bond of unity among all believers and as the abiding guarantee of the irrevocability of his covenant, but the very formula itself expresses the most fundamental truth of the whole Christian message, the truth of our redemption through the passion and death of Christ. As a result, the whole kerygmatic message of the Church actually proceeds from the sacramental words of consecration, prepares for them, and announces them. Let us reflect a bit on what this last statement implies.[32]

The eucharist is the sacrament of the Word as such. Not only is the incarnate Word present under the appearances of bread and wine after the words of consecration, he is also present by virtue of the words themselves. This does not imply that the words of the sacrament are the efficient cause of the sacrament. They are rather an enduring constitutive moment within the sacramental sign itself which continues to be constitutive of the sacrament even after the words themselves have been spoken.[33]

Moreover, because the word of God spoken to man in this eschatological age must be heard in faith, the eucharistic word which renders the incarnate Word present among us is in a real sense born of the belief of the Church which by her faith posits the words of the sacrament as an inner moment of her own self-realization as the primal sacrament. Conversely, belief in the Lord present under the appearances of bread and wine is perpetuated in the Church by the sacramental word which renders him thus present among us as our food and spiritual nourishment. In other words, the effective word of God proclaimed in the Mass is actually the primal kerygma in which all other effective words of the Church participate, be they formally sacramental or not.[34]

Moreover, because at the eucharistic banquet the Church as a whole is present in the sacramental offering of individual Christian communities, which are themselves present in the world as concrete manifestations of the whole people of God, communion cannot be a mere act of personal piety. It has an essentially ecclesial dimension: to receive the body of Christ is to become more perfectly incorporated into his Mystical Body which is the Church.[35]

Needless to say, baptism and confirmation, the Christian sacraments of initiation, necessarily involve a definitive, graced commitment of the Church to the individual who seeks formal and visible acceptance in God's people in order that he may by his subsequent life and death truly manifest the grace of Christ to the world. Incorporation into the Church by the protestation of the Church's common belief, and not of a personal worldview, is thus not only an effect of baptism, it is itself the baptismal character. Moreover, because the grace received by baptismal incorporation into Christ's death is also incarnational, confirmation, as the sacrament of initiation into adult Christian living, introduces the baptized Christian into a life of charismatic witness to, and defense of, the faith. This fuller incorporation of the individual into the community involves a new and definitive commitment of the Church to him.[36]

Similarly, every time the Church intervenes in the life of an individual to free him from his sins, there must be a definitive sacramental commitment of the Church to the sinner. This happens most notably in the sacraments of penance and extreme unction.[37]

When one fails to live up to the obligations of Christian living imposed by the sacraments of initiation, the Church cannot remain simply indifferent if she truly desires to manifest Christ's grace visibly to the world. The pardon of sin in the sacrament of penance comes through reconciling the individual sinner with the community of believers he has dishonored by his sin and so reconciling him with God.[38]

Similarly, by her visible intervention at times of serious illness, the Church dispels from the death of her members that darkness which is a consequence of sin and gives visible expression to their eschatological hope and trust in God. Such an act at such a moment necessarily involves the definitive commitment of the Church to the individual and so constitutes a sacramental sign of eschatological grace.[39]

Moreover, since man is essentially social and society has of necessity a salvific meaning, Christian marriage is also a sacramental moment in the life of the Church and manifests the eschatological relation of God to his people.[40]

The love of Christ for his Church symbolized in Christian marriage is not merely an interesting religious metaphor; the relation and conduct of Christ to his Church actually reaches a visible fulfillment in marriage itself. Man is by his nature monogamous. Monogamous marriage is, moreover, the foundation of human society, the same human society which Christ entered and transformed definitively by becoming himself a man born of a woman. Even more, God created this monogamous, bisexual human nature precisely with a view to the incarnation and to the Church as the sacramental prolongation of the incarnation in time and space. And this Church which proceeds from the incarnate Word as the real symbol of God's definitive offer of eschatological grace in Christ is truly the faithful bride of Christ. When, therefore, a man and woman commit themselves irrevocably to one another in Christian love, this commitment can only be a sacramental manifestation of the eternal commitment of Christ to his Church.[41]

The basic problem involved in discussing the sacramental nature of holy orders is to show why the conferral of the official powers of the hierarchy also necessarily involves a definitive sacramental commitment on the part of the Church to the individual to whom such powers are given. Why, in other words, does the conferral of ecclesiastical jurisdiction also have to imply the conferral of sacramental grace?[42]

The hierarchy through their share in the triple authority of Christ to teach, govern, and sanctify are constitutive of the very essence of the Church. It is, then, reasonable to suppose that whoever shares in this power needs the grace of God if he is not to use it sinfully. One might object, of course, that the validity of individual, official acts of the Church's ministers does not depend on the personal sanctity of the ministers themselves. On the other hand, if the Church of Christ is to be the holy Church, a living symbol of grace in the world, some of its members must actually possess personal sanctity; and holy laymen are not enough to make a holy Church. The very sanctity of the Church's laymen depends radically on the sanctity of the Church's clergy. Even though it is true that a sacrament can be administered validly by a priest who is in mortal sin, still, no one can pretend that the valid administration of the sacraments is wholly independent of the good will of the minister himself. Even a minister in mortal sin must still intend to administer the sacrament for validity. We may conclude, then, that though the sacramental nature of the Church can survive the occasional administration of the sacraments by an unworthy priest, still, in a truly holy Church such sacrileges could not become a general rule. Upon the general and prolonged holiness of the clergy as a body depends, then, the continuation of the sacramental system as such within the Church.[43]

Moreover, the Church's sacramental words, as we have seen, are continuous with and prepared by the preaching of the Church. Like the preacher, the minister of the sacrament does not, in speaking the sacramental words, proclaim his own philosophy of life. Rather, he proclaims the living faith of the Church. The sacramental word ought, then, to find its ideal fulfillment in the graced, personal encounter of minister and recipient in a joint, personal act of faith, hope, and love.[44]

We may conclude, then, that the Church's conferral of official power to administer the sacraments upon an individual must also involve the Church's graced commitment to that individual in order that he may be worthy of his office and that he may learn to work out his own salvation in dispensing to others the redemptive grace of Christ.[45]

Only these seven situations—the eucharist, initiation into the Church and into an adult witness to the faith, the forgiveness of sins, the anointing of the sick, marriage, and orders—actually fulfill the definition of a sacrament. In any other situation, the word spoken by the Church—as in preaching or in the sacramentals—either lacks the Church's definitive commitment as the primal sacrament or is not spoken to the individual in a decisive salvific situation of his life.[46]

But Christ did not institute the sacraments simply for them to be understood. He instituted them to be used by men as an efficacious means of growing in grace. In the following chapter we shall consider the important relationship which exists between personal and sacramental piety.

NOTES

1. S, IV, 313–314.
2. _Ibid._, 315–317.
3. _Ibid._, 318.
4. _Ibid._, 318–319.
5. _Ibid._, 320.
6. _Ibid._, 320–321.
7. _Ibid._, 321.
8. _Ibid._, 321–322.
9. _Ibid._, 322–325.
10. _Ibid._, 326–327.
11. _Ibid._, 329.
12. KS, 11–13.
13. _Ibid._, 13–16.
14. _Ibid._, 17–18.
15. _Ibid._, 18–21.
16. _Ibid._, 21–23.
17. _Ibid._, 23.
18. _Ibid._, 23–26.
19. _Ibid._, 26.
20. _Ibid._, 26–27.
21. _Ibid._, 27–28.
22. _Ibid._, 28–30.
23. _Ibid._, 31–34; S, IV, 299.
24. KS, 34–36; S, IV, 297–298, 301.
25. S, IV, 337–340.
26. KS, 37–38.
27. _Ibid._, 38–46.
28. _Ibid._, 46–51.
29. _Ibid._, 52–62.
30. _Ibid._, 37–38, 64.
31. KS, 62–67; S, IV, 341.
32. KS, 73–76; S, IV, 349–350.
33. S, IV, 351.
34. _Ibid._, 352–355.
35. KS, 76–78.
36. _Ibid._, 79–82; S, IV, 342.
37. S, IV, 343.
38. KS, 83–85; S, IV, 343.
39. KS, 100–102; S, IV, 343.
40. S, IV, 342.
41. S, IV, 342; KS, 95–99.
42. KS, 85–87.
43. _Ibid._, 87–91.
44. _Ibid._, 91–93.
45. KS, 94–95; S, IV, 342–343.
46. S, IV, 344.

SUGGESTED READINGS

The Church and the Sacraments, W. J. O'Hara (tr.), (New York: Herder, 1963).

VII. Personal and Sacramental Piety

Catholics, in speaking about their Church, are often accused of a certain "triumphalism." The accusation is not altogether without foundation. Triumphalism, where it exists, often stems at least in part from the failure of Catholics to reflect that their Church is not only a motive for their faith but an object of their fervent belief. As a result Catholics often tend to overlook the possibility of there being a difference between their own fiducial experience of what the Church stands for and the experience of other men who can see nothing in the Church besides its external visible structure. It is not surprising, then, that to empirical eyes many claims made by Catholics about the Church may indeed seem to smack of triumphalism.[1]

The Ecclesiastical Dimension of Christian Piety

To a great extent, Catholic piety is still living that experience of the Church which found official expression in the documents of the First Vatican Council. To be sure, First Vatican did in fact teach many important things about the Church; but no one, least of all the Council Fathers themselves, would maintain that First Vatican exhausted all the true and valid statements about the Church which one can or even should make. If, then, one is to agree with the Council Fathers that the splendor of the visible Church constitutes a major motive for belief in Christ, one must also acknowledge that the work of the Holy Spirit within the Church is clearly visible only to one who actually views the Church with the eyes of faith.[2]

Catholics should, therefore, be wary of speaking of the Church exclusively in idealized terms. These terms have real meaning, but they should not prevent us from experiencing the Church in her less ideal, more human aspects. For although the Church sanctified by the spirit of Christ is and must always be a holy Church, it is also a pilgrim Church of weak men in search of that fatherland which is the eternal kingdom of God. It is also a Church of poor sinners who all too imperfectly heed the call of Christ to holiness and grace. It is also a Church which looks forward constantly to the darkness of a death illumined only by faith in Christ.[3]

But we can go a step further. Not only do we believe the Church as a sign of God's truth, the Church is itself constituted as a visible sign of grace and as an object of faith through the belief of its members. This fact fully realized has important consequences for Christian piety.[4]

As we saw in the previous chapter, it is the transforming presence of grace which puts each Christian in actual possession of the reality of God who is the object of his faith. Grace, moreover, comes to men, not as individuals, but as members of a human community which was redeemed by the incarnate Word—as members, therefore, of that community of belief which is the Church.[5]

For this reason, unity of belief within the Church is much more than saying the same thing as the *magisterium*. It is opening oneself to the mystery of God, and more specifically to that mystery of God incarnate which is sacramentally prolonged and realized in the Church itself. Ecclesial piety is, therefore, much more than the sum total of the piety of individual Christians;

for the piety of individual Christians can exist and grow only in and through their incorporation into a visible community of belief.[6]

This means that when Christians believe in the Church as an object of faith, they actually believe in one another as partakers of the transforming grace of God. The Church, therefore, as the visible manifestation of God's grace becomes present both in the world and to each individual Christian as well, precisely because men have believed in the gift of God. Hence, not only is the Church an object of faith, it actually exists as an object of faith precisely because it is believed.[7]

This view of the Church as a visible sign of grace constituted in and through the belief of its members helps throw considerable light on the relation between personal and sacramental piety. For implied in it are both the fundamental distinction and the intimate relationship which exist between the sacraments considered as real symbols of grace and the sacraments considered as the personal acceptance of grace in and through the external sacramental rite.[8]

The Theory of the "Two Ways"

Although there is no actual conflict between personal and sacramental piety, it is not always easy to reconcile the two dogmatically. For example, it is solid Church teaching that through spiritual communion one can receive the grace of the holy eucharist without actually receiving the sacrament itself. Similarly, since sin can be forgiven outside the sacrament of penance, one might wonder why a sincere examination of conscience and an act of perfect contrition could not often serve as a sufficient substitute for the current practice of frequent confessions of devotion. Again, if the sacraments of penance and communion form such an integral part of Christian piety as current sacramental practice might lead us to believe, then how is one to explain the fact that the Church has allowed Christians to employ both of these sacraments relatively rarely at different periods in the development of Christian asceticism?[9]

With regard to this last question, we would do well to recall that though modern theologians have offered a number of reasons why the frequent reception of the sacraments of confession and communion constitutes an integral part of Christian piety, these reasons are not always completely satisfactory from a dogmatic point of view. Some theologians, for example, argue to frequent reception from the fact that sacraments produce grace *ex opere operato*. But, as we saw in the preceding chapter, the *opus operatum* of the sacraments does not simply prescind from the personal dispositions of the recipient. It does not mean that the sacraments produce grace mechanically or even that the more often one receives a sacrament the more grace grows automatically in the soul. The amount of sacramental grace received depends radically on the dispositions of the recipient himself; and even then it need not be mathematically proportioned to the frequency of reception.[10]

Other theologians have urged frequent reception on the grounds that each sacrament gives a special sacramental grace which can be received only in the sacrament itself. Now, it is true that each of the seven sacraments produces its own special effect which distinguishes it from the other sacraments; but it is theologically questionable whether there are really any graces, whether sanctifying or actual, which cannot be received outside the sacraments. For it is one thing to speak of those effects which distinguish the sacraments from one another and quite another to say that God cannot produce these effects outside the sacraments themselves.[11]

Theologians have also argued for frequent reception of the sacraments by pointing out that God instituted the sacraments to be used and that whoever neglects the sacraments thwarts the express will of God. But even granted that the slothful neglect of the sacraments is sinful, what constitutes slothful neglect in a given situation? Are we to assume that the Church was herself guilty of sinful neglect when in past ages she deliberately countenanced the relatively rare reception of the sacraments?[12]

Part of the difficulty in giving a satisfactory dogmatic explanation of the relation between personal and sacramental piety comes from the tendency of many theologians to speak as though there were two completely different "ways" of acquiring and increasing grace: the "objective way" and the "subjective way" of individual sanctification.

The objective way is the way of the sacraments. Here the tendency is to use baptism as a model sacrament, and infant baptism as a model baptism. In such an approach, one's major theological preoccupation becomes the effort to establish the minimal dispositions necessary for the reception of any given sacrament and to treat these minimal dispositions as constitutive of the essence of the sacrament itself. In addition, the dispositions of the recipient tend to be represented as the minimal prerequisites which must be already present prior to the actual conferring of the sacrament itself.[13]

Theologians of the subjective way, on the other hand, tend to speak of the extra-sacramental reception of grace as if it were a purely subjective event without reference to the Church and to the sacraments.[14]

The proponents of the theory of "two ways" have got hold of a genuine theological problem: infant baptism is true and valid baptism, perfect contrition outside confession does restore one to the state of grace. But one can question whether the "two ways" constitute as rigid a dualism as their proponents sometimes seem to infer.[15]

The Incarnational Dimension of Christian Piety

In his own discussion of the relationship of personal and sacramental piety, Rahner insists first of all upon the incarnational character of grace. The grace of God which we now possess is that grace which is given to us in Christ. This grace, which flows from the hypostatic union of the Word of God with human flesh, is itself dynamically incarnational. It is the root source of the ultimate glorification of our human bodies and, as we shall see in a later chapter, of the gradual integration of nature into person. It transforms the whole of man, not just his soul.[16]

Now it is a metaphysical fact that because the soul is the form of the body, man is incapable of performing a purely spiritual action. Even man's acts of intellect and will depend upon electro-physical, corporeal changes in the human organism. As a result, the grace of Christ which transforms man's spiritual activity must of its nature possess a quasi-sacramental structure.[17]

At the same time, since grace is essentially an act of God, any human act posited in grace is also of its nature a manifestation of God's action upon man.[18]

Because the grace of Christ is intended for mankind as a whole, it must also reach individual men precisely as members of a human community of salvation. Now, the community of the just, precisely because it is visible, requires a hierarchical structure through whose personal actions of teaching and sanctification grace achieves incarnational visibility. The sacraments are just such actions. In other words, grace is present in the sacramental sign precisely because Christ chooses to deal symbolically with men in the sacramental actions of the Church. Thus, it is not the Church alone that confers the sacraments, it is Christ himself who acts within the gestures of the Church.[19]

In addition, the recipient of the sacrament must bring to the sacrament his personal desire to receive it. He must, in other words, personally will the historical manifestation of God's grace toward him through the sacramental action of the Church. The sacraments, therefore, are nothing else than a visible historical dialogue between Christ's Church and the individual Christian. They also constitute a more perfect incarnation of grace than any act of personal piety because in them the Church also speaks her effective words of grace to an individual in the name of Jesus Christ.[20]

It is false, then, to distinguish the subjective and objective ways of justification as if they were two separate and unrelated entities. Even when grace comes to man through the "subjective way," it comes to him in and through the Church. It is not an isolated event but the action of Christ upon a member of his body. Even spiritual communion and perfect contrition imply a desire for the sacrament.[21]

Similarly, the sacraments are the living embodiment of the charity and faith of the individual who receives them. One does not make a confession of devotion or go to communion, for example, just so that the Church may strengthen one's wavering faith. Rather, by incorporating himself into the Church's visible sacramental action, the individual Christian manifests and embodies his faith more intensely than he would by a spiritual communion or by a purely internal act of contrition. Even more, within the sacrament he encounters Christ's own response to his faith in the form of the sacramental action of the Church. Hence the sacramental action actually unites perfectly within itself both the objective and the subjective ways. For not only is it the visible, graced manifestation of a personal act of the recipient (*opus operantis*), it is also the visible manifestation of Christ's action upon the soul in the sacramental action of the minister (*opus operatum*).[22]

This insight into the continuity and interdependence of the "two ways" should underly any intelligent use of the sacraments. For just as the mutual love of a husband and wife which is implicitly present in their daily contacts with one another still seeks spontaneous expression from time to time in explicit manifestations of mutual affection, so in an analogous fashion the personal piety of good Christians should spontaneously seek formal expression in actions which are explicitly liturgical and sacramental, even when these actions are not of strict obligation.

The Practice of Frequent Confession

Hence, in dealing with the matter of frequent confession and communion, spiritual directors should avoid giving the impression that subjective dispositions are of no consequence in approaching the sacrament. Moreover, just as in marriage the full and solemn expressions of love can occur with greater or less frequency, so in the devotional use of the sacraments, frequency can depend on the personal spiritual needs and piety of the individual. Rahner wishes in no way to discourage the frequent reception of the sacraments, since this is in fact the approved modern usage. He is merely seeking to introduce an element of freedom and adaptability into their use by taking into account the personal spiritual needs of individual Christians.[23]

From a number of statements made above, the reader may have gotten the impression that Rahner would like to discourage the practice of frequent confessions of devotion. To avoid any misunderstanding, we might do well to clarify his thoughts on this particular point before proceeding any further. Far from discouraging frequent confessions, he is in fact quite concerned with keeping the devotion from degenerating into a mechanical practice devoid of personal meaning.[24]

One point perhaps needs clarification at the outset. The problem of frequent confessions of devotion is theologically quite different from the problem of the confession of venial sins. True enough, in a confession of devotion one confesses either venial sins or mortal sins already confessed and forgiven through sacramental absolution. Still, to say that venial sins and forgiven mortal sins are valid matter for confession does not prove either the need for or the advisability of making such confessions frequently.[25]

The problem here is much more that of the relationship between frequent confession and advancement in perfection. Ascetical writers all teach that advancement in Christian perfection brings with it the increasing realization of one's own sinfulness. Without questioning this teaching, some modern theologians have begun to wonder whether this increased self-knowledge need necessarily find expression in the practice of frequent confession. Some have even gone so far as to question the advisability of this practice at all.[26]

For Rahner, this latter suggestion seems exaggerated in view of the Church's official sanction of the practice. A more constructive approach to the problem, he suggests, would be to attempt to demonstrate modern man's special need for the frequent use of the sacrament.[27]

But in attempting such a demonstration, one would do well to question some of the traditional justifications for confessions of devotion proposed by spiritual writers. We refer specifically to the need for spiritual direction, the forgiveness of sins, and the sacramental increase of grace.[28]

As far as the need for spiritual direction goes, it could hardly be the decisive reason for the Church's encouragement of confessions of devotion. True, frequent confession may be an occasion for regular spiritual direction; and many actually prefer to seek direction in confession because of the sacramental seal of silence and because of the anonymous relationship of penitent to confessor. But confession is much more than an occasion to receive direction. It is a sacrament whose frequent reception, if it is to be justified, must take into explicit account the sacramental nature of the act itself.[29]

Nor is the problem solved simply by appealing to the power of the sacrament to forgive sins, since the sins confessed in confessions of devotion are either serious sins which have already been forgiven or venial sins which can also be forgiven outside the sacrament. Serious sins once forgiven cannot be forgiven again; and there is solid theological ground for our supposing that the eucharist is the ordinary sacrament of forgiveness for venial sin.[30]

Finally, there are too many ways of increasing in grace for one to attempt to justify frequent confessions of devotion exclusively on that basis.[31]

Frequent confessions can, of course, actually be a fruitful source of spiritual direction, of forgiveness, and of grace. What Rahner is questioning is whether these three benefits sufficiently explain confessions of devotion when they are viewed within the context of the concrete spiritual needs of modern man.[32]

Rahner suggests that a modern justification for frequent confessions of devotion can be found in a consideration of the nature of the sacraments in general and of the sacrament of penance in particular. As we have already seen, the adult reception of the sacrament involves a personal act on the part of the recipient by which he accepts the grace of Christ offered him in the sacrament. Hence the sacramental act is a visible, concrete manifestation not only of God's definitive offer of grace in Christ but also of man's free, personal acceptance thereof. Now, the sacrament of penance, because it is the visible manifestation of the grace of repentance and of reconciliation with God and with his Church, can and should be an especially potent force in forming the personal piety of modern Christians. For since penance, unlike the eucharist, is explicitly a sacrament of reconciliation, it manifests man's need for God's forgiveness with greater clarity than does the mere reception of holy communion. Rahner argues that modern man, surrounded as he is by a rationalistic and naturalistic milieu, has a special need to acknowledge frequently the primacy of God's forgiving grace over his own acts of sorrow and contrition. He also suggests that frequent confession can be an efficacious means of bringing modern Catholics to a realization that all sin, even venial, is an offense not only against God but against one's fellow Christians. In an age when men are tending more and more to react against an exaggerated individualism, such a realization is of no small ascetical advantage.[33]

These reflections help to throw considerable light on the present use of sacramental confession in the Church. We say the present use because in its historical evolution confession has assumed such diverse forms that theologians of the sacrament are often hard put in their efforts to rule out different types of confession as being of their nature contrary to the substance of the sacrament. It is a simple fact, for instance, that St. Augustine never went to confession, that for many years confessions of devotion did not exist in the Church, that in the early Church confessions were as a rule postponed until one was on one's deathbed, that the early Christians frequently advised a young person in danger of death to postpone his confession until he was certain to die, since in the event of his recovery he would certainly lose the grace of confession by sins of the flesh, and that for centuries Christians were allowed to confess only once in their lifetime. The medieval theologians of confession, we know, did not bother to distinguish between perfect and imperfect contrition; and St. Thomas held that no one in the state of grace was obliged to make an annual confession.[34]

These facts should not scandalize modern Christians, for they merely prove that the sacrament of penance is a living institution, which, precisely because it is living, is in a constant state of development. On the other hand, this development imposes upon confessors and pastors of souls the serious obligation of seeing to it that the future evolution of the sacrament proceeds along healthy lines. Unfortunately, we have constant reason to be alarmed at the possible course that such an evolution might take, for the popular piety of the simple and uneducated tends universally to degenerate into legalism, magic, and taboo. These three tendencies spring from our all too human limitations; more specifically, they are rooted in the inability of the unreflective mind to distinguish between personal perfection and the objective performance of ritual acts. In the sophisticated atmosphere of the twentieth century, such abuses, never healthy or justified, are even more dangerous, because they also tend to bring the sacrament itself into disrepute. In order to realize that the problem is a real one, confessors need only think of those pious penitents who either feel the need to invent sins in order to go to confession or cannot distinguish concretely the difference between material and formal sin.[35]

To counteract these magical tendencies, pastors of souls must work to deepen in their spiritual charges a realization of the theological as well as the personal meaning of the sacrament of penance. For instance, on the personal side, they must make sure penitents understand that the *opus operatum* is not the automatic, magical conferral of grace and that the full effectiveness of the sacrament is measured by the personal dispositions of the penitent. Penitents must be made to realize that Christ did not institute the sacrament just to save men the effort of personal contrition; that where there is no genuine contrition, sacramental absolution is impotent to work forgiveness; and that true contrition is the vital transformation of one's life and not just the cheap regret contained in a weak "if only I hadn't." Finally, pastors of souls must themselves realize that unless they train our Christian youth in a personal and meaningful use of the sacrament, these same young people in later life will almost certainly be repulsed by the semi-magical practices they have learned and will eventually abandon the sacraments altogether, simply for the lack of proper spiritual formation.[36]

Not only must Christian pastors make sure that their penitents make of their confessions meaningful personal acts, they must also see to it that our Christian people understand the nature of the sacrament of penance in all its aspects. For instance, penitents must learn to regard the sacrament as a genuine mystery, as the judgment of the cross upon the sins of the world and upon their own sins, as, therefore, a part of an abiding salvific dialogue between God and man.[37]

Some Forgotten Aspects of Penance

In addition, modern sacramental catechesis almost always tends to overlook a number of important aspects of confession. For instance, how many Christians consciously reflect that the sacrament of penance is a manifestation of the fact that sin is an offense not only against the will of God but also against the Christian community itself? When an individual assumes membership in the Church, he simultaneously assumes as his own personal trust and obligation the Church's duty as the primal sacrament to manifest existentially the holiness that has come to men through the grace of Christ. When, therefore, a Christian sins seriously, he not only sins against God; he also fails seriously in the living testimony which is his duty as a member of the Christian community.[38]

Although it is frequently overlooked, this ecclesial aspect of sin is clearly testified to both by Scripture and by the early confessional practice of the Church. The rarity of confession among the early Christians was simply an expression of their vivid consciousness of serious sin as a betrayal on the part of the sinner of the trust which the rest of the Church had lovingly placed in him.[39]

Although the confession of venial sins does not involve as total a reconciliation, even it has a communitarian aspect. Needless to say, because venial sins are qualitatively different from mortal sins they are to a lesser degree offenses against God and the Church. Nevertheless, they still constitute a visible failure of holiness in a member of Christ's body; and as such they are also valid matter for the visible reconciliation of sacramental absolution.[40]

Rahner feels that modern Catholics have much to learn on this score. They are too little conscious of the fundamental fact that neither justification nor the loss of grace is a purely private event. Since the coming of Christ, both sin and justification are essentially communal realities. Although the Old Testament psalmist could lament that he had sinned against God alone, the Christian of the new and definitive covenant who sins against God is by that very fact a source of scandal and offense to his brothers who share with him the sanctifying grace of Christ.[41]

This ecclesial aspect of sin was much clearer to early Christians than it is to their modern descendants, owing to the Church's primitive practice of publicly "binding" prospective penitents. This practice has now largely fallen into disuse, so that modern theologians usually explain that the Church "binds" a penitent nowadays when she refuses him absolution, the idea being that by this refusal the Church obliges the penitent to return to confession when he is properly disposed.[42]

But in the early Church binding had a very different meaning. It was a kind of excommunication, though not in the modern canonical sense of the term. It consisted in the solemn liturgical exclusion of penitents from the official worship and life of the Church for the period preceding their sacramental absolution. During this time of ritual separation, they were also bound to perform public acts of penance.[43]

In thus binding a baptized Christian who had had the misfortune to fall into serious sin, the primitive Church was attempting to manifest visibly the true communal significance of the penitent's guilt, that by betraying the grace of baptism the fallen Christian had actually placed himself outside the communion of the just.[44]

Needless to say, the Church bound penitents only in order to loose and absolve them; binding and loosing are two phases in one and the same process. But both of them must be taken into account in order to reach a full appreciation of the Church's official attitude towards sin. For it is not alone through absolution but also through the public manifestation of the sinner's guilt as an offense against both the Church and God that his sin is ultimately removed.[45]

This practice of binding still survives in the Church, but in an obscurer and more diluted form. The main source of its obscurity lies in the fact that nowadays many people go to confession who do not need to, while many do not go to communion who should. For the modern equivalent of binding consists basically in the serious obligation incumbent on all baptized Christians of submitting any serious sin they may commit to sacramental absolution before they are allowed to approach the communion table. In a hypothetical parish where everyone in the state of grace would go to communion and no one but those in mortal sin would go to confession, the visibility of this "binding" would be more manifest. Still, neither the obscurity of the binding nor the fact that it now takes place *latae sententiae* instead of *ferendae* in any way alters its essential meaning.[46]

What *is* important is that this binding is still a visible, liturgical manifestation of the communal aspects of sin. The only real difference is that the visibility of binding in its present form exists in the sacramental rather than in the external forum.[47]

Nor is this sacramental binding as ineffectual a means of disposing the sinner to repentance as one might suppose. One need only speak to those living in serious sin to know that being barred from the common eucharistic table can mean a great deal to the sinner himself.[48]

At this point a possible difficulty may well occur to the reader. How, he may ask, can this sacramental binding belong to the essence of the sacrament of penance when the sacrament can be validly received without such binding actually being present? In a confession of devotion, for instance, in which a penitent accuses himself of venial sins only, the penitent is not only not barred from the eucharist prior to sacramental absolution, but he knows that the very reception of the eucharist can itself forgive his sins.[49]

In attempting to handle this objection, Rahner admits quite frankly that the Church does not bind a penitent in the case of unconfessed venial sins as she does in the case of unconfessed mortal sins. But on the other hand, even though venial sin does not separate one from the inner life of faith, it does separate one from the perfection of charity which comes to us from God through the Church. Moreover, even though one can restore the fervor of charity through prayer, the eucharist, or good works, nevertheless, when an individual in venial sin comes to the Church because he takes his guilt seriously as an offense against the Church as well as against God, he freely places himself in a situation which is analogous to the Church's obligatory binding of serious sin. In a sense, then, the penitent binds himself because he realizes that there is no sin which is not in some sense also a sin against one's neighbor.[50]

An interesting remnant of this primitive penitential liturgy of binding are the two prayers which the priest recites before he begins the formula of absolution. The liturgical meaning of these prayers was more evident in the early Church when the bishop, in binding the penitents to a period of public mortification, laid his hands upon them and prayed for them in the name of the Church before barring them temporarily from the common life of the Christian community. These two prayers still survive in the present formula for confession as a permanent symbolic manifestation of the fact that it is the Church who goes forth to meet the penitent by her prayers long before he approaches her for absolution.[51]

But the Church, as we have already said, binds the penitent sacramentally only that she may loose him through the words of absolution. Theologians have long disputed the relationship between the formula of absolution and the acts of the penitent in constituting the sacramental sign of penance. Scotists regard the acts of the penitent—his self-accusation, contrition, and resolution of amendment—as a necessary condition for absolution, but as nothing more than a condition. Thomists, on the other hand, maintain that the acts of the penitent are related to the absolution of the priest as matter is to form. The genuine insight which underlies the scholastic terminology of the Thomists is that the sacramental sign of confession is constituted in its essential integrity by both the acts of the penitent and the absolution of the priest. In other words, the penitent is not himself utterly passive before the grace-bringing sacramental sign. Instead, he himself contributes positively to that sign by the penitential acts he himself performs, even though it is the absolution of the priest which gives to those acts their ultimate meaning and sacramental efficacy.[52]

Moreover, according to the promise of Christ, the absolution of the priest looses sin "on earth" and "in heaven." What this promise of the Savior actually means is that the ecclesiastical act of binding and loosing, of exclusion from the Church and reconciliation to the communion of the just through absolution, is a sacramental event in and through which the guilt of the baptized sinner is remitted before God. In other words, it is the act of reconciliation with the Church which constitutes the essence of the sacrament of penance. For through the external sign of reconciliation one begins to share once again in the justifying spirit of Christ and becomes capable once more of manifesting visibly that holiness which comes from the presence of God within the soul.[53]

Theologians have long disputed whether or not the penance imposed in confession is also an integral part of the sacramental sign. Rahner is inclined to think that it is; for it would seem that the liturgy of repentance and reconciliation is not ended simply when the penitent leaves the confessional. The penance imposed is not just an external punishment; it is a personal act of the penitent by which he consciously acknowledges the burden of his guilt. It actually completes the process of his total conversion to God and reconciliation with the community. His penance may be said to take away the temporal punishment due to sin inasmuch as his action contributes to that complete personal integration in grace which the good Christian must achieve either in this world or in purgatory.[54]

The Theological and the
Psychological Dimensions of Guilt

Once modern Catholics have realized the deep personal and theological meaning of the sacrament of penance, pastors of souls will have no reason to fear the competition of psychotherapists. For though both priest and psychotherapist are concerned with the problem of human guilt, they approach it from completely different though complementary viewpoints.[55]

As a basic theological concept, guilt means something quite different from the psychic phenomena, such as states of depression and mental unbalance, which preoccupy the psychotherapist and go by the same name. For the theologian guilt does not designate a sickness but a free, personal act according to its particular degree of truth or falsity, justice or injustice. It exists, therefore, at the level of free spirit and not at the level of psychic mechanisms.[56]

Similarly, for the theologian guilt means much more than the violation of community conventions. Theological guilt goes much deeper than mere taboo. It exists at the most fundamental level of man's personal dealings with God.[57]

Theologically, therefore, there can be guilt only where man knowingly and deliberately sins against God. Where there is no knowledge and will present, there may be material sin; but there is no guilt.[58]

Moreover, for the theologian guilt is primarily an event rather than a state. The state of sinfulness merely results from the guilty act, although the personal act is not, of course, always clearly separable from the state of sin and may even on occasion become the expression of the abiding malice of that state.[59]

The concretization of human guilt in an external act is a part of the constant dialectic of matter and spirit. Because man is an incarnated spirit who knows himself only insofar as he knows that which is distinct from himself, he needs the material world in order to achieve personal fulfillment in the exercise of freedom. When he freely posits a sinful act, he closes himself to God by resting in the good things of this world to the exclusion of God. The external act in which his choice is incorporated is the sign, the visible manifestation, of his spiritual abandonment of God. This external manifestation of guilt is not identical with personal guilt, it is rather that visible reality through which man sees himself and recognizes himself as a sinner. Moreover, this dialectic is present in every sinful act, inasmuch as every sin, even those we regard as purely "internal," finds expression in physical changes within the human composite.[60]

But even though man is a being constructed from the inside outward, he still possesses a personal center of spiritual transcendence by which he is ordered to being as such, and hence ultimately to God. Because of his inner transcendence, every man must maintain a state of existential openness to the whole of reality if he is to achieve complete personal fulfillment. In its perfection, this spiritual openness also includes a readiness to hear and accept the word of God. But because man is spirit incarnated, he cannot express even this deepest center of his being except through constant interchange with his environment. As a result, even though his actions are objectifications of his person, they never express his person exclusively. They always contain within themselves environmental elements which are foreign to the person as such.[61]

In speaking of human actions, then, we must distinguish carefully between the person insofar as he is spirit and freedom before God, the partially assimilated material medium in which the human person must seek perfection and fulfillment, and the definitive person who through his activity has achieved a particular degree of concrete perfection. It is important to note in this context that a concrete remnant of one's personal self-expression in matter remains within the self even after the personal act which constituted it has ceased.[62]

These reflections may help us to understand a bit more clearly the distinction between sin and suffering. Sin is a free act of the primal person in the center of his being, where he lives in openness to God and through which he transforms the material medium of his actions in its relation to God himself. Suffering is a constitutive element of sin insofar as it transforms the material medium of a sinful action. It is the material expression of an inner contradiction between the sinful action and the human person who posits it. Note well, however, that suffering as the material expression of a personal act can outlast the personal act of which it is the expression. Moreover, as an objective transformation of man's material environment, it can affect even those innocent of its existence. When a Christian encounters innocent suffering, he can react to it in one of two ways. If he himself accepts the suffering in innocence, he unites himself to the innocent Christ in his passion and death. But if he responds to suffering guiltily, even though he himself was not its original guilty cause, he becomes himself the source of new guilt and contributes freshly to his own burden of suffering and to that of his fellow men.[63]

At this point it would be well to point out the ambiguous nature of any external action as an expression of personal guilt. For even though our subjective awareness of personal guilt becomes objectified in our awareness of our own external sinful action, still because every external act takes place in a medium which can be formed by passivity as well as by action, the external actions of men always remain ambiguous signs of guilt. We have no clear-cut norm for determining with any absolute certainty the extent to which an apparent sinner is the victim of suffering or the agent of guilt. We can, of course, assess our own guilt with greater certitude than that of others; but it is really only God who searches the depths of the human heart.[64]

This fundamental distinction between guilt and suffering helps us to distinguish the respective roles of the confessor and the psychotherapist with greater precision. Suffering is a constitutive sign of guilt, not the same thing as guilt, not even always the result of personal guilt. If it is accepted properly, it can even become a source of sanctification by uniting us with the innocent Christ in his passion.[65]

Freedom from guilt, on the other hand, can come only from God. It involves an act of personal conversion which is essentially the assumption of a position, a stand, with regard to God. More-over, because it has God as its object, only God can take away man's guilt.[66]

The forgiveness of guilt is, therefore, essentially different from the elimination of suffering; for even when sickness and suffering result from guilt, they remain essentially distinct from it. As a result, even after theological guilt has been forgiven, one may still have to cope with its residue of personal suffering. But however praiseworthy the fight to eliminate suffering of any sort may be, it should not blind us either to the inevitability of some suffering in human life or to its redemptive value in Christ.[67]

There should, however, never really be any cause for conflict between the priest and the psychotherapist provided each is careful to respect the limits of his own proper activity. The function of the priest is to mediate God's forgiving word to guilty men. The function of the psychotherapist is to eliminate the suffering which lies at the root of psychic illness. Both seek to heal the soul, but each does so in his own manner. This common goal of healing, far from separating them, should be a source of mutual and enlightened cooperation.[68]

Catholic devotion to the eucharist has traditionally centered around the dogma of the Real Presence. But under the impact of both the liturgical and the ecumenical movements, Catholic theologians have begun to re-examine the old controversies of the Protestant Reformation about the Real Presence. Rahner himself feels that the inter-faith polemics which have long surrounded this dogma have sometimes tended to obscure rather than to clarify the Church's true teaching concerning it.[69]

The Doctrine of Transubstantiation

In explaining the Catholic dogma of transubstantiation, Rahner makes a fundamental distinction which he hopes will render the doctrine more palatable to Protestant theologians. He states that the dogmatic explanation of a truth of faith may be either logical or ontic. A logical explanation translates the truth—say, a statement of Scripture—into terms less open to misunderstanding, but without altering or expanding the content of the original statement. An ontic explanation, on the other hand, preserves the content of the original statement from misunderstanding precisely by expanding and developing its explicit content. The distinction appears to be fundamentally the same as that between a formal and virtual implicit.[70]

Rahner feels that the divergence of opinion among Catholic theologians as to the meaning of the dogma of transubstantiation is an indication that the dogma as found in the Council of Trent is only a logical, not an ontic, explanation of the words Christ used in instituting the sacrament, "This is my body, this is my blood." In confirmation of this suggestion, he points out that the council itself in defining transubstantiation declared the dogma to be taken from Christ's words and carefully avoided giving approval to any philosophical interpretation of the term "transubstantiation." When, therefore, the council states that the substance of the bread is changed though the species of the bread remain, it is not defining any philosophical concept of substance and accidents but merely asserting in terms less equivocal to the Renaissance mind that the consecrated bread is truly Christ's body even though it still looks like bread. Rahner feels that once transubstantiation is understood in this light, the doctrine itself should offer no great difficulty to orthodox Lutheran theology, which itself defends a doctrine of the Real Presence, even though Catholics and Lutherans may still remain divided concerning the binding force of such a conciliar pronouncement.[71]

Unfortunately, Catholic emphasis on the doctrine of the Real Presence has sometimes tended to obscure the true meaning of the eucharist in Christian piety. We know, for instance, that in the past Catholics have sometimes overlooked the fact that the sacrament was instituted primarily to be received, not primarily to be venerated.[72] Pastors of souls should protect their spiritual charges from any misconceptions in this regard by seeing to it that they are properly formed in a eucharistic piety which is theologically sound.[73]

Thanksgiving After Mass

For instance, not a few Catholics believe that the real reason one should make thanksgiving after Mass is in order to honor Christ, who continues to be present through the sacramental species in the stomachs of communicants. Now, though Rahner believes that thanksgiving after Mass is a meaningful and recommendable devotion, he questions whether there is a solid basis for the devotion in the continued sacramental presence of Christ in the communicant through the sacred species. Although his suggestion to the contrary has scandalized some pious souls, he advances some solid arguments in favor of his position.[74]

One should be clear on what is the basic problem here. Rahner in no way questions the doctrine of the Real Presence or the advisability of thanksgiving after Mass. What he questions is the appropriateness of the traditional theological justification for thanksgiving.[75]

All theologians agree that the Real Presence of Christ continues as long as the eucharistic species are present. The difficulty in understanding this doctrine, Rahner feels, stems in part from the medieval concept of substance. Trent, in speaking of the eucharist, actually talks of the substance of bread and wine being changed into the body and blood of Christ, but we should be wary of interpreting the word "substance" anachronistically, in a modern, scientific sense. Through modern science we know today that there are in fact many substances in bread, not just one, as one might surmise from reading Trent. When the council Fathers spoke of the substance and of the species of bread and wine, they were talking in much less sophisticated and in more common-sense terms than does the modern scientist. In using the terms substance and species, the council merely wished to assert that Christ is truly present in the eucharist as long as the consecrated appearances of bread and wine continue to exist by the standards of an ordinary common-sense judgment. For example, consecrated wine, when mixed with unconsecrated wine, ceases to be consecrated because in the eyes of common sense it ceases to have a separate existence of its own. Consecrated hosts which are so pulverized that they are no longer recognizably bread are no longer consecrated even though they retain the same chemical composition.[76]

By the same token, masticated bread ceases almost immediately to be bread in any recognizable sense of the term. Hence, once the consecrated host has been consumed, the Real Presence of Christ also ceases almost immediately. The mere fact that the chemical components of the bread may remain in the communicant for some time after the reception of the sacrament is by itself insufficient grounds to justify the conclusion that Christ is still sacramentally present under the species of bread.[77]

Not only is the continuing sacramental presence of Christ in the communicant for any length of time extremely questionable, the theory that the grace of communion increases *ex opere operato* as long as the sacred species are chemically present within the communicant is also open to serious doubt. The *opus operatum* of a sacrament is found in the sacramental sign itself. The sacramental sign of communion is its actual reception. The mere chemical presence of the sacred species in the stomach of the communicant is not a sacramentally meaningful sign.[78]

The basic weakness of attempting to justify thanksgiving after Mass by appealing to the sacramental presence of Christ in the communicant lies in a failure to distinguish Christ's sacramental presence from his pneumatic presence in the hearts of men. Those who propose such a theory seem to forget that the eucharistic presence is actually meaningful as the effective sacramental sign of Christ's pneumatic presence in the soul and that without that pneumatic presence through grace the mere eucharistic presence of Christ in the communicant becomes a sacrilege.[79]

Symptomatic of this same theological imprecision is the tendency to speak of Christ's presence in the communicant as "beginning" with communion. Logically, then, Christ should also "leave" as soon as the sacred species cease to be chemically present in the communicant's stomach. The fact that this conclusion is (fortunately) seldom reached does not eliminate the dogmatic imprecision implicit in its premise.[80]

These dogmatic criticisms of some of the pious justifications for thanksgiving after Mass are in no way intended to discourage the practice itself, which can be both praiseworthy and meaningful. For instance, for many priests it may be the only regular opportunity they have to spend time in meditation before the

Blessed Sacrament. Many souls may also find the practice a
useful counterweight to the sobriety and brevity of the Roman
liturgy.[81]

Moreover, every individual as an individual needs an extra-
liturgical outlet for his personal devotion. Of the many private
devotions in use in the Church today, the practice of thanksgiving
after Mass is perhaps the most liturgically meaningful. In the
liturgy of the Mass, we consecrate our day-to-day living to God
and receive from him the strength to conduct ourselves as
children of the light. The moments spent in thanksgiving after
Mass offer a useful transition from the sacred and somewhat
abstract solemnity of the liturgy to the hubbub and brutality of
modern living. Viewed in this light, thanksgiving after Mass is
simply a personal effort to apply the fruits of liturgical worship
to our daily lives.[82]

Visits to the Blessed Sacrament

Another aspect of popular devotion to the Blessed Sacrament
deserves serious consideration here, the practice of visits to the
Blessed Sacrament. The problem here is somewhat analogous
to thanksgiving after Mass, namely, the need for a solid theological explanation of the devotion's meaning and validity.

Here again theologians have tended to think exclusively in
terms of the real and adorable presence of Christ in the eucharist.
The trouble with such an explanation is that it overlooks the
fact that Christ is present in the eucharist not primarily to be
adored but to be received. Originally, the sacrament was kept
in the Church not as an object of veneration but in order to be
available for distribution to the sick who could not attend the
liturgical celebration of the Mass.[83]

If, then, visits to the Blessed Sacrament are to have genuine
meaning, they must have as their object the person of Christ
present in the sacrament as the food and life of our souls. A visit

to the Blessed Sacrament places the Christian in the presence of the sacramental sign of the death-offering of Jesus for our salvation. A visit to the Blessed Sacrament should, therefore, be a prolongation of one's participation in the Mass and an anticipation of one's reception of holy communion. Since, moreover, the eucharist is the sacrament of Christian unity, visiting the Blessed Sacrament need not lead to ascetical individualism.[84]

Such visits can also be the healthy manifestation of an altar-centered piety. In sacrificial religions the altar is always an object of special veneration. In the Christian tradition the altar is not just an instrument of sacrifice, it is itself a sacred thing, the spatio-temporal continuity of the sacrifice of Christ. Visits to the Blessed Sacrament can be an expression of this reverence for the altar; tabernacle piety is basically altar piety.[85]

Visits to the Blessed Sacrament can also be joined with the practice of spiritual communion. Not that spiritual communion should ever replace sacramental communion, to which it is essentially subordinated. But the practice of spiritual communion can become an expression of one's abiding union with Christ through faith and love. Every visit to the Blessed Sacrament should in fact be a spiritual communion. For the individual Christian, the practice of spiritual communion can thus become a vital link between tabernacle piety and sacramental piety.[86]

Education for Eucharistic Piety

Rahner feels that spiritual directors should pay special attention to the proper formation of the young in eucharistic piety. Such formation is as important as it is difficult, for it concerns the central mystery of Christian belief, the *mysterium fidei* par excellence. The problem is even further complicated by the fact that eucharistic devotion, like the liturgy of penance, has undergone an elaborate historical evolution which has a claim to our respect. In spite of the brasher assertions of some liturgists, no one can claim to have formulated *the* eucharistic devotion. Eucharistic piety cannot be dictated *a priori*. Each generation of Christians must find its own personal relationship to the eucharist, upon which theologians have a subsequent duty to reflect.[87]

Before addressing ourselves to the specific problem of training young people in eucharistic piety, we would do well to pause a bit and reflect upon the meaning of the Mass for Christian living in general. First of all, the Mass is not Christianity. People today would like to have simple and easy solutions to their religious problems; but there is no single formula, not even a liturgical one, which can claim to be a sure-fire recipe for religious success. No single devotion, not even the Mass, can claim to be the only key to Christian living, even though the Mass is at the very center of Christian belief and cult.[88]

This last statement may seem shocking, particularly to liturgical zealots, but it is nevertheless true. The Mass symbolizes and even contains our redemption in Christ; but important as it is, it is not so important that it precludes the existence of the other six sacraments. Moreover, the grace of God which comes to us in Christ transcends even the sacramental order and is present to us at every moment of our existence. In a very real sense, Christians approach the altar of sacrifice to do there what their day-to-day Christian living has made them worthy to do.[89]

Indeed, God alone is the true and ultimate center of our religious life. We reach God, of course, through the sacramental order; but it is important to focus our piety upon God himself, lest we fall into different forms of religious monomania. Our devotion to the Mass, to be truly liturgical, must be realistically viewed in the total context of Christian living. In forming our young people in liturgical piety, this fact is of cardinal importance and must never be lost sight of. Young people indeed must learn to look upon the Mass as the center of their faith, but their faith can have a genuine center only if they have also learned to live a full and complete Christian life.[90]

In speaking of the Mass as well as of the other sacraments, we must, of course, avoid any mechanical notions of the *opus operatum*. Even sacramental grace *ex opere operato* must be received in a prepared human subjectivity. There is, of course, room for a genuine reciprocity here. For instance, though imperfect contrition suffices for the reception of the sacrament of penance, it does not suffice as a permanent attitude of living. The sacramental order exists to lead men to perfect love and to convert that love to a permanent attitude of soul.[91]

Hence education for full participation in the Mass cannot be simply education for liturgical and community worship. It must also be education for personal piety and for integral Christian living. Only by being a complete individual formed in grace can a Christian truly participate in the explicitly liturgical, communitarian aspects of worship. Our liturgical instruction of the young must, therefore, awaken in them a vivid awareness of the majesty and mystery of God's eruption into human affairs. They must learn in their day-to-day living the meaning of thanksgiving, of the presence of God, of abandonment to him, of contrition, etc. Otherwise their presence at Mass will necessarily degenerate into a meaningless ritual formalism. The Mass of daily living is an irreplaceable preparation for the Mass of the Church.[92]

Education for full participation in the Mast must, therefore, also be education for inner personal fulfillment. Communal participation in the Mass is liturgically meaningful only if it is the personal participation of every member of the community. By the same token, any liturgical reforms undertaken in the Church will have their ultimate justification to the extent that they actually foster inner personal piety. This means in the concrete that in order to educate young people to full participation in the Mass, we cannot limit their education to liturgical acts themselves.[93]

How, then, in the concrete order is one to go about forming

young people in meaningful eucharistic piety? By young people we mean here those between the ages of fifteen and twenty-five. Rahner's suggestions, without exhausting the subject, provide an interesting point of departure.[94]

The Process of Spiritual Growth

He feels, first of all, that we need to introduce a certain amount of suppleness into our traditional concepts of human progress in Christian perfection. Although Scripture frequently speaks of conversion and change of heart, the sacred writers make no attempt to reduce progress in perfection to distinct stages or steps. St. Paul speaks of perfection in terms of the fullness of the knowledge of God, but knowledge for Paul is not the speculative gnosis of the Greeks. It is knowledge in the scriptural sense of the total, personal, affective experience of God.[95]

With the development of Christian thought, we find two fundamental approaches to progress in perfection. One tradition, beginning with Clement of Alexandria and culminating in the Pseudo-Dionysius, distinguishes three stages in perfection: the purgative, the illuminative, and the unitive. St. Thomas, on the other hand, distinguishes the beginner, the proficient, and the perfect. Post-Thomistic theology tends to parallel these two doctrines by equating the purgative way with that of beginners, the illuminative with that of proficients, and the unitive with that of the perfect. But this synthesis has never received any official sanction by the Church.[96]

Hence a historical investigation of the development of Christian ascetical theory reveals that though there exists something like degrees of Christian perfection, no one has yet elaborated a definitive explanation of what these levels or stages of perfection might be.[97]

There are a number of theories which aim to explain how progress in perfection comes about. Some theologians equate perfection with the amount of sanctifying grace in the soul, but they are hard put to explain why a fundamentally holy person need not start from scratch in his quest for perfection after falling into an isolated mortal sin. This approach suffers basically from an excessively quantitative notion of grace and tends to overlook the fact that moral growth is in fact a qualitative integration of the whole personality. It fails to explain, for instance, why a long life lived in the state of grace does not necessarily find fruition in personal perfection; or why a pious novice who has never sinned mortally during his life can grow into a cranky, intolerant, and thoroughly unbearable old priest.[98]

Another theological explanation of progress in perfection identifies spiritual growth with the degree of significance, worth, and perfection of different classes of moral acts. In this explanation beginners in the spiritual life, or those in the purgative way, are occupied with the fight against serious sin; the proficients, or those in the illuminative way, with the conquest of venial sin and imperfection; and the perfect, or those in the unitive way, with the practice of the counsels and the quest of what is more perfect. Corresponding to these three ways are the three degrees of prayer, discursive, affective, and contemplative.[99]

Although this theory is useful as far as it goes and can perhaps be verified in isolated cases of spiritual development, it is, Rahner feels, too rigid a conceptual structure to apply point by point to every individual Christian. In order to introduce more suppleness into this particular scheme of spiritual development, Rahner insists on the importance of taking into account the concrete situation of individual Christians.[100]

The term "situation" in this context is a broad and extremely analogous one. It includes such diverse concepts as the life-cycle of each individual, his age, degree of physical development, his abiding state of health, his nearness to death. Situation also includes one's fate, that is, those circumstances which set the *a priori* limits of free choice but which themselves lie outside the control of human freedom. It is also, and more concretely, a previous situation insofar as it forms and determines our present situation. For instance, whether or not I have already experienced a particular object can make a great deal of difference in the quality of my present experience of the same object. A religious conversion late in life is quite different from the conversion of an adolescent.[101]

The "Situation" of Christian Youth

Rahner feels that the spiritual formation of young people should take into account their concrete situation. Our present effort to explain spiritual progress as a facility in virtue which comes from the repetition of moral actions leaves much to be desired. This approach fails to distinguish adequately between a free act of virtue and psychic automatisms. Automatic reflexes are not virtues, though they can serve as an extra-moral basis for virtuous action. But instead of trying to develop virtuous automatisms, we should instead recognize the possibility of concrete variations in the practice of virtue according to the concrete situation in which a particular Christian may find himself. Now, the situation of young people is quite different from the situation of adults.[102]

The concrete receptivity of men to different religious truths varies considerably according to their physical, psychological and situational development. At one stage of his development, a man's piety may be more spontaneously trinitarian or sacramental than at another. We must also reckon with the possibility that the meaning of certain religious truths lies beyond the grasp of young people.[103]

Young people are optimistic. They look to the future with hope. In their growing awareness of themselves as persons, they are more conscious of their capacities than of their limitations.

They tend to approach life as though it were an athletic competition. In his concrete situation, the young person needs an asceticism which is active and constructive. God is for youth the highest formulation of its bursting optimism rather than the goal of its final submission in death. As a result, young people by reason of their situation are actually not quite capable of grasping the meaning of Christianity in its fullness. They tend to have little understanding of a commitment to God in the darkness of faith, or of the mystery of the cross with its hope against all hope and with its ultimate triumph through suffering.[104]

What young people can understand is God, the loving creator and father of all life, who sends each man into the world with a particular mission to perform. They can understand Christ as a friend and companion, a leader and conqueror, a brave and true brother protector. They can understand the Church as a community of men with the highest aspirations, bound together in faith to work for a better world.[105]

Eucharistic Piety and Spiritual Growth

Hence, although in forming the eucharistic piety of the young we cannot, and should not, omit the cross with all it implies, still we need not make the cross the focal point of our young people's piety. The Mass should be for them an Easter celebration of the new and effective alliance of God with men. It should be the sacrificial feast of Christian brotherhood and friendship.[106]

If this analysis of the spiritual needs of young people is accurate, then we must, in addition to training them in eucharistic piety, adapt the traditional liturgical form of the Mass to meet the needs of their concrete situation. The Mass as we have it now is too full of obscurities and repetitions to appeal to the young. We must change its basic structure and content so that it can become a genuinely personal expression of youthful self-offering to Christ. By thus training our young people in self-dedication to the hardship and sacrifice of full Christian living, we shall give them the best possible existential introduction to the mystery of Christian dying in the darkness of faith.[107]

But with growth in maturity there should also come a growth in one's awareness of the meaning of Christian suffering and of its relationship to the holy eucharist. For the eucharist as an offering is not merely the re-presentation of the saving death of Christ, it is our own personal participation in that death, in which the total self-offering of Christ in submission to the redemptive will of the Father found its most perfect expression. The Christian who participates in the Mass and receives the body and blood of Christ so joins his will to the will of Christ that the suffering of the crucified Savior transforms and elevates his own attitude towards suffering.[108]

Moreover, just as the Christian through the grace of baptism is drawn into the death and resurrection of Christ in such a way that his sufferings, precisely because they are transformed into a share in Christ's suffering and into a spiritual death to sin, become a sign of the inner presence of grace, so too the eucharist as the sacrament of the daily increase in grace draws the baptized Christian ever more deeply into the mystery of redemptive suffering.[109]

Finally, because the reception of the eucharist involves the more perfect incorporation of each Christian into the Mystical Body of Christ, and because the whole body shares in the suffering of one of its members, particularly when that member is its head, so participation in the eucharistic sacrifice must be for each Christian an expression of his inner willingness to suffer with his crucified Lord, and through the acceptance of suffering to prepare himself for the ultimate acceptance of death in the darkness of faith.[110]

The Mass and TV

We will conclude this rather lengthy chapter with a few remarks concerning Rahner's reflections on televising the Mass. It must be admitted that the tasteful televising of the sacred mysteries of the Mass presents certain problems, but Rahner assumes an exceedingly negative attitude toward any introduction of the TV camera into the church. He feels that the Mass is too sacred and personally intimate a thing to be exposed to common view on every television screen. He regards television as too profane and public a medium of communication to be compatible with personal participation in the sacrifice of the Mass through faith and love. It is interesting to note that the Constitution on the Sacred Liturgy adopted by the Second Vatican Council takes a much more balanced attitude toward modern means of communication. The council Fathers are content to stipulate that broadcasts of sacred rites, and especially of the Mass, be done "with discretion and dignity, under the leadership and direction of a suitable person appointed for this office by the bishops."[111]

NOTES

1. S, V, 379–380, 385.
2. *Ibid.*, 384–385.
3. *Ibid.*, 380–384.
4. *Ibid.*, 386.
5. *Ibid.*, 386–388.
6. *Ibid.*, 390–393.
7. *Ibid.*, 393–396.
8. KS, 67.
9. S, II, 115.
10. *Ibid.*, 115–116.
11. *Ibid.*, 116.
12. *Ibid.*, 117–118.
13. *Ibid.*, 119–120.
14. *Ibid.*, 120.
15. *Ibid.*, 121.
16. *Ibid.*, 126–127.
17. *Ibid.*, 127–128.
18. *Ibid.*, 128.
19. *Ibid.*, 129–132.
20. *Ibid.*, 132–133.
21. *Ibid.*, 135–136, 140–141.
22. *Ibid.*, 136–137.
23. *Ibid.*, 137–140.
24. S, III, 213–214, 234–237.
25. *Ibid.*, 211.
26. *Ibid.*, 211–213.

27. *Ibid.*, 213–214.
28. *Ibid.*, 214.
29. *Ibid.*, 214–215.
30. *Ibid.*, 215–217.
31. *Ibid.*, 217.
32. *Ibid.*, 217–218.
33. *Ibid.*, 221–223.
34. *Ibid.*, 227–229.
35. *Ibid.*, 229–233.
36. *Ibid.*, 234–237.
37. *Ibid.*, 237–238.
38. S, II, 143–145.
39. *Ibid.*, 145–146.
40. *Ibid.*, 146–147.
41. *Ibid.*, 147–148.
42. *Ibid.*, 148–149.
43. *Ibid.*, 150.
44. *Ibid.*
45. *Ibid.*, 150–152.
46. *Ibid.*, 152–155.
47. *Ibid.*, 155–156.
48. *Ibid.*, 156.
49. *Ibid.*, 157–158.
50. *Ibid.*, 158–160.
51. *Ibid.*, 171–175.
52. *Ibid.*, 161–167.
53. *Ibid.*, 177–180.
54. S, II, 182; III, 241–243.
55. S, II, 279–280; III, 244.
56. S, II, 280.
57. *Ibid.*, 280–281.
58. *Ibid.*, 281–282.
59. *Ibid.*, 282–283.
60. *Ibid.*, 284–286.
61. *Ibid.*, 286–287.
62. *Ibid.*, 287–288.
63. *Ibid.*, 289–290.
64. *Ibid.*, 290–292.
65. *Ibid.*, 293.
66. *Ibid.*, 293–294.
67. *Ibid.*, 294–296.
68. S, II, 296–297; III, 244.
69. S, IV, 357–358.

70. *Ibid.*, 372–374.
71. *Ibid.*, 374–378.
72. *Ibid.*, 383–384.
73. SG, 198.
74. *Ibid.*, 199–206.
75. S, IV, 387–388.
76. *Ibid.*, 389–392.
77. S, IV, 393–394; SG, 207.
78. S, IV, 394–395; SG, 207–209.
79. S, IV, 395–396.
80. *Ibid.*, 396.
81. SG, 199–201.
82. *Ibid.*, 202–206.
83. *Ibid.*, 215–220.
84. *Ibid.*, 223–224.
85. *Ibid.*, 226.
86. *Ibid.*, 227–231.
87. *Ibid.*, 148–150.
88. *Ibid.*, 150.
89. *Ibid.*, 150–152.
90. *Ibid.*, 152–155.
91. *Ibid.*, 155–157.
92. *Ibid.*, 157–160.
93. *Ibid.*, 160–162.
94. *Ibid.*, 162.
95. S, III, 11–14; SG, 162–163.
96. *Ibid.*, 14–19.
97. *Ibid.*, 19.
98. *Ibid.*, 19–21.
99. *Ibid.*, 22–23.
100. *Ibid.*, 23–24.
101. *Ibid.*, 24–26.
102. *Ibid.*, 26–30.
103. SG, 164–167.
104. *Ibid.*, 169–171.
105. *Ibid.*, 171–172.
106. *Ibid.*, 164–167.
107. *Ibid.*, 172–183.
108. S, III, 191–195.
109. *Ibid.*, 195–199.
110. *Ibid.*, 199–202.
111. SG, 185–197.

SUGGESTED READINGS

"Personal and Sacramental Piety," *Theological Investigations,* Karl Kruger (tr.), (Baltimore: Helicon, 1963), Vol. II, pp. 109–134.

"Forgotten Truths Concerning the Sacrament of Penance," *Theological Investigations,* Karl Kruger (tr.), (Baltimore: Helicon, 1963), Vol. II, pp. 135–174.

"Guilt and its Remission: The Borderline between Theology and Psychology," *Theological Investigations,* Karl Kruger (tr.), (Baltimore: Helicon, 1963), Vol. II, pp. 265–282.

"The Sacrifice of the Mass and an Ascesis for Youth," *The Christian Commitment,* Cecily Hastings (tr), (New York: Sheed and Ward, 1963), pp. 136–170.

"Developing Eucharistic Devotion," *The Christian Commitment,* Cecily Hastings (tr.), (New York: Sheed and Ward, 1963), pp. 171–204.

VIII. The Church of the Diaspora

Because it is the primal sacrament, the Church has the mission of manifesting to each succeeding generation of men the presence of eschatological grace in the world. Such has been the purpose of the Church in the past; it is the purpose of the Church today.

Hence, the problem of what it means to be a Christian in modern times is not merely a political, a historical, or a philosophical one. It is a theological problem with vast implications, for it involves the careful interpretation of the present situation of the Church in the light of revelation and Church tradition.[1]

The Church and the Modern World

Still, one might be inclined to wonder whether there can be such a thing as a theological problem which is concerned with the modern world. Can we really hope to find anything which treats the modern world in its modernity in a revelation which was made two thousand years ago? However one may go about giving a positive answer to this question, this much is sure: a revelation relevant for modern times would have to take the form of a prophecy, not in the sense of a prediction of specific events, but in the sense of a supernatural enlightenment which reveals the true inner nature of events.[2]

In attempting to assess the present situation of the Church

theologically, we should recall a few ideas presented in previous chapters. We have already seen that Christian time is not simply identical with world history and that the history of salvation in the strict sense is not simply identical with the history of human culture. Because this is so, no single historical age can be the definitive time of the Church. Rather the Church, precisely because it is the temporal manifestation of grace, must in its development find a variety of cultural expressions. Christianity, then, cannot be identified with a particular political party or cultural ideal. Instead, it must be vitally aware of the shifting patterns of human culture and of the human and religious implications of such current issues as modern technological progress and governmental centralization.[3]

Rahner himself feels that the present situation of the Church can be best characterized as a diaspora, an enduring situation which is a necessary, if not completely desirable, moment in the history of salvation and one full of consequences for contemporary Christian behavior.[4]

In evaluating the present situation of the Church, he suggests that we be careful to distinguish three types of historical situation: one which is as it should be, one which is without relation to the norms of equity, and one which is not as it should be but which must still be accepted because it cannot at present be changed. Situations of the last type, though they are unjust in themselves and involve some violation of equity, nevertheless have their positive meaning in the total history of salvation.[5]

The present diaspora is such a situation. The Middle Ages in Europe produced a cultural synthesis in which the role of the Church was dominant. But as soon as the Church in God's salvific providence was strong enough to survive the shock of dispersal throughout the world, the medieval cultural complex dissolved, and with it the temporal power of the Church. This temporal diminishment and political weakness was and is in conformity with the promise of Christ to his disciples that they would fall heir to sufferings and persecutions.[6]

The Meaning of the Diaspora Situation

What, then, does it really mean to speak of a diaspora situation? It means primarily that the cultural milieu of the modern Christian does not have a specifically Christian character. But this fact, though simply stated, entails a number of important practical consequences. First of all, it means that the faith of modern Christians, subject as it is to constant challenge, must depend radically upon the personal commitment of the individual under grace rather than upon the external support of institutions and social pressures. It means that the clergy, which in the Middle Ages was part of the upper class, is so no longer, and hence that Church and State are no longer in disastrous competition for political supremacy. It means too that modern laymen must assume increasing importance in the affairs of the Church.[7]

Ghetto Catholicism is for Rahner a failure to recognize the existence of a diaspora situation, the pretense that by some historical miracle the Middle Ages continue to exist in modern times. At its worst, ghettoism is the rejection of the divine mission to go and preach the gospel to every living creature. It is an attempt to abandon the New Testament conception of a missionary Church for the Old Testament conception of a chosen people.[8]

Acceptance of the diaspora situation as a necessary, if not ideal, moment in salvation history has other important consequences in the concrete handling of the business of the Church. For instance, where Catholic universities exist in a predominantly Protestant country, it means that these universities cannot be modeled on a Roman university if they are to avoid becoming ghetto universities. It means that direct ecclesiastical intervention into political matters is a thing of the past. It means that the time of Mass should be adapted to the rhythm of modern living: when men today have leisure time in the afternoon, the afternoon should be the time for Mass. It is fruitless to preach the mortifying advantages of an early rise to laymen for whom an early rise is physically impossible. It means that in moral matters we must make room for cultural as well as individual excusing circumstances. It means, finally, that the Catholic press and hierarchy must be sensitive to non-Catholic opinion.[9]

A realistic acceptance of the diaspora situation is something quite different from defeatism. On the contrary, only by accepting our situation as it really is can we effectively Christianize it. Ghettoism, where it exists, is apostolically ineffective precisely because it wastes its energies in defending the indefensible instead of adapting to a situation and mastering it.[10]

It is, then, in this diaspora Church that each individual Christian, be he pope or bishop, priest or deacon, pastor, religious, or layman, must bear witness to the grace that is his in Christ. Yet the kind of concrete witness each Christian is called upon to bear depends upon his role within the hierarchical Church. We are, in the figure of St. Paul, one body and many members. In the present chapter we will consider briefly the diversity of roles that different Christians have come to play within the visible Church in her efforts to manifest to the world the grace that is hers in Christ. We shall begin with a consideration of the role of those Christians who constitute the Catholic hierarchy.

The Pope and the Bishops: Collegiality

Perhaps one of the most important problems in modern theology is the problem of the relationship between papal and episcopal authority. Its answer, though of necessity difficult, is full of implications for the nature of the Church itself and for its pastoral practice in the contemporary world.[11]

Traditional Catholic theology speaks of the Church as hierarchical and monarchical in structure. Although this is a defensible position, Rahner suggests a certain amount of care in applying the term "monarchical" to the Church. If by a monarchical Church we mean one in which the pope as an individual has primacy of jurisdiction over the entire Church, including the bishops themselves, then the Church is truly monarchical.[12]

But if by a monarchical Church we mean something in the nature of an absolute monarchy, then our conception of the Church simply does not fit the facts. The pope is not an absolute monarch in the ordinary sense of the term.[13] There are in the Church official structural elements which exist independently of the pope and which constitute a genuine limit upon papal authority. Not the least of these elements is the college of bishops itself, which like the papacy is of divine institution. Thus, though the pope is superior in authority to any individual bishop as an individual, even to the point of being able to appoint and depose him, still the pope can never abolish the episcopacy as such. The power of the bishops as a college comes to them from God, not from the pope; and that power not even the pope can abrogate.[14]

Hence it is clear that the bishops are something more than officials in the papal court. Although their concrete relation to the pope is still in need of much more speculative clarification, this much at least is clear: on the one hand the pope can do whatever the bishops can do, and on the other hand whatever the bishops can do is always done under the pope and in union with him.[15]

Unfortunately the problem has been rendered even more complex by the definition of papal infallibility at the First Vatican Council. Non-Catholic historians of the Church tend to regard the theology of papal primacy, which followed upon Vatican I, as irreconcilable with the previous practice of the Church. According to this prior practice, they argue, bishops enjoyed a power of jurisdiction independent of papal authority. Hence they tend to regard Vatican I as a serious departure from an earlier and authentic Church tradition.[16]

Rahner suggests that a possible way out of this theological impasse lies in a conception of the Church as something more than a juridical entity. Individual episcopal sees, he suggests, are something more than jurisdictional areas within the total juridical complex of the Church. Could not, then, the answer to the problem of the relation between papal and episcopal authority lie in the clarification of the relationship between individual churches and the universal Church?[17]

The Church redeemed by Christ is, of course, the whole Church; but in ancient times local churches were also called "the Church." This usage was more than a *lapsus linguae*; it stems from the biblical concept that the true Israel was present wherever God's faithful remnant was to be found, that the whole of Israel lives in each part, and that that part is more than just a portion of the whole. When we apply these notions to the Church, we can conclude that the Church as a whole exists where she is an event of grace in the fullest sense of the term. As an event of grace, the local church is nothing else than a particular manifestation in time and place of the whole universal Church.[18]

It is extremely important in this context not to think of the Church as though it were the static substance of a decadent scholastic philosophy. The visible Church is more an event than a substance. Not that events alone constitute the essence of the Church; but when we speak of the Church as an event, we are forced to take into account her need for constant self-realization and self-renewal.[19]

Now, then, if the Church is an event, she is most fully an event when she achieves self-realization as a society, as a communion of saints. It is for this reason that the communal celebration of the Eucharist has occupied such a central position in the worship of the Church. It is the central action of the total complex reality which is the Church, that act by which the Church as the sacramental continuation of the presence of God incarnate among men brings to an explicitly sacramental realization the saving presence of Christ in her midst as an abiding bond of union and of love.[20]

Now, when the eucharist is celebrated by a local church, there exists an important reciprocal causality between the local community and the universal Church. It is because there is a universal Church that Christ is present sacramentally in the local community, while on the other hand the local community in turn through its sacramental act is a concrete manifestation and self-realization at a particular moment of space and time of the universal communion of saints.[21]

If we attempt to rethink the relation of pope and bishops in this larger, more universal context, many problems receive considerable clarification. The papacy exists because there is and must be one universal Church until the end of time; but because the universal Church must also exist as a multiplicity of local events if it is to exist at all, there must also be an episcopacy which through the eucharistic sacrifice and the administration of the sacraments transforms the local community into a self-realization of the universal Church. Thus, just as the universal Church is present in the local community, so too is the jurisdictional and sanctifying power of the Church present in the local bishop.[22]

The superiority of the papacy to the episcopacy lies in the fact that the jurisdictional and sanctifying power of the pope is a manifestation of the unity of the universal Church as such, whereas that of the bishop is a manifestation of the presence of the universal Church in some local community. But here one should note well that though the pope remains jurisdictionally superior to the bishops, he possesses no power of orders which is intrinsically superior to that of the bishops: he is himself the Bishop of Rome. Moreover, because the universal Church must exist in its local manifestations, the episcopacy like the papacy is truly of divine institution. Hence, when a bishop teaches, it is with his own authority that he does so. He is not simply a messenger of the papacy.[23]

The local bishop is, then, by reason of his office much more than a Vatican official. He possesses his own special charism. Though he must always recognize and respect the unity of the Church which is manifest in papal decrees, he must become in his own right a dynamic source of initiative within the Church, and most especially within his own diocese. All of this must seem very complicated to those who are content with nothing but simple solutions, but the fact remains that the Church is itself a very complex entity. Any oversimplification of its structure is of necessity a falsification.[24]

But we are still far from a complete explanation of the relationship of pope and bishops. For the more juridical aspects of the problem are complex in the extreme. For instance, what does it mean concretely to say that the bishops have unconditional rights which are of divine institution and hence cannot be abrogated by the pope, when the pope does in fact have the right in particular instances to intervene in individual dioceses and even to depose individual bishops? This is a very thorny problem and one which needs precise handling if it is to find an answer at all. So it might be well in the interests of precision to make a few preliminary remarks before proceeding to the heart of the matter.[25]

First of all, it is well to point out that in any well-ordered state, although a good part of natural law finds incorporation in positive law, positive law alone cannot be taken as an adequate expression of the whole of the natural law. The same is true in an analogous sense of the Church. The fact that the rights of the bishops may not in the past have found clear expression in canon law does not mean that those rights do not exist at all. More important than in any codex of laws, they exist vitally in the Church as a lived reality even though they may not at a given moment in time be reflexively comprehended as of divine institution.[26]

Secondly, the divine institution of the episcopate cannot be explained adequately by the questionable affirmation that although the pope cannot abolish the episcopacy as such, everything else in the relationship between pope and bishop is of purely human institution. For the divinely instituted episcopacy cannot be constituted by the power of orders alone (even ordinary priests can with special permission confirm); it is constituted rather by the jurisdictional power of the bishop as such. But if the episcopate is constituted essentially by its proper power of jurisdiction, then it follows that episcopal jurisdiction is not just a subdelegation of papal jurisdiction. It exists in its own right.[27]

Still, it is one thing to assert that episcopal jurisdiction exists side by side with that of the pope and quite another to determine the proper content of the jurisdiction of the individual bishop. Rahner suggests that one way to determine the concrete content of the divinely constituted authority of individual bishops is to define more precisely the divinely constituted authority of the episcopacy as a whole; for just as it is the essence of the Church which is the basis of the authority within her, so too it must be the essence of the episcopal college which is the basis for defining the rights of individual bishops.[28]

The Scriptural Basis of Collegiality

Our basic starting point in this discussion is, then, that the episcopal college as a whole is the rightful successor to the apostolic college (without, of course, implying the necessity of individual bishops succeeding to individual apostles). Now in the primitive Christian community, it was the apostolic college as a body which bore the full burden of authority within the

Church and not the individual apostles as such. For had the apostles received their authority individually from Christ and not as a group, then there could have been no question of their being subordinate to Peter as their head. A jurisdictional head implies a jurisdictional body. Hence we may conclude that the very primacy of Peter is itself meaningful only in the context of a group conferral of authority upon the apostolic college as a whole.[29]

Thus it is that Scripture refers to the apostolic college as a new Israel, a vital unity in which each member shares in the authority of the group in subordination to Peter, who is its head. But unfortunately Scripture gives us no neat juridical principle with which to settle the jurisdictional relationship between Peter and the other apostles. For the sacred authors, it is the Spirit of love and of truth who must by his unifying presence forestall any absolute conflict of authorities.[30]

The picture of the apostolic college which emerges from a reading of Scripture is, then, a complex one. Each member of the apostolic college actively rules the Church along with the other members. Even though he can seek to win the approval of the rest of the college for his ideas and policies, he possesses no domain of power which is exclusively his. But he can represent the other members of the college when they are not themselves physically present. This collegial sharing of authority also means that each member of the apostolic college has the serious obligation of giving a hearing to his colleagues; for each apostle must assume responsibility for the action taken by the college as a whole. Finally, the physical dispersal of the college in no way affects either the authority of the college as a whole or the jurisdictional primacy of Peter within the college.[31]

Now, we have said that the college of bishops taken as a group is the legitimate successor of the primitive apostolic college. This means among other things that the college of bishops as such is prior to individual bishops considered precisely as individuals. The college is not just the sum total of the individual bishops who make it up. It is itself the constitutive reality in which all of its members somehow participate in subordination to the pope, who in turn is not only a member of the college but its head and source of unity.[32]

The Function of Ecumenical Councils

One important consequence of the priority of the college as such over the bishops as individuals is the fact that the ecumenical council constitutes the highest governing power in the Church. Thus, bishops as individuals not only do not exercise the same powers as they do when acting in council, but in union with the pope they constitute in council a single supreme authority within the Church. Let us reflect a bit on what this means.[33]

Human experience shows us that there cannot be two supreme powers in any given society; and in this the Church is no exception. We must not make the mistake, then, of conceiving papal authority in such a way that it seems to replace that of the college of bishops. But while there is only one authority in the Church, namely, the episcopal college, it is the pope who is the source of unity within the college.[34]

The ecumenical council is, then, the visible expression of the basic structure of authority within the Church. The bishops in council do not receive new powers from the pope; by acting in assembly they visibly manifest a single authority which as a college they always possess but which outside of council they could not exercise with the same visible unity.[35]

The action of the bishops in union with the pope in council is, therefore, representative of all the faithful, though in a manner different from a democratic congress. The bishops are not elected representatives who must simply follow the will of their electorates; they are pastors of souls with responsibilities both to God and to their spiritual charges. The bond of unity which links the bishops with their faithful is the gratuitous decision of God to found one Church in Christ, not the will of Christians to establish a religious society of their own. It is this salvific intervention of God in human history which grounds both the faith of all Christians (which includes faith in the legitimate authority of the Church) and the authority of the hierarchy (which presupposes the faith of those who wield it).[36]

It follows from these reflections that there can be only one infallible teaching authority within the Church. As supreme authority in the Church, Rahner argues, the council possesses an active infallibility granted to it immediately by Christ. The problem with such a position is, of course, to reconcile the infallibility of the pope with conciliar infallibility.[37]

We know, of course, that the action of the pope is required in any conciliar definition. But if, on the other hand, the action of the college is also included in a "purely papal" definition (like that of the Assumption), then we may legitimately conclude that there is in fact only one infallible authority within the Church, the college of bishops acting in union with the pope, who is its head. Rahner maintains that this is in fact true; that when the pope defines "alone," he speaks as the head of the college and in its name. A papal definition, then, is in fact another way of the whole college exercising its authority in and through its head.[38]

We may conclude, then, that the same basic relationship exists between the pope and the bishops as between Peter and the apostles. The pope is pope insofar as he is head of the college of bishops at least in this sense, that the college of bishops, being of divine institution, is unthinkable without the pope as its head, while the pope can be acknowledged as pope only if there is a college of bishops of which he is the head. Moreover, Rahner argues, only if the pope is pope insofar as he is head of the episcopal college can we explain why the pope does not exercise the same jurisdictional authority over the bishops as over other Church officials, or why indeed the power of the pope over all members of the universal Church is the concrete fulfillment of what it means to be head of the episcopal college.[39]

The existence of important paracanonical influences of the episcopacy upon the government of the Church should by now be clear enough. Still, it is perhaps worthwhile to insist again that the actual co-effectiveness of the episcopal college in conducting the past affairs of the Church need not always have been explicitly and reflexively acknowledged in Church law in order to be real. If in fact the pope rules the Church as the head of the episcopal college, then in the official actions of the pope, the college is already actually ruling. The precise paracanonical influence of individual bishops on the government of the Church has assumed a multiplicity of forms in the course of history. What is essential is that the constant mutual give-and-take between the pope and the bishops in the government of the universal Church has constituted a genuine (yet paracanonical) right which is quite distinct from the jurisdictional rights of individual bishops within their own dioceses.[40]

The Bishop and His Diocese

We are now in a position to draw some tentative practical conclusions as to the nature of the episcopacy. First of all, it is clear that the rights of individual bishops can never be so limited practically and concretely as to abolish the divinely constituted rights of the episcopacy as such. Moreover, the pope as head of the episcopal college has the obligation to encourage individuality and legitimate pluralism among the bishops. Obviously this obligation in no way implies that in matters of diversity the rights of individual bishops are simply to be presumed, while those of the pope are to be proved. But it does mean that legitimate pluralism within a fundamental unity belongs to the essential structure of the Church and is the business of both pope and bishops. Not only must the pope as source and manifestation of unity in the Church foster multiplicity and the free discussion of disputed points, the episcopal college as the concrete manifestation of multiplicity and diversity within the Church must always manifest an overriding concern for the unity of all Christians under the pope.[41]

But in ruling their dioceses in and for the Church, individual bishops must be allowed to exercise a genuine autonomy. This has in fact been the constant practice of the Church in the past, but we have reached a point in the development of the Church in which this practice needs more explicit enunciation. Precisely because we are today a diaspora Church, we can no longer afford to give the world the impression of being an exclusively European or even an exclusively occidental Church. We cannot afford to confuse unity with uniformity if we intend to renew all things in Christ. Indeed the ecumenical importance alone of an explicit recognition of the local authority of the bishops should be so evident as to need no further comment.[42]

More specifically, we are in need today of a thorough re-examination of the mutual paracanonical obligations which exist between the pope and his bishops. For example, might it not be advisable to give official canonical status to the actually existing national councils of bishops? Or again, might it not be advisable to draw up more specific regulations for the conduct of Church councils? Is it really necessary that a bishop be obliged to raise problems in council mediately through a papal commission? Might it not be useful and advisable to have general councils for pastoral and doctrinal renewal at fixed and regular intervals?[43]

Secondly, we may draw some conclusions from all that has gone before as to the nature and structure of an episcopal diocese. The diocese has as its function to manifest at a particular time and place the presence within a particular community of the universal Church of Christ. A diocese must, then, be large enough to embrace all of the manifold aspects of the Church's life. In this context Rahner questions whether the tendency towards small dioceses current in Europe is altogether justified. A diocese must be large and complex enough to possess a meaningful character of its own if it is to fulfill its basic function within the total life and structure of the Church.[44]

Thirdly, because he is a member of the episcopal college, no bishop can govern his diocese as though it were a separate entity cut off from the life of the universal Church. Cooperation among the bishops and sympathy with the problems of other dioceses should be the natural consequence of membership in the Church's ruling body.[45]

Finally, those in a position of authority within the Church should reflect prayerfully and constantly upon the sensitivity, adaptability, tact, humanity, and charity which their office demands of them. For when those in authority assume rashly that every legal use of authority is automatically and in every circumstance also a moral use, the consequences can only be disastrous. It is quite conceivable, for instance, that in a concrete circumstance a particular jurisdictional act of the pope or the bishop might be juridically correct but morally unjustifiable in view of the concrete situation in which the action is taken.[46]

These few remarks concerning collegiality hardly exhaust everything that might be said about the relation of pope and bishop in the diaspora Church; but for the moment they will have to suffice. For it is time for us to come down a step in the hierarchical ladder of Church structure and focus our attention on the priest and his proper function within the complex life of Catholicism.

The Priestly Vocation

The priesthood is a very special type of vocation. It is not just a job. It is not even a simple profession like that of the doctor and lawyer. Nor does the priesthood essentially involve a life of formal asceticism as does the vocation of the monk. This last fact has perhaps been obscured in the west by the practice of clerical celibacy, but the mitigation of celibacy in eastern churches would seem to indicate that there is no absolutely necessary connection between celibacy and the priestly state.[47]

From a dogmatic point of view, the priesthood implies two basic functions. It implies, first of all, cultic powers, the power to administer the sacraments and offer sacrifice. Second, it implies a mission to preach: the priest is an apostle. Both of these functions have considerable foundation in Scripture, but they were not always united in the same office.[48]

In the Old Testament acts of cult appear as visible expressions of man's inner attitudes and needs before God. Prophecy, on the other hand, appears as the free self-revelation of God to man through chosen charismatic messengers. In other words, in Old Testament cult, the initiative for the dialogue between God and man lay with man rather than with God; but in genuine prophecy it is God himself who takes the initiative. A clear sign of this basic difference between the two offices was the fact that the priesthood of the Old Testament was an inherited office and underwent considerable human organization, while prophecy always lay outside the power of man to control. Prophetic schools preserved the word of God freely revealed through the true prophets he had chosen; but the schools did not and could not create the prophets themselves.[49]

But in the priesthood of Christ, the cultic and the prophetic offices of the old dispensation are permanently united. For Christ, the unique highpriest and prophet of the new law, is himself the sacramental reality which the Church proclaims in her worship and preaching.[50]

As we have already seen, the Word made flesh is our only mediator before the Father. Because of his redemptive death, our salvation has been definitively accomplished, the age of the Church is an eschatological age, and the sacramental words of the Church are eschatological words.[51]

As a result, the cultic priesthood of the new law is nothing else than the power of rendering the eschatological reality of Christ sacramentally present to men, both through the Mass, which prolongs his sacrificial offering of definitive reconciliation with the Father, and through the sacraments, which are real symbols of eschatological grace. We should also note that the priesthood of the New Testament is no longer limited to a particular class or group within the new Israel. The cultic priesthood of the New Testament is an extension and perfection of the priesthood of the faithful themselves. When, therefore, the ordained priest, who alone is actively empowered to pronounce the words of consecration, offers the Mass, he does not speak for himself alone but in the name of the whole Christian community, which with him and through him offers to God a sacrifice of praise.[52]

As in the case of the cultic priesthood, New Testament prophecy has likewise undergone a radical transformation in Christ. God inspired the Old Testament prophets to speak to men in his name, but in the New Testament God has spoken his definitive word to man in the person of his Son. Hence, New Testament prophecy, unlike that of the old dispensation, cannot announce any radical change in the relationship of God and man. The Christian "prophet" can only prolong in time the prophetic witness of Christ himself, who proclaimed the good news of salvation realized eschatologically in his own incarnate person.[53]

Now, as we have already seen in a previous chapter, there is real continuity between the prophetic and the sacramental words of the Church. The words of Christian prophecy do not only tell of salvation; in their most perfect form, they actually render salvation present in the hearts of men. Conversely, the formally sacramental words pronounced by the Church constitute an act of public prophetic witness to the salvation which is ours in Christ. Thus, the Mass is sacrament, sacrifice, and prophetic proclamation of the good news of redemption. The very words of consecration pronounced by the priest at Mass are the primal kerygma from which all other sacramental and prophetic words of the Church derive.[54]

The ordained priest of God, then, exercises a liturgical and a prophetic function more perfect than that found in any other religion. In his cultic functions, the priest of Christ not only symbolizes but actually brings to sacramental realization the prophetic words spoken to us in the incarnate Word of God. In so doing, he shows himself the minister both of the priesthood of Christ and of the priesthood of Christ's faithful as well. He is the minister of Christ's priesthood because his cultic acts (and most particularly the Mass) prolong in time the eschatological offering of Christ; he is the minister of the priesthood of the faithful because as sacramental spokesman for the priestly people of God he makes possible the cultic participation of all the faithful in the eschatological offering of Christ. In his prophetic function, the priest of Christ prolongs the prophetic mission of Christ himself by bearing witness to the truth of his message. In so doing, he also serves the faithful children of God in whose fiducial assent to the message of salvation the proclamation of the good news finds its perfection and fruition.[55]

We said at the beginning of this discussion that the priesthood is not just an ordinary human profession. The fact that holy orders (like marriage) is a vocational sacrament is a clear sign that the priesthood changes man radically and existentially. But if this is so, then one may legitimately ask which aspect of the priesthood produces the profounder existential transformation in a man: Is it his cultic powers? Or his prophetic powers? Or do both transform him equally?[56]

A bit of reflection will reveal that the cultic priesthood has less existential impact upon the priest as an individual than does his prophetic office. For one thing, the cultic acts the priest performs consume a relatively small proportion of his time. Moreover, although the priestly exercise of cultic powers imposes the serious obligation of worthiness on the part of the sacramental minister, for the rest the valid administration of the sacraments takes place independently of the existential state of soul of the priest himself: even a priest in serious sin can validly administer the sacraments. One might object that because the valid administration of the sacraments does at least depend on the right intention of the administering priest, it is not completely independent of his state of soul at the time of administration. Although this is true, a right intention is implied in any act of cult, and hence even in the cultic priesthood common to all Christians. It alone, therefore, can hardly be the source of greatest existential impact in the priestly vocation. The cultic priesthood, therefore, while imposing new obligations upon the priest, involves no new vocation as such. It is rather a further development of an old calling.[57]

The prophetic priesthood on the other hand, although inseparably bound in Christianity to the cultic priesthood, does involve a new vocation, a new calling. For the prophet is a man specially chosen from among God's people. He is marked as the messenger of God's word, and this in a way that transforms him radically and existentially. For the prophetic proclamation of the word of God absorbs the whole of a man; the very life of the prophet is an integral part of his message.[58]

The prophetic witness demanded of the priest is, then, fruitless without his personal assimilation of the message he proclaims. Not that the objective truth of the message depends on his personal assimilation of it. But his ability to touch the hearts of men, and hence his ability to bear effective prophetic witness to the message of salvation, will be proportionate to the degree to which the priest is himself possessed by God's prophetic word.[59]

The prophetic mission of the priest, then, launches him into a whole new way of existing. The ordained priest proclaims the truths of salvation, not as an ordinary Christian, but as one who is empowered to render the reality of Christ sacramentally present in the central act of Christian worship. Unlike the ordinary Christian whose vocation it is to bear witness to his living faith in various situations of daily living, the ordained priest is summoned by God to bear witness through his faith to the very word of God itself. And because his vocation comes, not from the concrete situation in which he finds himself, but from God, who summons him to proclaim the message of salvation and to defend its truth, the priestly vocation gives a whole new existential dimension and meaning to the Christian life.[60]

The Priest and the Poet

Indeed, the priest as minister of God's word is in a sense called upon to be the poet of God's truth, to pronounce those basic words of human speech which lead the soul of man to the full experience of its own transcendence in grace. Of course, the office of the priest and of the poet differ in a number of ways, but there are also significant points of contact between them.[61]

In every language there are words which may be described as basic words. In general such words escape precise verbal definition; but though we cannot always define their individual meanings with clarity, basic words do manifest at least two common characteristics. First of all, they always concern human transcendence, the openness of the soul to the infinite as such. When fully comprehended, therefore, they are concerned ultimately with our salvation. Second, basic words always place us face to face with reality itself; they do not interpose themselves between us and the real.[62]

Now as the minister of God's word, the priest does not proclaim his own personal religious experience. Instead, his words must lead souls to the acknowledgment in faith of that unique salvific reality which is the source of all salvation, God's Word made flesh. This divine word spoken to men by God in Christ is a free word, the product of free and gratuitous love. And because it is a definitive word spoken to all generations of men, it is a word which must be proclaimed to each succeeding age until the end of time. Now, as we have seen, the sacramental words of salvation pronounced by the priest are effective words. In them God's word is truly present and capable of being responded to by men.[63]

To the extent that his words are truly prophetic and truly effective, therefore, the priest can never be just a poet of the word of God. Indeed, one need only experience a few Sunday sermons to realize that not every priest is in fact a poet. Even more, the sacramental efficaciousness of priestly words marks them as coming from God himself instead of merely from the poetic heart of man. The priest, then, is in truth simultaneously both more than a poet and less than one. Yet the two vocations call out to one another.[64]

The vocation of the priest calls to that of the poet insofar as the words of the priest must also come from the heart. Not that the ultimate efficaciousness of his explicitly sacramental words depends on being in the state of grace, but rather that the very efficaciousness of the sacramental words of God imposes on him the obligation of speaking them and the prophetic words which flow from them with all his heart and soul. The poetic word is, therefore, the natural tool of his prophetic mission. For what human words can better express the sentiments of the human heart in its graced openness to God than the words of the poet?[65]

On the other hand, the vocation of the poet also calls to that of the priest. For in speaking the basic words of human transcendence, the poet longs implicitly for the word of God which unlocks the innermost secrets of the human heart. Thus, in the charismatic fusion of the powers of the poet with the mission of the priest, the grace of God is singularly manifest.[66]

Moreover, not only do the prophetic and sacramental words of the priest call for a response in faith on the part of men, but this response itself finds its best expression in the basic words of poetry. For the openness of the heart to the divine mystery of God-made-man implies of its nature the mystery of human transcendence, a willingness to hear those unifying words which penetrate to the center of human existence.[67]

The poetic, in the sense in which we use the term here, is, then, presupposed in the Christian experience. Not that one must be a poet in order to be a Christian. Rather, by the very fact of human transcendence, all men are existentially open to understanding the basic words which touch a man at the very center of his being. Conversely, openness to the Christian message implies a receptiveness to the poetic word.[68]

Moreover, what is true of the poetic is true of humanism in general. Both find their ultimate meaning in the grace of Christ. Hence, just as the truly Christian includes the truly human as an essential element, so too the struggle of the word of God against the forces of darkness parallels the struggle of the genuine poetic word against the forces of anti-humanism.[69]

Training for Priestly Work

Because of the priest's special prophetic mission, the Church today has got to do some serious rethinking of the problems of educating men for a priestly apostolate in the prevailing diaspora. Unfortunately, not all the problems have simple answers.[70]

Although it is evident that priests, like everyone else today, have need of some sort of academic education in addition to theological studies, the problem of deciding what sort of academic education is suitable for diaspora priests has been complicated by the fact that university studies are themselves undergoing a crisis as a result of extreme specialization. The centers of creative thought seem to be shifting from the universities to the laboratories. Yet just how this academic shift should affect the intellectual, and especially the theological, formation of priests is not yet at all clear.[71]

Even the specifically theological formation of priests presents numerous problems. Theology today is split into so many specialized disciplines that the ordinary seminarian can do little more than skim the surface of most of them. That this specialization within theology has to some extent hurt theology itself is clear from the current estrangement between biblical and dogmatic theology and between philosophy and dogma.[72]

In all our curriculum reforms, our guiding norm should be the formation of priests who are genuine pastors of souls and not just theologically learned men. Those engaged in seminary work should be especially on their guard against the dangers of complacency and inbreeding. Seminary teachers are invariably themselves ex-seminarians, whose natural human tendency is to hand on what they themselves have learned. When seminaries become theological ghettos the inevitable result is irrelevance and inner stagnation. In addition, a theological formation for a twentieth-century apostolate cannot afford to be purely "speculative," if by "speculative" we mean a theology which is not genuinely pastoral in its orientation. The modern seminarian needs to be trained to be articulate in his faith, to communicate it to others in terms which are intelligible to men and women today. This need will not be filled simply by adding a course in pastoral theology to the already bulging seminary curriculum. There is need rather for a change in attitude and approach within the courses already taught.[73]

Pastorally oriented theology does not mean a lowering of intellectual standards in our seminaries. On the contrary, it means that Catholic theologians today must begin to train their scholarly research more and more upon problems that actually trouble the souls of modern men. Above all, seminary teachers should not let preoccupation with "regulations" force them to compromise either the content or the relevance of their courses.[74]

The Role of the Pastor

Although every pastor is a priest, not every priest is a pastor. So before moving on to a consideration of the place of the diaconate in the diaspora Church, we might do well to reflect a bit on what the office of the pastor adds specifically to that of the priesthood. For the role of the pastor, in Rahner's analysis, is a very specific one within contemporary Catholicism.

The pastor is a priest who is bound in his apostolic mission to a particular place. This simple fact has a number of important consequences. The diaspora situation means, among other things, that the kingdom of God has been dispersed over the face of the earth. Just as the local bishop and the diocese he rules are together a concrete manifestation in a particular community and at a particular moment of space and time of the whole universal Church, so too the pastor and the parish whose head he is manifest in an analogous though less perfect fashion the same universal Church at a local, subdiocesan level.[75]

But the office of pastor labors under a number of concrete limitations. For example, the pastor's duties prevent him from engaging in any explicitly missionary activities. Because he is locally bound to the service of a particular community, the pastor cannot go marching off to the conquest of new lands for Christ. His concern is of necessity with the local community of which he is the priest, the liturgist, intercessor, shepherd, preacher, doctor, and helper in every need. For it is his office to consecrate this place, this portion of God's earth, completely to him and to make of it a true spiritual home for those who live in it.[76]

Although there is no denying the importance of the pastor's contribution to the work of the Church, the complexity of modern society makes any effort to organize all the Church's multiform activities at a parish level pastorally unrealistic. This is particularly true in large cities, where the complexity of the social structure has reached staggering proportions.[77]

Parishes and dioceses exist in the Church not because they are of supernatural origin but because men, if they are to live at all, must live in a particular place. Hence, although it is true that the parish is one of the oldest organizations in the Church, still, the parish as such is of human, not of divine, origin and can be replaced by more effective structures should the need arise. Hence, if parishes continue to exist in the Church, it is because they are still effective and vital centers of a variety of apostolic activities. At the heart of the parish is the altar; it is, therefore, the local center of liturgical worship and serves as the natural means of coordinating apostolic activity at a local territorial level. Still, the parish is not the only organization in the Church with the sanction of tradition. Although canon law makes every baptized Christian a member of a parish, the pastor has never been the only person in the Church charged with the spiritual care of souls.[78]

Although a local church does fill man's need for a spiritual home, unfortunately this need is not the only spiritual need which modern man experiences. Men of today face a number of individual, social, and moral problems of religious significance which the parish as such is not always capable of handling. First of all, modern travel has made the parish less of a spiritual home than it was in the less mobile society of the Middle Ages. Second, modern urban society with its complex stratification is no longer organized on a purely territorial level. Finally, the increasing secularization of society has made it imperative that individual Christians have the effective right to undertake apostolic activity on their own initiative without this activity being necessarily subject to the control of the local pastor.[79]

All of these facts point to the conclusion that the parish principle, while still a valid principle of pastoral practice, needs considerable supplementation if the Church is to adapt realistically to the structure of twentieth-century society and to the religious needs of the people who live in it.[80] It is precisely here that the religious orders can make a unique contribution to the pastoral work of the Church. For although religious orders can and should work within the parish structure, they enjoy the special advantage of being a supraterritorial organization, not bound within the spatial limits of parish work. This fact makes them an apt tool for meeting those individual and social needs of modern man which are not in fact provided for by membership in a spiritual home.[81]

To be more specific, the complex economic structure of modern society provides an interesting example of a pastoral need no longer adequately answered by the parish as such. Until the development of modern industrial society, the local center of religious activity, the parish, coincided with the local center of economic activity. Today the economic structure of society has far outgrown the local parish level and has reached national and even international proportions. To assume, then, that the local parish is still as capable as it was in the Middle Ages of the meeting of spiritual problems posed by these new and complex economic structures is simply to close one's eyes to the facts of life and to retire into an unrealistic ghettoism.[82] Similarly, in addition to Catholic organizations to meet problems posed by labor and management, we also need Catholic professional groups to meet the needs and problems of doctors, lawyers and other professional men. Such organizations would complement, not supplant, activities undertaken at a local parish level.[83]

The Renewal of the Diaconate

Perhaps one of the clearest symptoms of the fact that the Church of today faces a diaspora situation is the decision taken at Vatican II to revive the office of diaconate. For this decision has resulted in large measure from the increasing secularization of society as well as from the desperate lack of priests. It is also the fruit of the pioneering thought of theologians like Karl Rahner.

But before we consider the meaning of the revival, there are three facts which we would do well to recall. First of all, the diaconate involves a share in the authority of sacred orders with which Christ invested his Church.[84] This authority is conferred upon a deacon through a rite whose sacramentality is commonly regarded as certain by most theologians. The purpose of the diaconate is to help priests and bishops carry out the mission of the hierarchy itself. The works which the deacon performs must, therefore, be of greater moment than the cooperation offered the hierarchy both officially and unofficially by ordinary laymen. Third, although the diaconate can be a step on the way toward the priesthood, it need not be. A vocation to the diaconate does not necessarily imply a vocation to the priesthood.[85]

When, therefore, we speak about the renewal of the diaconate, we are speaking of a diaconate which is to be conferred by the sacramental ritual now employed in the Church. It is a permanent office and not just a step on the way to the priesthood. (Needless to say, the establishment of a permanent diaconate in no way calls into question the present practice of conferring the diaconate as a necessary preliminary to priestly ordination.) Moreover, the new diaconate would not bring with it the obligation of celibacy (although the present practice of conferring a celibate diaconate on those destined to be priests would remain unchanged).[86]

Of course, the revival of the diaconate may not be equally opportune in every part of the world, but we have good reason to think that in many places it would indeed be most suitable. For example, in many dioceses of the Church today, the office of deacon already exists, even though it does not now enjoy the advantages of sacramental consecration. We are thinking especially of mission areas, where lay catechists, in spite of the fact that they may be already married, are frequently employed to perform many of the functions proper to the office of deacon.[87] But in many other countries which are not technically mission areas, the frequent lack of priests, the many new apostolic needs of the Church arising from social changes and shifting social patterns, the need to acknowledge officially and to reward the good offices of many devoted married people, the crying need to give relief to the already overburdened clergy—all these things and more point to the apostolic advantage of reviving the diaconate in some form or other.[88]

Now where the need for such a revival exists, it is also fitting (though not absolutely necessary) that the revived diaconate take the form of a sacramental ordination. For not only does the Church have the power to impart such an ordination, but for solid theological reasons she has always been inclined to prefer the sacramental conferral of grace whenever possible. Her reasons are twofold: not only does the grace of the sacraments deepen and perfect the dispositions of the recipient, but the grace of Christ is itself incarnational and finds its most fitting expression in explicitly sacramental acts.[89]

Before Vatican II the matter of celibacy was for many a serious stumbling block in the way of renewal; but it need not have been. For one thing, it is theologically questionable whether the diaconate as a permanent office in the Church has the same affinity to the celibate state as does the sacred priesthood. Moreover, non-celibate deacons could act as a useful link between the regular celibate clergy and married laymen. They could also help to manifest more clearly the real distinction which exists between the office of deacon and that of priest. Then again, since marriage is not simply a concession to human weakness but is a sacrament with a positive meaning and consecration all its own, it is difficult to see any intrinsic incompatibility between Christian marriage and sacramental ordination to the diaconate. Finally, one could easily avoid the problem of switching from one form of the diaconate to another by restricting the non-celibate diaconate to people who are already married.[90]

The new deacons can serve the Church in a variety of ways. In the past the diaconate has assumed a number of different concrete forms, so that there is in the office room for considerable suppleness and adaptability. In the case of non-celibate deacons, one could perhaps de-emphasize the liturgical aspects of the office and insist more on directly apostolic activities and works of charity. But even so, the new deacons' activities would differ essentially from those of lay collaborators in the work of the hierarchy. Unlike laymen engaged in Catholic action, the new deacons through their sacramental consecration will share explicitly in the universal mission of the hierarchy itself.[91]

The work of the new deacons will, of course, need to be coordinated with the priestly apostolate. There is even the possibility of a certain amount of overlapping, since the office of priest contains that of the deacon within itself in an eminent manner. Sometimes in the past deacons have acted in direct dependence on the local bishop; at other times they have been placed under the direction of priests themselves. The simple fact of the matter is that the Church can interrelate the activities of her priests and deacons differently according to need. But one important pastoral division of labor between the two might certainly derive from the prophetic mission of the priest. The priest, as we saw above, is constituted a prophet of God's word by his power to pronounce the sacrificial words of consecration, which are the primal kerygma of the Church. Deacons have no such

power. Their mission in the Church is primarily one of service
to others in works of charity.[92]

Of course, there are a number of practical problems connected
with the revival of the diaconate which are still to be settled.
Not the least of these is whether married deacons should support
themselves by some sort of job or profession in addition to the
work of the apostolate. Rahner feels that the diaconate deserves
sacramental consecration only when it is a call in the full theological sense of the term, that is, when the diaconate constitutes
the basic structuring principle of a man's life. Hence, he feels
that for the sacramentally consecrated deacon, the apostolate
itself should be a full-time job. Ordained deacons and their fam-
ilies should, then, live from the altar in the manner of the present
ordained clergy.[93]

At a more juridical level the renewal of the diaconate need
not involve any changes in present laws for celibate deacons,
whose office is unaffected by the renewal. But canon law must
be expanded to include the diaconate in a new form. Eligible for
the non-celibate diaconate would be married men who in addition to other qualifications would be willing to consecrate themselves on a permanent basis to the service of the Church. There
should be a suitable time of testing for candidates; and regulations permitting return to the lay state should not be too strin-
gent. Even married deacons, Rahner suggests, should be allowed
to perform certain liturgical functions, particularly those indicated
in canons 741; 845, § 2; 1147, § 4; 1342, § 1. Their canonical obedience to the local bishop would include two basic elements:
(1) the duty to perform liturgical and apostolic functions within
the limits laid down by the local bishop; (2) the duty to lead a
life both proportionate in its external forms to the office they
profess and regulated in its particulars by the local ordinary.
Preparation for the new diaconate would include the normal
religious instruction of an educated Christian plus any special
formation needed for the immediate exercise of the concrete

duties of the office. This latter should include a period of practice
in the office before consecration and proper liturgical instruction
in the rites to be administered by the deacon. In all things the
local bishop would see to the proper assistance of his deacons
in matters personal and religious as well as to the coordination
of the apostolic endeavors of the deacons with those of the
regular clergy.[94]

The Religious Vocation

Religious have a very special function to perform in the Church
of the diaspora. By consecrating themselves to the practice of
the evangelical counsels of poverty, chastity and obedience, they
attempt to manifest to the world in a visible, existential manner
the truly transcendent and eschatological character of the grace
that is ours in Christ.

Christian perfection consists in the love which is given to us
through the Spirit of Christ. This love is Christological in its
source, ecclesial in its redemptive purpose, and transcendent and
eschatological in its character. That is to say, Christian love is
eschatological because it has been given to the Church in the
incarnate reality of Christ himself, in whom our redemption has
been definitively accomplished.[95]

Because Christian love is eschatological, it is not just one
virtue among others; it seeks man's complete personal fulfillment
in grace. And for this reason any good act can become for the
Christian a means of expressing the love which is his in Christ.[96]

It follows, therefore, that the life of renunciation represented
in the evangelical counsels is also an expression of this same all-
informing love. But in Christian renunciation divine love assumes
a very special form of expression. Unlike other acts informed by
the love of God, renunciation cannot be explained by means of
human ethical principles; it is not aimed at establishing the
moral harmony and balance which characterize ordinary obedi-

ence to the natural law. The life of the counsels demands the
deliberate renunciation of positively good, this-worldly values
with the full realization that these values are both good in themselves and a potential means of achieving perfection in grace.[97]

Now, such a loving renunciation can be truly meaningful only
where love awaits its final fulfillment in perfect union with God.
Why is this so? Renunciation for its own sake is always meaningless. It becomes meaningful only when it exists in function of
some higher good; and this higher good is truly Christian when
it is grasped only in and through faith in Christ. Hence, the real
meaning of a life of Christian renunciation must lie in the precise connection which exists between the renunciation of a this-
worldly good and the perfection of Christian love.[98]

How, then, are we to explain this connection? Simply to say
that renunciation is a manifestation of Christian love because it
is more difficult than an ordinary life of virtue, in the last analysis
explains nothing. For the real question is why is it truly meaningful for a Christian to choose precisely what is more difficult
as an expression of his love for God? To claim that the life of
the counsels manifests Christian love because by it one freely
withdraws from the temptations of the world overlooks the fact
that the religious life brings with it its own very subtle forms of
danger and temptation. Nor does the example of Christ provide
us with an adequate explanation of the meaning of renunciation,
since one must still explain why Christ himself chose the way of
poverty, chastity and obedience.[99]

The answer to the problem of the connection between Christian love and Christian renunciation lies rather in the fact that
Christian renunciation expresses a love which reaches out in
hope and in faith to a good which transcends our experience of
any purely human good. This transcendent character of Christian love, which is implicit in any act performed in grace, appears less clearly in acts which are in themselves naturally good
and humanly meaningful. Such acts contain within themselves

their own intelligibility. But where love takes the form of renunciation, it is unintelligible except in the light of Christian faith and hope.[100]

But why, one might ask, should God, who is the author of all good things, call upon men to renounce the good things he has made? The reason is simply this. Christian renunciation is a lived participation in the visible eschatological mission of Christ in his Church. By embracing a life of renunciation, the religious visibly manifests in an existential, quasi-sacramental way the same transcendence of eschatological grace which the Church, the primal sacrament and real symbol of grace, manifests sacramentally in baptism and the eucharist. It is a more perfect way of life than the way of the commandments, not because the counsels are better for man as he is or should be in himself (for this would imply that non-religious live at a kind of subhuman level), but because in embracing a form of life which through its triple renunciation does not of its nature involve the natural perfection of the individual as such, religious bear witness more perfectly to the transcendent, eschatological character of Christian love.[101]

Evangelical Poverty in a Changing World

But apart from the intrinsic difficulty involved in a life of renunication, religious of the diaspora face a number of perplexing problems. Perhaps poverty presents the greatest number of difficulties.

If we look to Sacred Scripture to discover the meaning of evangelical poverty, we find that the theme of the kingdom of God is dominant. The poverty recommended by Jesus for the sake of the kingdom is not a plan for social reform. Entering the kingdom means for him entering an eschatological situation in which riches become a dangerous source of distraction from the things of God and from the final hope of the true Christian, whose treasure is laid up in heaven. Much more than a simple expression of class consciousness, the counsel of Christ to sell one's possessions and give them to the poor is a manifestation of the Christian's living hope that all men may be united one day through love in the kingdom of God. It is, then, for these reasons as well as for the sake of liberty of action in the apostolate that Jesus demands a life of poverty of all those who are sent to preach the good news of God's kingdom.[102]

The epistles of St. Paul and that of St. James add some further reflections of the primitive Church concerning the meaning of true Christian poverty. They insist more explicitly on the ecclesial dimensions of Christian renunciation. For them, the renunciation of temporal possessions is part of the Church's public acknowledgment of the fact that while the things God has made are indeed good in themselves, redemption comes, not from them, but from God alone. By the same token, this same renunciation proclaims the Church's constant expectation of the final coming of the Lord when the whole of creation shall be made new in love and in grace.[103]

All of this is clear enough in the abstract, but the problem of adapting the evangelical ideals of poverty to the needs of religious orders in the twentieth century is an extremely complicated one. A large part of its complexity derives from the fact that poverty and riches are in some measure relative terms which admit of considerable concrete variation according to the social and economic differences of place and time.[104]

There is a gnawing feeling among a number of today's religious that somehow the orders are gradually growing "laxer" in matters of poverty. Unfortunately, verifying and evaluating this "laxity" is not such an easy matter. If we measure poverty in terms of the power which results from the economic control of productive goods, then one might argue that the orders have never been as poor as they are today. Moreover, if it is true that religious do not go hungry today as much as in previous ages, that they possess wristwatches and typewriters, and enjoy other conveniences in modern living, it is also true that the standard of living of people in general is higher in Christian countries than it has ever been and that these new conveniences need not necessarily be symptomatic of "laxity."[105]

On the other hand, religious today, in spite of the austerities they practice, do enjoy a rather high degree of economic security. For today's religious to support themselves through begging, as they did in former ages, is simply impossible. Not only must the orders be remunerated in some way for their services if they are to survive economically, they frequently find themselves in competition with secular institutions for money, donations, and gifts.[106]

As a result of these changes, religious poverty has tended to become identified in practice with the willingness of religious to be satisfied with a simple manner of life. Less fortunately, within religious communities themselves, more and more emphasis has come to be placed on the least important aspects of poverty, namely, its organizational and legalistic aspects.[107]

Nevertheless, simple dependence upon a superior cannot of itself constitute the essence of religious poverty. Instead, the genuine problem which the orders must face today is making such dependence an instrument of truly poor living. Hence, the fact that religious today use more things than in former ages is of itself not nearly so dangerous as the unrealistic and all too frequent tendency among some religious to regard the use of many of the benefits of technological progress as "concessions" to poor living justified by the legal fiction of the superior's permission. Such an attitude tends to deprive legitimate permissions of their real meaning. It reduces religious life to a kind of bureaucracy and encourages lack of responsibility and of simplicity among religious themselves by fostering the self-deception of thinking that anything at all is justified in the name of poverty which is covered by the proper permission.[108]

What, then, are religious orders to do about the diminished impact of evangelical poverty upon the lives of religious themselves and upon society in general? One could perhaps argue that in preserving a certain degree of asceticism in the enjoyment and consumption of material goods, religious orders preserve the essentials of poverty. But is this really the case? Might it not be true instead that one of the really serious threats to the preservation of religious poverty is an exaggerated traditionalism which regards any effort at adapting religious poverty to the contemporary situation as necessarily involving a "compromise" with the ideals of religious life? It is precisely because there is no pat solution to the problem of adaptation that religious superiors must encourage more variation and freedom of experimentation in the quest for a more acceptable and meaningful formula for living as poor men in the modern world. But in this, as in all things, the orders must be realists. Particularly in active orders, general adaptation cannot be imposed artificially; it must take into realistic account the concrete needs of an apostolate in twentieth-century society.[109]

The Meaning of Religious Chastity

The virginity of the mother of God helps to give some insight into the meaning of the religious vow of chastity. Paradoxically, we can understand the true meaning of Mary's virginity only if we see it as a consequence of the grace of her divine maternity. The reason why the Son of God did not have an earthly father was not that he already had one in heaven but that the grace of his incarnation was completely and utterly gratuitous. To say that the incarnation is gratuitous means that it transcends utterly whatever man is by his nature or can produce or merit by his natural activity alone. The miraculous virginity of Mary is nothing else than the visible manifestation in her flesh of the transcendent origin of her divine son and of her own total transformation in grace.[110]

The religious who vows a life of celibacy to God imitates in a less perfect fashion the virginity of Our Lady; but he bears witness in his own way to the same transcendent origin of grace and to his hope for eventual transformation in glory. As in the case of Mary, the chastity of the religious in no way flows from a contempt of Christian marriage. But by deliberately choosing a life of physical sterility in order more perfectly and freely to devote himself to the things of God, the religious proclaims that his only hope and love are found in the transcendent grace of Christ, who shall come again to judge all men and to reward the faithful servants of his kingdom.[111]

The Practice of Religious Obedience

Rahner feels that the third vow of religion, that of obedience, is sometimes distorted in practice by a number of popular misconceptions. First of all, religious obedience has nothing to do with the obedience of children to their parents. Unlike religious obedience, that of the child is ultimately aimed at its own elimination, since the real goal of his submission to his parents is to prepare him for an independent adult life. This is not true of religious obedience. Religious, moreover, are not children, although at times they can act childishly. Also, although the parent by reason of his age and experience is automatically endowed with a greater degree of wisdom and intelligence than is the child, the same is not necessarily true of the religious superior with regard to his subjects.[112]

A religious superior should, then, avoid trying to play "daddy" or "mama" to his or her community. He must recognize the possibility that his subjects may in fact be more competent than he in many fields, particularly in this modern age of specialization;

and he must be willing to profit from their knowledge. For while religious obedience cannot itself be "democratized," the democratic process can be extremely useful to superiors in reaching competent judgments.[113]

Second, religious obedience must be much more than the observance of the "traffic laws" of religious life. Superiors and subjects alike must recognize that ordinary house regulations are intended to be nothing more than an intelligent way of living together in a group. In what concerns the daily order, then, superiors should avoid claiming direct divine inspiration for every minor decision and regulation they make, while subjects should guard against all forms of petty carping and rebellion, which accomplish nothing and inevitably dwarf and distort the human soul.[114]

Finally, the practical place of obedience in religious life should not be exaggerated. Commands from the superior are not the only source of divine initiative within religious communities. Only God exercises that absolute creative authority which has as its correlate pure passivity. Hence, there is always room for subjects to express to their superiors their own personal preferences and contrary opinions. Moreover, subjects should be ready and able to act on their own initiative when the situation requires them to do so. In true obedience, the subject and the superior are co-responsible for what is actually done in their community. For no superior can pretend that he is able to see and arrange everything; nor can he truthfully claim that his office makes him the only source of light and order within the community.[115]

It is traditionally said that true religious obedience consists in doing the will of God, which is manifest in the will of the superior. Although this statement is clear enough in the abstract, in the concrete it can present a number of real problems. For instance, how can a subject conscientiously claim to be doing the will of God on those occasions when he finds himself called upon to execute orders which he recognizes to be inept and perhaps even culpable on the part of the superior himself, even though they may involve no sin on the part of the subject? Also, subjection to one who is not God is never good in itself. If, then, the superior is only the interpreter of God's will, where does he derive the light and the authority to say what God wants or does not want in a given situation? The fact that a superior wields ecclesiastical authority is no assurance that his every command will be in accord with the will of God. Nor does it help matters to say that a religious by his obedience imitates the obedience of Christ; for while Christ was always obedient to his Father's will, the concrete problem facing the religious is that of deciding when in any given circumstance God approves a particular human command.[116]

In attempting to provide an answer to these preplexing problems, Rahner suggests that they are in fact false ones based on a false interpretation of the meaning of religious obedience. Religious obedience is not submission to another for its own sake. Hence, it is misleading to place the essence of religious obedience in the letter-perfect fulfillment of this or that command or even in an abstract readiness to do anything superiors may ask. Religious obedience is not an end in itself. It is a means of binding oneself to the public and permanent renunciation of property and family for the love of God.[117]

Both religious authority and religious submission, therefore, exist for the sake of public witness in the Church. The rules of a religious institute limit the authority of religious superiors by defining the concrete form that religious renunciation will take in a particular order or congregation. By the same token, religious subjects in freely renouncing property and family must for that very reason also bind themselves to obey their legitimate superiors in matters concerning the evangelical counsels where there is no question of sin as such.[118]

Of course, in embracing a life of evangelical perfection, a religious cannot foresee all the consequences of his initial commitment any more than a young couple can foresee all the consequences of their marriage vows. But he knows in advance that not all the consequences will be pleasant. Religious obedience, therefore, also implies a willingness to imitate Christ our Lord, who was obedient to the death of the cross. Hence, when commands given in a religious context are difficult or meaningless, obedience can take on positive meaning through the mystery of the cross, which is itself the manifestation of the presence of God's saving grace in the world. Still, there is always the possibility that what a superior commands may be so false and inept as to be positively sinful. The subject has the serious obligation to test the morality of any command from the superior. Moreover, he must constantly suspect the selflessness of his own motives. For true religious obedience is always the offering of oneself to God in love, and it anticipates the total offering of oneself to God which every man must make in that final renunciation which is death.[119]

Religious Renunciation and the Enjoyment of Creatures

One must not think, however, that a life of religious renunciation is incompatible with the enjoyment of God's creatures. Anyone familiar with the ascetical and mystical doctrine of St. Ignatius of Loyola will know that this is not so. Ignatian piety is truly a piety of renunciation and of the cross. Ignatius demands of his followers the triple renunciation of poverty, chastity, and obedience and holds up to them as their model Christ, poor, suffering, and humiliated. And yet, at the same time, Ignatius preaches a doctrine of joy in the creatures of God. This paradox of Ignatian spirituality is really very important, for it can give us a much deeper insight into the true meaning of Christian renunciation.[120]

For Ignatius, the religious's flight from the world is not a repudiation of God's creatures; it is a way of acknowledging publicly the fact that God is the transcendent goal of Christian existence. It is not a flight from created things as such; for to identify religious renunciation with the flight from creatures as such is to imply that salvation lies in the flight from materiality itself and not in the gratuitous eruption of God's grace into human history. For Ignatius, then, renunciation as the total response of an individual to that grace is nothing else than a necessary precondition for the encounter with God immanent in the world he has made and redeemed.[121]

Paradoxically, therefore, Ignatius's joy in the creatures of God is completely compatible with his doctrine of indifference, renunciation, and love of the cross. For Ignatian indifference is nothing else than the readiness to do whatever God may ask even if what God asks is the cross and Calvary. Far from closing one off from the world, such an indifference is itself an openness to God wherever and however he may choose to manifest himself in his creation.[122]

To the mind of Ignatius, then, a life of religious renunciation for the sake of penetrating more deeply into the mysteries of God's grace not only does not separate one from the things which God has made; such a life involves an ever deeper immersion in the mystery of God present everywhere in his creation. This is why Ignatius thought of his sons as contemplatives in action, men who were so completely familiar with the things of God that they were able to see his traces everywhere and to rejoice in the divine image wherever they encountered it. "For I greet him the days I meet him, and I bless when I understand."[123]

Secular Institutes

Secular institutes are the newest form of religious institutes in the Church. Their members, while living externally the lives of ordinary laymen, profess the three religious vows of poverty,

chastity, and obedience. Although the members of secular institutes do not live the life of ordinary religious in its external
trappings, they correspond substantially to the state of canonical
perfection. Hence their mission in the Church is the same as
that of religious and essentially different from that of lay Catholics. On the other hand, Rahner feels that because secular
institutes differ significantly in their manner of living in traditional religious institutes, they should beware of thoughtlessly
apeing the ways and customs of the established orders.[124]

The Emerging Layman and His Mission

Within recent years theologians, and even the hierarchy itself,
have laid increasing emphasis on the positive role which laymen
must play in the diaspora Church. This emphasis is still a relatively new thing in Catholic circles. Previously, whenever theologians and canonists thought of the layman, they conceived
of him in negative terms as a Catholic who was neither cleric
nor religious and who was the object of the pastoral care of the
hierarchy.[125]

Now as a matter of fact, all this is perfectly true. The layman
is neither a member of the hierarchy nor a religious. He does
not exercise either the power of orders or the power of jurisdiction proper to the hierarchy. He does not possess the habitual
liturgical faculties of those in minor orders or even the faculties
of permanent catechists. He has no vows of poverty, chastity,
and obedience and does not bear public witness to the saving
grace of Christ in the same way that religious do.[126]

But while all of this is true and serves to tell us what laymen
are *not*, it gives us precious little inkling of what their positive
vocation is within the total mission of the visible Church.[127]

A layman is a member of the visible Church in the fullest
sense of the term. That is to say, a layman is one who passes

from a state of sin to one of justification precisely by being in-corporated into the visible, hierarchical structure of the Church. Now, since justification can take place outside the sacrament of baptism, it must be that justification through the sacrament pos-sesses an added meaning of its own which is not found in extra-sacramental justification. This is in fact the case. Sacra-mental baptism adds to justification an explicitly social dimen-sion. It implies a special relationship to the visible Church which is not found in those souls who possess grace but are not as yet baptized. This special relationship is nothing else than a share in the sacramental mission of the Church. It consists in so living as to manifest visibly to the world the grace of which Christ is the living sacramental symbol. If, therefore, the layman is the object of the pastoral care of the hierarchy, it is precisely be-cause he must share with it a personal responsibility for the success or failure of the Church's salvific mission.[128]

Moreover, besides baptism, the other sacraments (with the exception of orders) are all designed to strengthen and confirm the layman in the accomplishment of his mission. The sacra-ment of confirmation, as the sacrament of initiation into adult Christian living, strengthens him against the pride and unbelief of the world in order that he may be true to his adult Christian calling. The sacrament of penance is the sacrament of public reconciliation with the Church for those who have failed to live up to the responsibilities incumbent upon baptized Christians. Through the reception of the eucharist, the layman (like the cleric and the religious) is vitally united with Christ and with the whole of the Church. In the bread of union he finds the daily strength he needs to perform the duties of his state of life in a manner worthy of his Christian vocation. The sacrament of marriage so consecrates the union of man and wife that it becomes a graced manifestation of the permanent union which exists between Christ and the Church. Finally, extreme unction so unites the dying Christian with the rest of the Church that his death in the Lord is transformed into a death with the Lord for all mankind.[129]

Nevertheless the mission of the layman remains essentially different from that of the hierarchy. Members of the hierarchy as official spokesmen for the Church are charged with the duty of preaching the gospel to every creature and of preserving it intact and free from the taint of error and abuse. As a result, a member of the hierarchy enjoys a fundamentally different relationship to the world from that of the layman; because of his total consecration to God, he ceases to be involved in worldly affairs as such. His all-absorbing mission is the universal proclamation of the good news of salvation, and that alone. The layman, on the other hand, does not change his relationship to the world through baptism. He keeps his role within human society and bears witness to Christ in carrying out that role in conformity with his Christian calling. Thus, while the mission of the hierarchy involves an explicit share in the universal teaching mission of the Church, the mission of the layman is particular and derives instead from the concrete situation in which he must live and work.[130]

It should by now be abundantly clear that the layman through his sacramental consecration receives a positive mission within the Church and is co-responsible with the hierarchy for her interior and exterior well-being. His is the mission of remaining in the world, of bearing witness to Christ in the concrete situations of day-to-day existence, and of transforming through a life of grace both himself and all the persons and things he may encounter.[131]

The mission of the layman is, then, in a very real sense a continuation of the redemptive work of Christ himself. For redemption is not something wholly extrinsic to the created order, although it is gratuitous. Grace, as we have seen, is essentially distinct from nature and raises nature to a supernatural end. But nature is not opposed to grace, nor is it closed to a supernatural destiny. In Christ, who is God incarnate, creation is drawn into a higher unity with the divine, which was foreseen by God from the beginning when he conceived and fashioned his universe. Moreover, in Christ, the unity of grace and nature is an eschatological unity which thrusts forward in a dynamic tension toward the day of the Lord when all things shall be finally made new.[132]

Now, because the layman is the Christian in the world, his apostolic mission is incarnational in the fullest possible sense. It is his sacred vocation to work for the re-creation of all things in Christ through a life lived in the fullness of grace. Not that he imposes on the world a prefabricated supernatural superstructure; his mission is instead truly incarnational, to save the world by bringing it to the fullness of its natural perfection in grace.[133]

If, then, the layman remains in the world, his life is not profane for all that. On the contrary, it is his position in the world which determines his personal salvific mission within the Church.[134]

For the charity which transforms every Christian as a result of his incorporation into the visible Church cannot remain hidden within him. It must find visible expression at every level of human activity. It must transform the material and spiritual achievements of a man; it must transform the Christian home. By his charity the Catholic layman must first of all act as the leaven which will gradually elevate the human effort to dominate the earth. Through his sensitivity to the material needs of his fellow man, he must work to change the achievements of modern technology into miracles of the healing love of the compassionate Christ.[135]

Moreover, by his charity, he must also work to transform the spiritual communion of mind and heart which unites all men into a communion of faith and Christian love. For not only is the goal of spiritual communion among men ultimately the communion of saints, but any genuinely human achievement in the conquest of truth and of beauty necessarily brings mankind closer to final fulfillment in the kingdom of God.[136]

In this context, it is perhaps worth reflecting parenthetically that certain professions hold a privileged place in the Christian transformation of society. As guardian and transmitter of our cultural heritage, the Catholic eductor has the awesome task of preparing the generations of the future for Christian living in a secularized world. He must, then, bring to his task a consciousness of the salvific providence of God manifest in the development of human culture as well as a liberating vision of the gospel of Christ as that truth which alone gives ultimate meaning and worth to all that is truly human. He must find in his faith an openness of the heart to the whole of reality, natural and supernatural; and he must see in the call of faith a summons to explore the whole of God's truth. Finally, by respecting the freedom and innate dignity of each of his pupils both as a human person and as a child of grace, he must seek to liberate within them the charismatic creativity of the spirit of God present in their hearts.[137]

Similarly, the Catholic scholar and intellectual should find in his vocation a commitment to the full articulation of God's truth. The investigation of the mysteries of the created universe should become for him an exploration into God. And for that very reason he must stand up for the right of truth to be heard and for that freedom of speech which Pius XII insisted is so necessary for the well-being of the Church.[138] Finally, he must learn to find in books the means of achieving that self-possession in silence and reflection which is as rare to modern man as it is necessary for solid, creative thought.[139]

Still, the Catholic intellectual cannot afford to minimize the contemporary problems inherent in the intellectual confession of Christ. Far from being scandalized at the apparent absence of God from modern life, he must seek instead ways to make the

Christian message meaningful to twentieth-century man. And if he recognizes the necessary limitations of human thought and the obstacles to communication imposed by modern rationalism and widespread ignorance of the more recent theological achievements, he also takes courage from the realization that the extreme claims of nineteenth-century scientific rationalism are at an end, that modern man is beginning to recognize the existence of metaphysical presuppositions at the basis of all scientific reflection and to grope beyond the limitations of scientific method for an explanation of human reality.[140]

Last of all, the Catholic layman must transform with the all-informing love of Christ the mutual and fruitful love of man and woman. United to his family by the spirit of Christ, the Catholic layman must find in his home a genuine field of apostolic endeavor. He must seek to make the love he bears those nearest to him a true vehicle of grace for himself and for them, so that united in this life by their mutual love and sacrifice for one another they may one day be united forever in the vision of God.[141]

It is, then, this vocation of lived Christianity which constitutes the true apostolate of the laity, and not the part- or full-time participation of laymen in the clergy's own mission of preaching and sanctification. We can even go a step further. Because the layman has an important salvific mission of his own to perform, as a layman he has no obligation to engage in the work of the hierarchy.[142]

Needless to say, in insisting on an apostolate proper to the layman, Rahner does not at all intend to discourage or disparage Catholic laymen who freely and generously give of their time to help the already overburdened clergy. Rather, his concern is to prevent such generosity from blinding us to the layman's true role in the total mission of the Church. The layman who takes an active part in the work of the hierarchy may be doing a wonderful and necessary thing, but he should not make the mistake of thinking that this sort of work is the only apostolate available to him or even that it is the one that best suits him as a layman.[143]

The Lay Apostolate: Some Practical Conclusions

We can perhaps draw a few practical conclusions from all these reflections. First of all, there can be no training for the lay apostolate without training for Christian living. Training people for the lay apostolate means training them to act as Catholics rather than to take part in Catholic action. Secondly, the lay apostolate includes the layman's own inner spiritual life and everything—Mass, the sacraments, personal piety—which tends to increase and perfect that life. Third, when laymen devote themselves full-time to organizations founded by the hierarchy to further the apostolate proper to the clergy (such as Third Orders, Marian congregations, Catholic action groups), they cease to be laymen in the strict sense of the term. Fourth, there is need in the Church for lay organizations which are extensions of the lay apostolate properly so called. We are thinking here of organizations like student and youth groups, academic and professional organizations, whose immediate goal is not specifically religious, although they recognize the pursuit of human goals as a Christian duty. These organizations should be projections of the daily personal and professional work of Catholic laymen and should lie outside the immediate control of ecclesiastical authority. Fifth, Catholic action, although it performs an excellent and important service in the Church today, is not a lay organization in the strict sense. It is an organization to which laymen belong who are interested in helping the clergy with the formation of lay apostles, with protecting the public rights of the Church, and with aiding and coordinating the activities of other Church groups.[144]

Sixth and last, although no man can touch another immediately at the center of his being, in his very openness to God,
there is such a thing as the care of souls; and it is an activity
to which the layman as a baptized Christian is automatically
consecrated. It consists in finding the way which leads in love
to God and from God to one's neighbor, so that in loving one
another as we are (for so God loves us), we may lead others
to that absolute and unconditioned love whose object is God
alone.[145]

The Male Christian and the Church

These reflections on the vocation of the Catholic layman would
not be complete without a few concluding thoughts about the
participation of Catholic men in the work of the Church. In
many places, particularly in Europe, Catholic men show a
singular diffidence to the affairs of the Church. And unfortunately this diffidence results in part from the failure of some
churchmen to recognize the specific religious needs of Catholic
men. Men and women manifest a number of important psychological differences. For one thing, the male of the species
tends to be more object-oriented than the female; he is analytic
rather than intuitive and is inclined to objectivity by preference.
He distinguishes more easily between things and persons than
women do; he lives from the head rather than from the heart.
Moreover, the normal male requires a certain amount of recognition of his achievements, although he is not ashamed of selling
his services. He tends to construct systems rather than visions
and to feel a bit uneasy in the face of emotional displays. He
bears contradictions between theory and practice less patiently
than women do and is often more emotionally inhibited in his
dealings with others.[146]

What the Christian male of the twentieth century needs to
attract him to the work of the Church is a manly version of

Christianity. The fact that he is bored by long sermons or less than thrilled by the prospect of marching in church processions does not mean that he is irreligious. His intellectualism actually gives him deeper insight into the transcendental aspect of religion, but his emotional reserve will make him balk at public displays of piety. What he needs, then, is a piety proportioned to his psychological makeup and to the rhythm and interests of his life.[147]

The modern male needs to find in his religion something to challenge his talents and capabilities. Priests and pastors of souls will find him approachable enough if they can convince him that they both need and respect him for his experience, his professional competence, and his expertise, and that they are willing to let him share with them genuine responsibility for the success or failure of church projects. Above all he must be made to feel that as a result of his work both he and the Church are experiencing simultaneously progress and growth.[148]

The Separated and Dissident Brethren

Perhaps one of the saddest symptoms of the present diaspora situation is the divisions which separate Christians from one another. These divisions pose for Catholics a number of human as well as theological problems. For instance, what should be the attitude of a Catholic toward his separated and dissident brethren? He is clearly bound to them by closer ties than he is to members of non-Christian religions. Yet the separation is also very real. Then too, what is the relationship of non-Catholic Christians to the Catholic Church? Are they members in any sense of the term? What constitutes a truly ecumenical attitude toward religious conversions? Before closing this rather long chapter, we shall try to indicate briefly Rahner's general approach to these difficult questions.

Rahner insists on the importance of approaching the problem of membership in the Church from the insights of sacramental theology rather than from a purely juridical context. The sacraments of the Church, like the Church itself, have a double aspect. Because they are external signs which produce grace, they can be considered either as merely verifiably valid and visible signs or in their totality as realities of grace.[149] The same is true analogously of the Church. The Church, as we have seen, is the primal sacrament; that is to say, in its very concrete, visible, and juridically graspable reality, it is a sign and incarnation of the salvific will of God and of the grace of Christ. As in the case of the sacraments, then, we can consider the Church either in its sacramental totality as the manifestation of the grace of Christ, or merely in its visibility, and prescind from the reality of grace as such.[150]

Now, if we consider the Church in its totality as a manifestation of grace, we can distinguish multiple levels within the total sacramental visibility of the Church. For anyone who lives his life in the possession of grace can be said to belong in a real sense to the Church's sacramental visibility. This is an important point; for though theologians are fond of talking of the hypothetical necessity of the Church as a means of salvation for non-Catholics in the state of grace, they usually become rather vague when they attempt to explain how precisely the Church can be a genuine means of salvation for those who are not members in the fullest possible sense. Once we recognize that anyone who possesses grace in a real sense belongs to the Church's sacramental visibility, then the problem becomes less acute.[151]

Men, after all, are not the descendants of Adam in the natural order alone. Through their common spiritual descent from Adam the sinner, and especially through their universal redemption in Christ, they are bound together in a common historical destiny of salvation or of perdition. As a result, it is the fate of man to work out his salvation in visible acts which manifest either his acceptance or his rejection of the grace of God. It follows, therefore, that all those who have accepted God's grace and who manifest their acceptance by a life lived in grace are historically united in the spiritual solidarity of God's people even before they come together in a visible hierarchical Church.[152]

To put the matter a bit more explicitly, when a human being freely opens himself under grace in a radical act of self-giving to God, his decision can only be the result of God's own salvific decision that he be justified. Now, such an act on the part of God and of man has of its nature a quasi-sacramental structure. It is more than just a manifestation of good will on the part of the one who is justified and lives in grace. It is the expression of his personal acceptance of a role in a visible and gratuitously constituted people of God. Implicit in such an acceptance of grace (which of course comes to us through Christ alone) must also be a desire for membership in the Church of Christ itself in which the same grace which unites the members of God's people reaches explicit self-consciousness and full sacramentality.[153]

The relationship of the visible hierarchical Church to the "people of God" in the special sense in which we use the term here is, therefore, similar to the relationship between the politically organized state and the nation. Both of them, the hierarchical Church as well as the "people of God," are expressions of God's universal salvific will; but the Church, proceeding as it does immediately from the incarnation, passion, and glorification of Christ, is in addition the visible expression of God's will that salvation take place in and through the incarnate Word of God. Since, therefore, no grace can ever come to men except through Christ, not only is the Church already radically present wherever the people of God exists, but the people of God finds in the Church its fullness of sacramental perfection.[154]

The Challenge of Ecumenism

But if it is true that non-Catholic Christians who have accepted the grace of God belong to the sacramental visibility of the Church more perfectly even than non-Christians who live in grace, then what should be one's attitude toward converting such people to Catholicism? This problem has been complicated somewhat by the progress of the ecumenical movement. Ecumenism has tended to shift our apostolic interests from the level of individual conversions to that of reunion among the churches themselves.[155]

Rahner feels that Catholics should beware of that form of exaggerated ecumenism which would regard individual conversions to Catholicism as meaningless. Looked at objectively, the baptized Catholic as a member of the visible Church in the full and perfect sense of the term has at his disposal greater means of sanctification than one who does not enjoy full membership.[156]

Of course, in the concrete order there always remains the somewhat difficult question of the extent to which a prospective convert can actually appreciate the means of salvation objectively offered him in the Church. When faced with popular misconceptions in the sacramental piety of some Catholics, those engaged in the apostolate may sometimes wonder whether Christians who rely more on the subjective means of growing in grace are at so great a disadvantage when compared with many Catholics. But there can be no question that a convert who is solidly instructed and cultivates a sound sacramental piety is in a better state than he was prior to his conversion. What Catholics need most, perhaps, is to adopt a more balanced attitude toward members of another faith. There is no longer need (if, indeed, there ever was one) to flaunt conversions to Catholicism publicly as though they were avenging acts of God performed to confound the adversaries of truth and justice.[157]

Moreover, Catholics should be positively concerned both to help separated and dissident Christians in their efforts to protect what is authentic in their faith from the inroads of secularism and to break down artificial and unnecessary obstacles to conversion and eventual reunion by encouraging the growing dialogue among the churches and cooperation with them in the work of re-Christianizing modern society.[158]

Needless to say, in all his dealings with his separated and dissident brethren, the Catholic should maintain an attitude of profound respect for the individual consciences of other people. We have no way of judging another individual's subjective ability to recognize either his need for the Church or an obligation to join her ranks.[159]

Still, Catholics cannot simply drop all convert work in the expectation of ultimate reunion among Christians. Their obligation to encourage those who are open to full membership in the visible Church is a real one and cannot be abrogated by the possibility of ecumenical work within the other churches.[160]

Moreover, Catholics should work so to improve their own Church that converts may truly find in it the fulfillment of all their previous belief. Here Catholics have much to learn from other Christians, particularly in liturgical and biblical matters. Converts themselves can contribute much to the inner reform of the Church. And where they find reform temporarily obstructed they should take whatever consolation they can in the realization that in accepting the grace of conversion they did before God what in their hearts they knew they had to do.[161]

One final point is worth mentioning. Not infrequently Catholics are faced with religious divisions within their own family. Although keeping one's faith alive and vigorous under such circumstances may not always be easy, Catholics must guard against denying their unbelieving relatives the love and the affection that is their due. Moreover, Catholics should never give up hope for the ultimate salvation even of the most apparently obdurate. For while Vatican I teaches that those who have accepted the faith have no objective justification for abandoning it, it is also true that one's faith can be so conditioned by environment and education as to deprive defection from the faith of any serious subjective guilt. Finally, though death in the Church is one more reason for hoping for the salvation of the departed, it is not the only reason we have to hope. We should never abandon our trust in the mercy of God, who has called all poor sinners to salvation in Christ.[162]

NOTES

1. SG, 13–14.
2. *Ibid.*, 14–16.
3. *Ibid.*, 16–24.
4. *Ibid.*, 24.
5. *Ibid.*, 24–27.
6. *Ibid.*, 28–32.
7. *Ibid.*, 32–36.
8. *Ibid.*, 38–39.
9. *Ibid.*, 39–44.
10. *Ibid.*, 44–47.
11. *Ibid.*, 235.
12. *Ibid.*, 237–238.
13. *Ibid.*, 239.
14. *Ibid.*, 239–241.
15. *Ibid.*, 242.
16. *Ibid.*, 242–243.
17. *Ibid.*, 243–245.
18. *Ibid.*, 245–246.
19. *Ibid.*, 247.
20. *Ibid.*, 247–248.
21. *Ibid.*, 248–249.
22. *Ibid.*, 250–251.
23. *Ibid.*, 251–252.
24. *Ibid.*, 253–255.
25. EP, 63–64.
26. *Ibid.*, 64.
27. *Ibid.*, 64–66.
28. *Ibid.*, 66–69.
29. *Ibid.*, 70–73.
30. *Ibid.*, 73–75.
31. *Ibid.*, 76–78.
32. *Ibid.*, 78.
33. *Ibid.*, 79–80.
34. S, V, 284–285.
35. *Ibid.*, 289–290.
36. *Ibid.*, 290–292.
37. EP, 86–88.
38. *Ibid.*, 88–89.
39. *Ibid.*, 80, 90–93.
40. *Ibid.*, 93–96.
41. *Ibid.*, 101–102.
42. *Ibid.*, 103–108.
43. *Ibid.*, 109–113.
44. *Ibid.*, 114–116.
45. *Ibid.*, 117–118.
46. *Ibid.*, 120–124.
47. S, III, 285–286.
48. *Ibid.*, 286–287.
49. *Ibid.*, 288–289.
50. S, III, 293; SG, 260–261.
51. S, III, 294.
52. S, III, 296–298; IV, 353; SG, 264–265.
53. S, II, 298–299.
54. S, III, 298–299; IV, 353–354; SG, 265–268.
55. S, III, 301.
56. *Ibid.*, 302–305.
57. *Ibid.*, 305–306.
58. *Ibid.*, 306–308.
59. *Ibid.*, 308–309.
60. *Ibid.*, 309–311.

61. *Ibid.*, 351–358.
62. *Ibid.*, 352–356.
63. *Ibid.*, 358–363.
64. *Ibid.*, 364–367.
65. *Ibid.*, 367–374.
66. *Ibid.*, 374–375.
67. S, IV, 144–150.
68. *Ibid.*, 448–450.
69. *Ibid.*, 450–453.
70. SG, 334.
71. *Ibid.*, 335–337.
72. *Ibid.*, 339–342.
73. *Ibid.*, 344–348.
74. *Ibid.*, 350–358.
75. *Ibid.*, 268–269.
76. *Ibid.*, 269–270.
77. S, II, 303–304.
78. *Ibid.*, 305–310.
79. S, I, 311–322.
80. S, II, 324–329.
81. *Ibid.*, 326–336.
82. SG, 438–442.
83. *Ibid.*, 442–445.
84. *Ibid.*, 272–274.
85. S, V, 304–307; SG, 279.
86. S, V, 313–314.
87. *Ibid.*, 314–321.
88. S, V, 314–323; SG, 379.
89. S, V, 323–325.
90. *Ibid.*, 331–335.
91. *Ibid.*, 335–340.
92. *Ibid.*, 341–344.
93. *Ibid.*, 345–347, 353.
94. *Ibid.*, 348–355.
95. S, III, 61–62.
96. *Ibid.*, 62–63.
97. *Ibid.*, 63–64.
98. *Ibid.*, 64–66.
99. *Ibid.*, 66–67.
100. *Ibid.*, 68–69.
101. *Ibid.*, 69–72.
102. "Die Armut des Ordenlebens in einer veränderten Welt," *Geist und Leben*, XXXIII, No. 2

(1960), pp. 270–272. Hereafter we shall refer to this article as "Armut."
103. *Ibid.*, 273–275.
104. SG, 275–276.
105. "Armut," 275–277.
106. *Ibid.*, 276–278.
107. *Ibid.*, 278–279.
108. *Ibid.*, 279–280.
109. *Ibid.*, 283–284.
110. MMH, 64–70.
111. *Ibid.*, 70–72.
112. SG, 487–488.
113. *Ibid.*, 489–490.
114. *Ibid.*, 491–492.
115. *Ibid.*, 492–497.
116. *Ibid.*, 497–498.
117. *Ibid.*, 500–501.
118. *Ibid.*, 502–503.
119. *Ibid.*, 503–509.
120. S, III, 329, 334–337.
121. *Ibid.*, 342–343.
122. *Ibid.*, 344–347.
123. *Ibid.*, 347–348.
124. SG, 369–380.
125. "Die Sakramentale Grundlegung des Laienstandes in der Kirche," *Geist und Leben*, XXXIII, No. 2 (1960), pp. 119–120. Hereafter we shall refer to this article as "Laienstandes"; S, II, 341–342.
126. S, II, 340–342.
127. "Laienstandes," 120–121.
128. *Ibid.*, 123–125.
129. *Ibid.*, 129–131.
130. *Ibid.*, 125–127.
131. *Ibid.*, 131–132.
132. SG, 58–75, *passim.*
133. *Ibid.*, 82–85.
134. S, II, 343–345.
135. S, III, 323–324.
136. *Ibid.*, 324–327.
137. SG, 317–333.

138. *Ibid.*, 307–312.
139. *Ibid.*, 475–480.
140. S, III, 461–471.
141. *Ibid.*, 327–328.
142. S, II, 352–357.
143. *Ibid.*, 323.
144. *Ibid.*, 364–369.
145. S, III, 316–322.
146. SG, 283, 286–291.
147. *Ibid.*, 292–295.
148. *Ibid.*, 296–303.
149. S, II, 77–78.
150. *Ibid.*, 80–81.

151. *Ibid.*, 83–84.
152. *Ibid.*, 84–89.
153. *Ibid.*, 89–94.
154. *Ibid.*
155. S, V, 356–359.
156. *Ibid.*, 365.
157. *Ibid.*, 366–367.
158. *Ibid.*, 369–372.
159. *Ibid.*, 377–378.
160. S, III, 446–450; S, V, 373, 378.
161. S, III, 451–453.
162. *Ibid.*, 419–434.

SUGGESTED READINGS

"Membership of the Church according to the Teaching of Pius XII's Encyclical 'Mystici Corporis Christi,'" *Theological Investigations*, Karl Kruger (tr.), (Baltimore: Helicon, 1963), Vol. II, pp. 1–88.

"Peaceful Reflections on the Parochial Principle," *Theological Investigations*, Karl Kruger (tr.), (Baltimore: Helicon, 1963), Vol. II, pp. 283–318.

"Notes on the Lay Apostolate," *Theological Investigations*, Karl Kruger (tr.), (Baltimore: Helicon, 1963), Vol. II, pp. 319 ff.

The Episcopate and the Primacy, Kenneth Barker et al. (trs.), (New York: Herder, 1962).

"The Sacramental Basis of the Layman's Position in the Church," *Nature and Grace*, Dinah Wharton (tr.), (New York: Sheed and Ward, 1964), pp. 83–113.

J. D. Gerkin, S.J., *Toward a Theology of the Layman* (New York: Herder, 1963).

IX. The Church Dynamic

When on the first Pentecost Sunday the apostles burst forth from the upper room upon a world enslaved and divided by sin, the message they proclaimed was one of liberation. For though men in their malice had put to death the Savior of the world, by his very crucifixion he had broken the bonds of sin and of death and ransomed mankind from the slavery of its own carnal appetites. As the real symbol of the liberating grace which is ours in Christ, the Church is also the visible sacramental manifestation of that unique freedom which Christ won for men through his redemptive death.[1]

Revelation and Human Dignity

Freedom is not an easy concept to define. Rational psychologists are fond of speaking of freedom as the possibility of choosing between two alternatives. Theologians sometimes sound a bit like rational psychologists when they speak of man's freedom to choose between salvation and damnation. But the freedom of a Christian goes much deeper than the freedom of choosing between this or that concrete possibility.[2] The Christian concept of freedom rests ultimately on the uniquely Christian experience of the dignity and worth of the human person in grace.[3]

For a Christian the essential worth and dignity of man consists in the fundamental fact that he alone of all God's creatures achieves spiritual self-possession in personal self-awareness and in the free exercise of self-determination within a historical community of personal beings who like himself are, in their very spiritual openness to the infinite God, capable of sharing in that love which is communicated to men in Jesus Christ.[4]

The intrinsic worth of the human person implies, therefore, a plurality of existentials within man himself. There is first of all a *corporeal existential* by which man achieves physical orientation to his biological environment. Because he is an embodied spirit, man exists in space and time and must achieve his perfection in a material world of extension and change. This corporeal existential also provides the material basis for man's spiritual, *social existential*. Man is by his nature ordered to personal communion with other men in a corporeally mediated society. He achieves his perfection as a human person to the extent that he opens himself in his unique spiritual individuality to an interpersonal communion of mind and heart with his fellow man. But man's spiritual existential also has a *transcendent, religious* dimension. Man is by his nature God-oriented. As a spiritual being which achieves self-possession in self-awareness and free self-determination, man is in his very metaphysical constitution a spiritual openness to the infinite. Finally, in the gratuitously established salvific order in which man exists, the human person also involves a *supernatural existential* by which man becomes explicitly Christ-oriented, gratuitously destined for immediate personal communion with the triune deity in the saving grace of an incarnate God.[5]

Needless to say, these different existentials are not spatially distinct within man. Though different, they are mutually dependent upon one another and so rooted in unity that it is the whole person, not just a portion of him, who expresses himself in each of his existential relationships.[6]

The Inner Threat to Freedom: Concupiscence

Now, the essential worth and dignity of man can be threatened not only from the outside, by impersonal forces or by human coercion, but also from forces from within the heart of man himself. For since the fall, man is inwardly divided against himself. Although he cannot in the last analysis destroy his own intrinsic worth, he can by his own sinful actions freely contradict it. Moreover, even before he acts, man is inwardly divided against himself by the fact of concupiscence. We would perhaps do well to dwell a bit on this last point before proceeding any further.[7]

Part of the difficulty of elaborating a speculative notion of concupiscence lies in the fact that any adequate explanation of its nature must reconcile two very different theological viewpoints. While on the one hand concupiscence must result from the sin of Adam, on the other hand it must be something natural to man from which he could be freed by a preternatural gift of God.[8]

Rahner feels that the traditional theological definition of concupiscence as sensible desires insofar as they are independent of spiritual control and ordered to an object which is morally evil labors under a number of difficulties. For one thing, this definition limits concupiscence to the sensible part of man alone. Rahner questions whether any human desire can in fact be purely sensible. In an incarnated spirit, he feels, every spontaneous sensible desire also involves a spontaneous spiritual movement of the soul, which, however, precedes the spiritual act of free choice itself. If, then, we define concupiscence in terms of sensible desires alone, we not only ignore the existence of these spontaneous spiritual acts, we also confuse the rebellion of concupiscence with that of the "lower," material part of man against his "higher," spiritual nature. Second, the traditional definition of concupiscence also labors under an awkward moral bias which makes it difficult to understand how an inclination to evil as such could belong to man by his very nature.[9]

Rahner distinguishes three possible senses of the word concupiscence. In its broadest, least technical sense, concupiscence means one's conscious reactive assumption of a position toward apprehended values. In a narrower sense, concupiscence is the combined movement of sensible and spiritual desire toward a determined goal or value insofar as this act takes place spontaneously and is the necessary preliminary to free choice. Finally, concupiscence in the technical theological sense means the spontaneous spiritual and sensible desires of man insofar as they both precede freedom of choice and resist it.[10]

Concupiscence, therefore, implies an inner division within man between person and nature. "Person" here means man insofar as he freely disposes of his own existence. "Nature" means everything within man which must be there as an object of this free self-disposition. As a result of concupiscence, man can never achieve in this life the perfect and total disposal of himself in freedom. Within him, "nature" and "person" remain two opposed polarities in a state of constant dynamic tension. While on the one hand, free decision tends to the total mastery of "nature," "nature," on the other hand, in its spontaneous resistance to freedom, maintains a constant autonomy.[11]

Note well, however, that in Rahner's approach concupiscence is itself without moral qualification. It appears as much in the unwilling blush of innocence as in the erotic impulses of the pervert. It can offer as much resistance to morally evil decisions as to morally good ones.[12]

Moreover, it is precisely because concupiscence is morally indifferent that it could be found in man in a state of pure nature. By the same token, Adam's freedom from concupiscence in the state of original justice did not involve a moral bias toward the good but the ability to dispose of himself freely with a totality and definitiveness impossible either to a purely natural man or to man after the fall.[13]

However, man after the fall does not exist in the state of pure nature. His consciousness has been transformed by a supernatural existential in which he must hear the word of God either as it has been spoken to us in Christ or as a terrible and inescapable silence. In the present order of salvation, therefore, concupiscence has conscious resonances not merely in the order of nature but in the order of grace as well. As a result, our experience of concupiscence is analogous to our experience of death discussed in a previous chapter. Both of them are natural to man. But in a nature intended for transformation in glory, both appear to be incongruous even where they are not explicitly recognized as consequences of the sin of Adam.[14]

The external threat to human freedom resulting from personal and impersonal forces outside man is not unrelated to the inner threat to human freedom which results from his own malice and concupiscence. The two threats mutually condition one another. The external threat is in large measure a consequence of man's own inner self-perversion, while the personal and environmental forces which work upon a man can so condition him as to make his own self-violation through sin morally certain.[15]

Redemptive Liberation in Christ

Thus menaced in the free disposition of himself, man in this life finds himself neither in a state of total guilt nor in one of complete redemption. His ultimate salvation and gradual liberation from every threat to his freedom both from within and from without lies in his progressive mastery of "nature" at every existential level of his being, through the acceptance of the gratuitous and liberating gift of divine love offered to him in Christ.[16]

Hence, not only is man's supernatural destiny dependent upon his acceptance of redemption, but even the preservation of his natural dignity and worth is impossible without the liberating grace of Christ. For without that grace no one can remain long without sin, which in all of its internal and external consequences is the only real threat to human liberty.[17]

The supernatural love of God and of one's neighbor which comes to us only in grace is not, therefore, just one virtue among others. It is man's only hope of ever becoming truly free. It is the actualization of man's supernatural existential, that radical commitment to God in grace which is the root source of human growth in personal self-possession.[18]

Moreover, because Christian love is the graced explicitation of the basic movement of the soul toward total freedom in grace, its formal object is concretely indistinguishable from the formal object of the will itself in its elevation to the supernatural order. Conversely, the other virtues have a specific formal object proper to each, because as particularized explicitations of man's initial commitment to God in love, they constitute the gradual conquest of "nature" and the partial achievement of freedom in self-possession.[19]

The Exercise of Freedom

We are perhaps now in a position to make a few practical conclusions concerning the concrete exercise of human freedom. First of all, freedom involves a number of internal and external presuppositions. Internally, freedom presupposes the basic structure of the human person in all of its existential dimensions. But it also presupposes a number of external circumstances which precede the act of free choice and limit its specific possibilities. In the concrete, then, freedom is the power of man to assume an attitude toward the infinite and absolute in the choice of what is limited and finite.[20]

Second, created freedom cannot be defined merely as fidelity to the universal norms of ethical conduct. These norms are valuable insofar as they define certain limits within which the exercise of freedom is possible. But precisely because they place limits upon the exercise of freedom, they cannot constitute the essence of freedom as such. In the last analysis this fact is the reason why any exaggerated emphasis upon the rights common to all men inevitably leads to infringement of the rights of the individual as an individual.[21]

Third, freedom is intrinsically valuable, it is not simply a means to an end. It is constitutive of the human person as such, which in its freedom pertains to the highest possible mode of being. Freedom, therefore, would have to be preserved for its own sake, even if the products of the free acts of men could be achieved without it.[22]

Hence, any effort to violate human freedom in the moral interests of society is itself an immoral act. Men have the inviolable right to decide their own salvific destinies. The unenlightened effort to make moral evil impossible for men at the sacrifice of their own personal liberty is not only utopian, it is itself evil.[23]

Fourth, man's inviolable right to the full exercise of his freedom extends to every dimension of human existence. The various existentials of human activity are interrelated and react upon one another. Economic, cultural, social, religious and Christian freedom are, therefore, so interconnected that to limit one is in the last analysis to limit them all.[24]

Fifth, the moral law as such imposes no limitations upon human freedom, since moral development and personal development in freedom are in the concrete order identical.[25]

Sixth, there is a hierarchy of values in the quest for freedom. Freedom of spirit is of greater intrinsic worth than certainty about one's physical existence. Hence, even though the material conditions of freedom belong to the intrinsic worth of man, they can never be secured at the sacrifice of spiritual freedom.[26]

Seventh, and here we are approaching the heart of the matter, individual freedoms limit one another in society. The very fact that man lives in a community of free persons leads necessarily to the limitation of the individual exercise of freedom. Moreover, legitimate limitation of the area in which another can exercise his freedom can take a variety of forms. One common form is the imprisonment of criminals in order to protect the legitimate freedom of innocent people. Another is the temporary pedagogical limitation of freedom in order to prepare individuals for greater liberty of action in the future.[27]

The fact, however, that human freedoms limit one another leads inevitably to the possibility of a social conflict of consciences. The classic case is that of the conscientious objector. In such a conflict any man who would seek to limit another's freedom is morally bound to reflect whether his own actions are both morally justifiable and morally necessary. If in fact his own act is morally unjustifiable or only morally justifiable but unnecessary, he has no concrete moral justification for limiting another man's exercise of freedom. But if after reflection he finds that he has a moral obligation to act even at the expense of another's exercise of freedom, then he has no choice but to follow his own conscience.[28]

Thus, the concrete confrontation of human freedoms in society leads inevitably to the problem of tracing a moral boundary between unrestricted freedom and its legitimate exercise. How, in other words, does one steer a course between anarchy and totalitarianism? There is no way of setting up such a boundary in the abstract, since any legitimate limitation of the exercise of freedom depends necessarily on the concrete circumstances which may justify such a limitation. By the same token, the possibility that past limitations of freedom may no longer be justified in the present circumstances imposes on men the obligation of constantly revising the structure of society.[29]

Eighth, the purpose of the state can only be the preservation of human freedom. The state is a necessary consequence of the growth and complexification of human society. It does not give man his rights; it exists rather for their preservation. Thus, in a democratic society only those laws are justified which do not prejudice the legitimate rights of minorities. Similarly, the right to vote can in many instances stand in the way of the vindication of human rights, although in other circumstances it may be the only way to secure their protection.[30]

Ninth, in a Christian view of the world, those forms of power which constitute a threat to human freedom are like concupiscence itself, a consequence of sin. For, if the purpose of power over others is the preservation of freedom, the use of power to contradict its own end can only be the result of human blindness and malice.[31]

On the other hand, the Christian cannot regard power itself as something intrinsically evil. Power is not itself a sin, although it can be used sinfully. Power is a necessary element in the human situation; it is the inevitable product of the social confrontation of many individual freedoms.[32]

But the human exercise of power is desperately in need of the healing grace of Christ if it is not to degenerate into man's oppression of his fellow man. Only a man who has comprehended the supernatural dimensions of human freedom can ever fully understand that the exercise of power can become an event of salvation only when it is transformed by the inner law of charity and love.[33]

As a result, a true Christian presumes to exercise power over others in any sphere only with the greatest fear and trembling. Suspicious of his own inner weakness and personal limitations, he is conscious of the danger of any human use of power becoming tainted by the effects of human malice and concupiscence. He feels the personal need of subjecting the use of power

to grace much as he feels the need of dominating his own per-
versity by the love of Christ. But he knows too that power
properly used in Christ can itself become a genuine event of
grace.[34]

The Church: The Source of Freedom

Finally, we may conclude from what has gone before that
the Church is a uniquely efficacious and unending source of
human freedom. Not only does she teach and defend the genuine
worth of the human person, but she is herself the primal sacrament, the unique source of the liberating grace of Christ which
alone can truly make man free.[35]

As the sacrament of God, Christ is himself the first and primary
manifestation of the liberating grace which comes to man in
faith and love. By his redemptive death, he has freed us from
sin, from the law, and from death itself: from sin, which is the
human effort to find salvation in nature alone or in oneself;
from the law, which without grace is only the occasion for
greater sin; and from that death which is the consequence of
sin.[36]

The Church as the sacrament of Christ prolongs in time the
salvific liberation of mankind effected in him. In her words of
prophetic witness to the events of salvation, she liberates the
hearts of men by enabling them to acknowledge that they are
now no longer slaves but sons in the love of their eternal Father.
Through her sacraments she pronounces the efficacious words
of liberating grace which sustain the wavering wills of her
children in the crucial situations of their lives. Finally, through
the holiness of her many saints, she manifests in a concrete,
existential manner the freedom which comes to men in Christ.[37]

Because the Church is the quasi-sacramental expression of
true freedom in the world, she must, even in her visible organizational structure, be careful to manifest the liberty of the children

of God. Unfortunately, at present, the Church is often in danger of appearing to modern men as a clerical version of the totalitarian state. In point of fact, nothing could be less true of her essential nature and mission.[38]

This false image of the Church is in large measure the product of an exaggerated legalism on the part of some Catholic clerics. Needless to say, the Church as a visible organization needs laws and has the right to enforce them. She not only has the right to proclaim abstract principles of conduct; she can legitimately bind the consciences of her subjects in particular circumstances. Moreover, this limitation of their freedom is justified even when individuals in the Church, without understanding why, obey the Church merely out of respect for authority.[39]

But the relationship of the individual Catholic to the Church must extend far beyond blind submission. Even where obedience is intelligent and not blind, the laws of the Church cannot spell out for Christians every decision they must make throughout their lives. Laws and universal ethical principles at best define the negative limits within which man can legitimately act. It remains for the individual to discover the best course of action available within the limits of the law.[40]

The Need for an Existential Ethics

Hence, in addition to a Christian deductive ethics based on universal laws and principles, Rahner feels that there is room in the Church for a Christian existential ethics of the individual as such.[41]

In recommending an existential ethics, Rahner is not endorsing situational ethics. The latter, he feels, is an extreme expression of existentialist bewilderment in the face of the growing uncertainty and complexity of modern society. Implicit in the situational approach to ethics is a certain bias against law and authority in any form. As a result, situation ethics rejects all universal moral principles and proposes instead the concrete situation alone as the only possible norm for forming the individual conscience. What situational ethics actually espouses, therefore, is a form of moral nominalism in which man is falsely reduced to a unique ethical individuality with nothing of moral significance in common with his fellow men.[42]

But while rejecting situational ethics, Rahner sees in it a kernel of truth which is instructive for an expanded notion of Christian ethics. Traditional Christian ethics arrives at moral imperatives by applying universal norms of conduct to particular situations. Rahner in no way questions the legitimacy or validity of the imperatives reached by this process, but he suggests that the deductive method of reaching moral imperatives suffers from real limitations. For it to be completely effective, not only must the principles be universal, but the concrete situations to which they are applied also must be typical.[43]

Let us suppose for the sake of argument an ideal moral situation from the point of view of a deductive ethics, one which has been so completely comprehended that we can articulate all the universal principles which do in fact apply to it. We can, therefore, without difficulty formulate a moral imperative by applying these universal norms to the situation in question. In such a case, will the moral imperative derived deductively necessarily express a man's complete concrete moral obligation?[44]

Rahner finds it very difficult to answer this question with an unqualified yes. For one thing, even if we can decide deductively what our moral goals must be in a particular set of circumstances, often we must still choose from a variety of legitimate means for reaching those goals. Which specific means we are to use need not necessarily follow deductively from our universal principles.[45]

And even if in the concrete there is only one possible way to handle a situation, the very fact that other ways of implementing one and the same moral imperative may be theoretically possible indicates that the concrete handling of the situation is not exclusively the result of a moral deduction.[46]

Moreover, according to Rahner, the ultimate reason why deduced moral imperatives are not always completely specified in the concrete lies in the very metaphysical structure of the spiritual person. An individual man is much more than just a particular instance of a universal idea of man. Human individuality is something positive; it is a personal individuality distinct both from mathematical and from ontological individuality. The mathematical individual is a construct of reason based on our experience of distinct objects in a series within the space-time continuum. The ontological individual is a relational complex which finds its distinctness by being related to other complexes within a whole. But the personal individual is a spiritual being, which is constituted in its individual reality by its openness to the infinite reality of God. Hence a man becomes a spiritual person to the extent that he approaches the unique individuality of God himself. Paradoxically, therefore, man is most an individual precisely when he is most open to all reality, to the reality of God and to the reality of all creation in God.[47]

Now, because the human soul is both personal and spiritual, it is not just the form of the body as in the case of the lower animals; it is a *forma subsistens*. Hence, Rahner argues, insofar as the subsistent human soul by its metaphysical constitution participates in the spiritual inseity of the angels, it must also to that extent participate in the same sort of moral individuality proper to angelic beings.[48]

Moreover, if man is the most uniquely individual of God's creatures by reason of his spiritual existential, then graced spirituality can only be the highest expression of created individuality; for it is through the actuation of his supernatural existential that man achieves a new kind of openness to God and to creation. Now, because human individuality is as much the will of God as those traits which all men share in common, it must also be of ethical significance and should have an impact upon the formation of our ethical imperatives along with those generalizable characteristics which ground valid universal moral principles.[49]

But here a serious difficulty arises. Even granting the possibility of an ethics of the individual as such, could one possibly go about developing and articulating it? Is the individual as such conceptually communicable? This much at least seems clear: Human knowledge is not limited to the application of universal concepts to particular facts. We are conscious of individual things in their individuality. As in our knowledge of individual objects, then, the articulation of concrete moral imperatives would seem to involve a kind of pointing, the concrete designation of a specific course of action which presents itself to us in all of its individual moral significance.[50]

But how does one go about forming such a concrete moral imperative? To answer this question in detail would take us far afield. A thorough answer would necessarily involve the investigation of a number of complicated problems: The peculiar nature of non-objective knowledge, the place of personal commitment in articulating moral imperatives, the possiblity of a concrete insight into free future acts, the impact of both grace and depth psychology upon the formation of moral imperatives.[51]

The Ignatian Logic of Existential Choice

Perhaps more to the point here would be a brief study of the logical process by which one might arrive existentially at such a concrete moral imperative. Rahner feels that the *Spiritual Exercises* of St. Ignatius offer us an interesting instance of such a process. The purpose of the *Spiritual Exercises* is to dispose the exercitant to make his personal choice of a state of life or to reach some other major decision in a state of spiritual detachment. Since the choice of a vocation is an individual matter and one which cannot be regulated on the basis of abstract moral principles alone, Ignatius's rules for making an election constitute an interesting study in the logic of arriving at a concrete moral imperative.[52]

Ignatius's approach to the problem of choosing a state of life is personal in the extreme. He directs the exercitant to seek the will of God primarily by reflection upon the interior movements of his own soul. To be sure, the universal principles of Christian ethics come into play here, especially as negative norms for discerning the suggestions of the evil spirit. But universal principles are not themselves the decisive element in the final decision of the exercitant. For Ignatius's major preoccupation is so to familiarize the exercitant with his subjective religious experiences that he can reach a concrete awareness of God's will for him by discerning and accepting those spiritual impulses which come from God and by rejecting those which have their origin either in his own self-love or in the evil spirit.[53]

To the modern Christian familiar with the achievements of depth psychology such a method of discovering the will of God must seem hazardous in the extreme. Even the fact that divine illumination can indeed exist side by side with movements of the unconscious does not make the problem of distinguishing one from the other any easier.[54] From a theological point of view, one must also face the classic objection of the manuals that such a divine intervention would have to be either supernatural or preternatural. If it is supernatural, then it is by definition beyond the limited powers of man to apprehend consciously; and if it is preternatural, it is useless for all but the mystics. Is it not better, then, to presuppose that all the interior motions of our soul are of natural origin until proved to be otherwise?[55]

Here it will be useful to recall what we said in an earlier chapter concerning the impact of the supernatural upon human consciousness. Although it is true that the human intellect cannot in this life apprehend the supernatural as supernatural, this

does not mean that the existence of a supernatural existential
has no impact whatever upon human awareness. The supernatural constitutes a horizon of consciousness within which particular objects may be grasped even though the horizon cannot
be consciously grasped as such.[56]

But even if the supernatural does transform human awareness,
is it possible for the ordinary Christian to discover in the movements of his heart evidence of a divine intervention without that
intervention being the equivalent of a preternatural revelation
of God such as we discover in the Old Testament prophets?[57]

In his rules for making an election, Ignatius answers this question with a strong affirmative. There is a religious experience of
consolation which is clearly distinguishable from the natural
movements of the soul or from the movements induced by
spirits other than God himself. When consolation comes in this
form, says Ignatius, it can come from God alone.[58]

Ignatius describes the consolation in question as being characterized by the fact that it is "without preceding cause." Rahner
interprets this descriptive phrase as meaning "without a specific,
concrete object of knowledge as the basis for the consolation."
The phrase describes, therefore, the direct experience of the
soul's very openness to the divine, an openness which of its
nature precedes any conceptual thought or pious reflection.[59]

In such an experience, God is simply given as the concrete,
personal, yet transcendent limit toward which we yearn in faith,
hope, and love. Being preconceptual, this experience of God is
free from the deceptions of words and particular concepts and
carries with it its own certainty and self-justification. This sort
of consolation is, then, nothing like the pleasant feelings which
may or may not accompany pious reflections. It is the personal
experience of transcendence itself.[60]

But can such an "objectless" experience serve as the basis for
discerning the concrete will of God for a particular individual?

For Ignatius, the practical usefulness of this experience lies in its certain divine origin. For since any possible object of a concrete personal election is by definition distinct from an "objectless" consolation, it is possible to confront the two within consciousness. If, in this confrontation, one continues to experience the same joy and peace as in the experience of graced transcendence itself, then that object of election which is compatible with the experience of God in transcendence must be the concrete will of God for the individual in question. As we have already indicated, Ignatius presupposes that the object in question is a morally good object in accord with the universal principles of Christian morality. But what is of interest to us here is that besides these general moral principles he evokes the exercitant's individual experience of grace as an additional norm for reaching a personal moral decision.[61]

Needless to say, only a truly holy and exceptional Christian is capable of experiencing such spiritual consolations, although he need not be a mystic to do so. Perhaps this is one reason why Ignatius insists that the *Exercises* in their entirety are not meant for the ordinary individual. It is also not surprising that many holy people spontaneously employ St. Ignatius's logic of existential choice without reflecting on what they are actually doing.[62]

The Role of the Individual in the Church

The possibility of supplementing our present ethics of universal principles with an existential ethics of the individual as such also helps throw light on a number of other theological problems. It helps us to understand, for instance, the importance of the individual Christian within the Church.[63]

For since man's religious acts must take place within a community of worship, the very reality of the Church is in a real sense constituted by the religious acts of individual Christians.

Hence, not only was the Church founded by the uniquely individual redemptive act of Christ, but the history of the Church
is in a very real sense a history of the saints.[64]

Because this is so, the hierarchy exists for the sake of the individual Christian, not the individual Christian for the sake of
the hierarchy. The unique goal of the Church's pastoral concern
must, therefore, be to help the individual Christian, as far as
possible, in his efforts to understand and to fulfill God's will for
him as an individual.[65]

If the pastors of souls would become more conscious of the
fact that all the needs and problems of their spiritual charges
cannot be answered by the universal principles of Christian
ethics alone, they would do both their charges and the Church
as a whole a great service. For by exaggerating the primacy of
the typical and the organizational over the individual, the spiritual leaders of the Church run the grave risk of stifling in Catholics that individual dynamism which is the soul of genuine
growth and spiritual renewal at either the personal or the organizational level.[66]

General consciousness among Catholics of the spiritual rights
and needs of individual Christians as individuals can also have
considerable impact upon the dealings of individual members of
the hierarchy either with individual Catholics or with groups of
individuals within the Church.[67]

For if the individual as such is of moral significance in the
Church, then Catholicism is truly charismatic not only in its
laity but in its hierarchy as well. The Pentecostal spirit has been
given not to isolated individuals but to the whole Church, so
that it may manifest the liberating grace of Christ to men until
the end of time. Those, then, who direct the Church have
special need of his charismatic gifts; for in spite of their high
office they still remain in part the weak and sinful children of
Adam. By the same token, since the mission of the hierarchy

is truly spontaneous and charismatic, it cannot be reduced exclusively to what is institutional, governable, calculable, and legally comprehensible. Indeed, to suppose otherwise is to endanger the Church's essential mission to manifest Christ's liberating grace to sinful men. For since the presence of the spirit in the hearts of men can find at best imperfect expression in a code of canon law, to divorce Church law from the informing spirit of Christ's love is ultimately to reduce Catholicism to a kind of tyranny. It was in order to prevent this Christian version of Phariseeism from ever petrifying his Church that Christ sent his liberating, gift-bringing spirit into the hearts of the Church's rulers.[68]

The Church Charismatic

By the same token, if Christ had ever intended his Church to be totalitarian in its structure, he never would have sent his charismatic spirit into the hearts of each individual Christian to enlighten him for his own benefit and for that of the whole Church. For a true charism is never merely a personal gift; it must also be genuinely ecclesial in its scope. Moreover, by also giving his liberating spirit to the Church's rulers, the Savior not only ensured the charismatic quality of their authority but also guaranteed a basic spiritual harmony between the hierarchy and the charismatic individual. Not that the truly charismatic individual can be recognized only by his immediate capitulation before official hierarchical pressures; rather, the same spirit which unites both hierarchy and individual in the love of Christ is the single dynamic source of their joint charismatic inspiration.[69]

We may conclude, then, that the charismatic belongs to the very essence of the Church as the primal sacrament. Charisms are not necessarily miraculous or mystical in their nature, but they should be striking enough to partake of the nature of a visible sign. Moreover, though the charisms of the primitive Church involved special graces, the Church in her subsequent development has never lost her charismatic spirit. Two clear indications of this fact have been the constant longing of Christians to bear witness to Christ through a martyr's death and the continual birth of new religious orders which give institutional shape to the charismatic inspiration of their founders.[70]

Indeed, the very foundation of religious orders gives an important insight into the essential relationship of the charismatic and the organizational Church. For unless the charismatic has an impact upon the very organizational structure of the Church, it will have no lasting effect upon the history of salvation.[71]

Although charisms are visible signs of the presence of grace in the Church, they need not be sensational for all that. Many truly charismatic figures lead lives in obscurity and humility. Moreover, since, as we have seen, anyone who lives a life in grace belongs in some sense to the visibility of the Church, even though he may not be a baptized Catholic, there is no reason to suppose that the Catholic Church has a monopoly on charismatic gifts.[72]

Since, moreover, the Church exists for the sake of the individual, the purpose of the hierarchical Church is in a very real sense to foster the charisms of each of her members. Conversely, the charisms of individual Christians must in their turn foster the harmonious growth of the whole Church as the primal sacrament. For not only do charisms manifest the faith and love of true believers; as signs of grace they are intelligible only in the light of faith and invite the belief of all those who witness them.[73]

But even though there can be no essential conflict between the hierarchical and the charismatic, harmony between the two does not come automatically. It would be a grotesque caricature of the Church to imagine that all movement within her must begin at the top and move downward. Differences of opinion between the hierarchy and individuals in the Church are not only inevitable; within limits they are even healthy.[74]

Still, because the Church is of divine institution, her structure cannot be in the last analysis democratic. The authority of the hierarchy derives from Christ himself and not from the will of individual Catholics to be governed in religious matters. Nevertheless, the same divine power which gave authority to the apostles also placed moral limits upon its legitimate exercise and abides constantly with the Church to make sure that both the authority and the rights of those subject to it are protected. The fact, therefore, that one is not a member of the hierarchy in no way excuses him from voicing his opinion in the conduct of Church affairs. As we have already seen, every individual Christian by the very fact of his baptism is co-responsible for the welfare of the Church along with the hierarchy.[75]

The discord which would apparently threaten to disrupt the Church as a result of the presence of many different charismatic figures among her members need not be a real cause for concern. One and the same God inspires every genuinely charismatic voice whether it be individual or hierarchical. And who, after all, are we, to seek to place limits upon the activity of the Spirit and the gifts he imparts? Every true charism is, moreover, informed by the same Spirit of love who unifies and vitalizes the Mystical Body of Christ. Just as love is the source of unity and wholeness in the heart of fallen man, so must it also be within the universal Church. As long, therefore, as an individual Christian strengthens this universal bond of faith and of love, he has the right to pursue his own charismatic spirit to the benefit of the whole Christian community. By the same token, the mark of the true Christian will always be a tolerance for and joy in the charisms of others, even when he himself does not fully understand them.[76]

But as in the case of the apostles and the prophets, every charismatic mission necessarily brings with it a portion of the cross. By the very fact that a charismatic mission is personal and individual, it is apt to meet with incomprehension or even coldness or opposition from those whose interests lie in other directions. The truly charismatic person must learn, therefore, to find strength in him who sends both the suffering of the charism and the grace to bear it patiently. He should avoid discouragement by reflecting that the mere fact that opposition to an individual charism may come initially from the hierarchy is not necessarily a sign that the charism is not from God. The ability to distinguish a true charism form stubbornness is itself a charism not necessarily granted to every member of the clergy. Needless to say, the fact that a true charism always brings suffering with it in no way justifies the opposition of Church officialdom to genuinely charismatic individuals. The hierarchy has no right to play the part of a modern Gamaliel by challenging the Spirit to prove himself in spite of their resistance. For although it is good for the Church to canonize a charismatic figure after his death, it is even better for her to recognize him while he is still alive and to foster his charismatic gifts to the benefit of all Christians.[77]

Still, the truly charismatic figure will always need to find in his union with the suffering Christ the courage he needs to accomplish his charismatic mission. He should not hesitate, therefore, to challenge those human structures in the Church which stand in the way of her healthy development, even though such institutional accretions have the strength that comes from continuity with the past, while the charismatic, because it is new and spontaneous, often appears to the limited viewpoint of the *status quo* as disturbing and incomprehensible. For it is precisely through the mediation of such charismatic disturbances that the Church comes to a fuller realization of her essential nature and mission.[78]

The Changing Form of Heresy

Symptomatic of the increasing importance of the individual and the charismatic in the Church is the changing form of heresy in contemporary Christianity. Not only has the Church never lacked for heresies, but the very term "heresy" is a Christian phenomenon. Indeed, there is a sense in which the whole history of the Church has been a history of heresy, the reaction of the Christian community to deviations and abuses in its midst. For, strictly speaking, heresy is possible only in a religious community which claims to preserve God's definitive self-revelation to men. Heresy implies, therefore, a conflict between personal belief and official Church doctrine; and to the extent that it threatens the authority of those who have received a mission from Christ to go and teach all nations, heresy actually places in jeopardy the very fact of divine revelation.[79]

Part of the contemporary problem posed by heresy lies in the tendency of modern men to reduce every affirmation except those based on immediate perceptual experience to a shadowland of hypothesis, opinion, and environmental preconditioning. We are told that one religious hypothesis is as good as another and that God, after all, looks only to a man's personal sincerity on the day of judgment.[80] In contrast to this modern version of religious indifferentism, the Church has always insisted on the need for belief in divinely revealed truth if man is to be saved. Implied in this insistence is the realization that the assent of faith is not just a matter of the mind but of the heart as well. For the Church knows all too well that men do not think about reality as though it were something completely outside them. Every affirmation a man makes also involves his assumption of a personal attitude towards the objective world.[81]

As a result, the Church should never treat a genuine heresy as though it were just another religious opinion. As deplorable as were the religious persecutions of the Middle Ages and the

Renaissance, they become a bit more intelligible when seen as an expression of the Christian conviction that error concerning one's own salvation is the worst possible evil that can befall a man. When a particular truth involves a matter of eternal life and death, deviations from it are bound to be matters of grave concern to the believing community.[82]

Canon law defines a heretic as one who after baptism into the Church obstinately doubts a truth of defined Catholic faith. Now, although to be a true heretic one must have been first baptized, in the concrete we obviously have to distinguish the case of the formal heretic who is first baptized a Catholic and then renounces culpably an article of faith from that of a person who is baptized and reared in good faith in another Christian Church. Moreover, in traditional terminology a heretic is also distinguished from an apostate. The reason for this distinction is that a heretic still remains in fiducial contact with many truths of salvation, while an apostate is a baptized Catholic who has renounced all belief in Christ whatsoever.[83]

But even if this distinction between a heretic and an apostate is valid in the abstract, one might legitimately question whether apostasy is concretely possible in a society under the influence of Christianity. For when a nation's very way of life bears the imprint of revelation, it is difficult to see how any person can live like the people around him and still claim to renounce the faith in its entirety. Is it not much more likely that social contacts and pressures will have such an impact upon the presumed apostate's personal attitudes that they will keep him in some sort of living contact with at least some truths of the faith even without his being reflexively conscious of the fact?[84]

But if this is the case with contemporary apostates, then *a fortiori* a heretic, who denies one or more isolated dogmatic truths but continues to affirm the rest of Christian belief, can retain vital contact with the main body of revelation. Moreover, even though one in heresy offends against the faith as a whole to the extent that his erroneous affirmations, taken to their logical conclusion, threaten the whole of Christian belief, still it is possible to find within heresy a positive inner dynamism, not precisely as error, but as an exaggerated and somewhat distorted affirmation of revealed truth. On the other hand, it is also possible for one in heresy so to make his erroneous affirmations the center of his religious belief as to relegate the rest of Christian truth to the periphery of his existential being. When this happens, he may indeed be in serious danger of losing all meaningful contact with the truths of revelation. Needless to say, in the concrete, we have no way of measuring with absolute certitude a particular heretic's degree of personal contact with the truths of salvation.[85]

The changing form of contemporary heresy, like heresy in its more traditional form, finds its roots in man's inner division from himself by concupiscence. Because we are never perfect masters of our spiritual situation, our concrete state of soul is always partially determined by factors beyond our control. These factors need not be just physical. They can also take the form of theories, ideas, and opinions prevalent in the society in which we live. The specialization of modern science, with its inevitable mixture of fact and hypothesis, brilliant insight and blind stupidity, only serves to complicate the problem. We can no longer think of man as a whole; we must see him rather through the fragmented reflections of innumerable special disciplines. Our very institutions reflect our modes of thought until our world is shattered into pluralistic islands of partial truths.[86]

When we consider the impact of this situation on concrete Christian beliefs, the possibility of innumerable, unnoticed crypto-heretics within the very Church becomes apparent. Mere membership in the Church is no guarantee against the impact of a secularized society upon one's religious faith. Note well, however, that the crypto-heretic is not merely one who believes one thing but does another; a crypto-heresy is a genuine dogmatic error which is affirmed implicitly and unthematically within the human consciousness but which nonetheless has a serious impact upon the religious life of a believer.[87]

In addition to the secularization of modern society, there are two other factors which contribute to the present prevalence of crypto-heresies. One is modern man's shyness in the face of serious religious reflection: when belief remains unthematic, heresy is likely to do the same. Another important factor is a prevailing mistrust of clerical authority. When fear of suppression becomes the prevailing intellectual temper among Catholics, it is all too easy to fall into private error as the only practical means of "getting along" with the hierarchy.[88]

Evidently, a revival of heretic hunts is no solution to the problem. On the other hand, just what a proper solution might be is not at all easy to determine. Crypto-heresies are hard to come to grips with. Because they are hidden and unthematic, mere condemnation has little effect upon them. As a result, and because they are simply another symptom of the existence of a diaspora situation, the burden of combating crypto-heresies lies with the consciences of individual Christians.[89]

Still, a concrete understanding on the part of the hierarchy of the real problems faced by modern diaspora Catholics will go far toward eliminating a number of crypto-heresies. Because they are unthematic attitudes implicit in consciousness, crypto-heresies demand in many instances solutions of wisdom and of tact rather than speculative refutation.[90]

Of course, when the need arises, the Church retains the right to condemn even crypto-heresies publicly by explicitating them and manifesting their falsehood. When this takes place, Christians must be careful, for their part, not to confuse the issue by reading into Church pronouncements distortions which were never intended by those in authority. Similarly, the responsibility of individual Christians to fight against the presence of crypto-heresies should not be interpreted in an individualistic or atomistic sense. The work in question is truly one of thinking with the Church and of understanding the events of salvation in the light of her teaching.[91]

The Eccesial Dimensions of Private Revelations

These reflections on the place of the charismatic in the Church can also give us an important insight into the meaning and ecclesial dimensions of private revelations.

Christianity has always regarded private revelations as possible. God can speak to man not only through the universe he has created but through private illuminations as well. But even though visions of divine origin are as possible now as they were in the Old Testament, since the coming of Christ their basic character and function in the history of salvation has changed radically. In contrast to the revelations made to the Old Testament prophets, private revelations of the New Testament can add nothing to the content of belief.[92]

On the other hand, Christians are not free to ignore private revelations either. If God truly speaks to us through the religious experiences of an elected messenger, we have no choice but to listen to what he has to say. But precisely because private revelations can add nothing new to the deposit of faith, the divine message contained in them will take on the character of a concrete moral imperative. Authentic private revelations in the New Testament, therefore, serve the important function of calling the attention of Christians to certain moral aspects of revelation which are important for the concrete situation in which the Church may happen to find itself but which are not strictly deducible from universal principles.[93]

The Authenticity of Private Revelations

Needless to say, it is extremely difficult to elaborate concrete rules for deciding when a particular private revelation is authentic. For purposes of discussion and from the evidence we now possess, we may assume that in private revelations imaginative visions are the normal case. We say the normal case, for there are exceptions: for example, one must still explain instances of visions shared by more than one person or cases in which profane observers see, not the vision itself, but other accompanying phenomena. Moreover, in considering imaginative visions as normal, Rahner in no way excludes the possibility of corporeal visions in the case of the risen Christ.[94]

Significantly enough, the problem of evaluating imaginative visions is similar to the one we encountered in discussing the existential logic of choice in the *Spiritual Exercises* of St. Ignatius; for in private revelations one can exclude *a priori* neither the possibility of self-induced hallucinations nor the fact of God's using visionary phenomena as the vehicle for a genuine revelation. Given, then, the possibility of divine revelations through imaginative visions, how do such religious experiences come about? We know that they must come from God in some sense, but the precise meaning of their divine origin is not always clear. For example, although it is theoretically possible in a private vision for God to act upon a human soul so immediately that he ignores all the established laws of nature, still, since an imaginative vision also involves activity on the part of the visionary himself, it seems likely that his personal psychological structure will also enter into the very constitution of the vision. As a result, the line dividing the natural from the supernatural in such experiences is often quite obscure.[95]

Moreover, the very statement that this particular vision is the work of God can have a number of meanings. In a broad sense, everything in the world is the work of God, except for sin. On the other hand, events in the history of salvation deserve to be called the work of God in a special manner. It is in this latter sense that authentic visions may be truly said to be of divine origin.[96]

But we are not out of the woods yet. For one thing, we have no reason to suppose that the indwelling of God in the soul should not lead ultimately to some sort of mystical experience which, nevertheless, need not be miraculous in the strict sense of the term. And at the same time, we must also allow for the possibility of a truly miraculous mysticism which transcends all the psychic and physical laws of nature. Note well, however, that because both miraculous and non-miraculous visions can be imaginative, the mere fact that the Church calls a particular imaginative vision genuine does not necessarily mean that it is miraculous.[97]

How, then, does God cause a non-miraculous vision? Since the imaginative vision involves an awareness of a localized, sensible object, theologians are quite justified in explaining it by means of a "sensible species." When the vision is miraculous, this sensible species must by definition be infused by God himself. In other cases, the species may be part of the visionary's psychic reaction to a spiritual grace and hence an illusion, a hallucination, the result of previous perceptions, etc.[98]

But how in the concrete does all of this come about? By way of preliminary we should note that the sensible object present in a vision is usually "objectified." That is to say, the visionary usually judges that the object of his vision is a reality actually existing outside himself. Objectivity, however, is always judged, never sensed. The fact that a visionary may "see," "hear," or even "touch" Jesus or his saints is of itself no proof that Jesus is really physically present. Also, criteria for objectivity must vary with the type of awareness in question. Since, then, imaginative visions manifest all the limitations of the imagination itself, the norms for their objectivity must lie outside the content of the sensible vision itself.[99]

We may conclude, therefore, that neither the content nor the vividness of a vision is a sure sign either of the objective existence of what appears to the visionary or of its supernatural origin. Not that a visionary can never validate his own religious experiences; but at the very least, his judgments taken alone lack the authority of proof in the external forum.[100]

It should be clear from the foregoing that any explanation of the divine origin of a non-miraculous, imaginative vision is necessarily bound up with the problem of how the sensible species is produced in the soul of the visionary. In a non-miraculous vision, the focal point of the divine activity need not be the visionary's sensible powers themselves. A direct divine illumination of the visionary's intellect and will could also provoke psychological resonances in his sensible psychic apparatus, in such a way that the sensible species, instead of being directly infused, would only accompany a much deeper movement of spiritual grace.[101]

The advantage of this explanation is that it throws light upon several difficult problems connected with imaginative visions. For instance, the indifference of the classical mystics to the sensible portion of their vision appears in this context to be based, not upon a Neoplatonic contempt for matter, but on their conviction, in the light of an even greater spiritual illumination, that the infinite God transcends any merely imaginative or sensible form. We can also understand why sensible visions which are unaccompanied by spiritual graces are automatically suspect (although an exception might be made here in the case of a prophetic vision which is confirmed by a miracle). Moreover, with this explanation, the disinclination of true visionaries to speak of the secondary sensible experiences involved in a vision together with their submissiveness to the judgment of legitimate authority upon the conceptual and imaginative content of their vision becomes more intelligible. It is also much easier to explain why the imaginative vision reflects the personal subjectivity of the visionary, why it is difficult to disengage the supernatural elements of the vision from the imaginative, or why it is possible for the imaginative element even of an authentic vision to contain factual details which are false and inaccurate. Moreover, if the sensible portion of a vision is only an echo within the visionary's subjectivity of a higher, spiritual illumination, there is no reason why a true visionary could not also be subject to ordinary hallucinations. In this context, we remark in passing that St. Teresa's observation that after the experience of a real vision one could never confuse it with an hallucination could be true of the vision's spiritual element but false of its imaginative echo.[102]

Is it possible then, on the basis of these reflections, to establish a certain number of concrete norms for judging the authenticity of imaginative visions? We can at least draw a certain number of general conclusions.[103]

First of all we can reject as irrelevant a number of criteria which are employed often enough by unreflective, pious folk for judging the authenticity of a vision. Even though the personal piety and sincerity of the visionary must always be presupposed for authenticity, they are by themselves no indication of the supernatural origin of a private revelation. Equally irrelevant is the degree of physical or psychological health of the visionary. Similarly, the clarity, the necessity, or the apparently perceptive quality of a vision are no indication of its genuineness and may even be a sign of the contrary. Finally, the habitual honesty of the visionary tells us nothing about the divine origin of his vision.[104]

But in addition to these negative criteria we can also establish some positive norms of authenticity useful both for the visionary himself and for those called upon to pass judgment on his experience. As far as the visionary himself is concerned, it is quite possible, as both St. Teresa and St. Ignatius have pointed out, to recognize the divine presence in a spiritual illumination while prescinding altogether from its imaginative echo. Such an experience of grace brings with it its own verification. But where there is question of real imaginative visions, the visionary should be extremely careful to guard against all attachment to the sensible and derivatory elements of his experience. He should seek exclusively the authentic grace of infused contemplation, which involves complete detachment of spirit from all sensible and conceptual forms. Except, however, in the case of genuine infused contemplation, and apart perhaps from some external miraculous confirmation, the visionary himself can reach no certitude concerning the supernatural origin of his vision.[105]

The problem is even more difficult for passive spectators to the vision. Within limits they can use the same norms as the visionary himself, although the possibility of actually verifying the authenticity of another person's experience is obviously very limited. At best the passive spectator must be content with a greater or lesser degree of probability. When in doubt he must preserve a healthy scepticism. Until there is sufficient evidence to the contrary, he can only presume the natural origin of extraordinary psychic phenomena.[106]

When, therefore, the Church approves of a vision as a passive spectator, she states no more than that belief in the vision's divine origin is not imprudent and that the content of the vision is not in conflict with revealed truth. But such a declaration on the part of the Church imposes no further obligation on the faithful than that of listening with respect.[107]

The Purpose of Prophetic Utterance

The evaluation of prophetic experiences poses something of a special problem. Prophecy can in the concrete take the most diverse forms. Fortune-telling, seances, and superstitious predictions are some of its degenerate manifestations. These practices are not prophecy in the strict sense, although they are in concrete instances open to diabolic influence.[108]

Clairvoyance and premonitions of distant or future events, such as the anticipation of death either for oneself or for others, provide us with a more complicated form of prophecy. For want of a better term we might call such experiences parapsychological prophecy. Because such phenomena do not ordinarily take place in a religious context, there is rarely ever any question of determining the presence within them of any supernatural influence. Their explanation is to be sought instead in the psychological, ethnic, and hereditary constitution of the visionary.[109]

We should also be careful to distinguish true prophecies from philosophical and theological anticipations of future events. Such "prophecies" are actually the result of personal study and insight into events, although in specific instances they need not be closed to the divine influence. But unlike supernatural prophecy they are worth no more than the arguments which support them.[110]

Finally, we should distinguish truly supernatural prophecies from fabricated ones. These pseudo-prophecies are cleverly concocted predictions whose purpose is to foster some religious or political goal. They are simply the human projection of past experience into the future in the hope of influencing people to favor a particular cause.[111]

But we can also speak of prophecies in the strict theological sense of the term. Because God transcends time and space, he can, if and when he so desires, reveal some future event to those to whom he chooses. Scripture also speaks of prophecy in this strict theological sense.[112]

The theological evaluation of these different forms of prophecy is no simple matter. The Church has condemned practices like fortune-telling, seances, etc., either because they attempt to tell the future with insufficient means or because they involve

the invocation of demons. The strange phenomena that sometimes accompany such practices are, however, generally admitted
to be the expression of the subconscious of the participants. By
contrast, parapsychological prophecies, when they actually take
place, pose no real moral problem since they are completely in-
voluntary. Fabricated, philosophical, and theological prophecies
are worth no more than the evidence offered to support them.[113]

When prophecies truly come from God, they manifest certain
clear characteristics. First of all, they precede the event to which
they refer, as did our Lord's prophecy of the destruction of
Jerusalem. Second, although they can be accompanied by a vision
or confirmed by miracles, they need not be. Third, and most
important, they always seek to place man before a basic existential choice with regard to God. Like eschatological statements,
their purpose is never simply to reveal a fact before it happens.
They do not seek to satisfy idle curiosity about the future.
Instead they proclaim to men in their freedom the awesome
truth that God, the sovereign master of history, is not only a God
who saves those who are faithful to him but is also powerful
enough to confound and to incorporate into his very salvific plan
the wickedness of those who reject him.[114]

Moreover, as in the case of visions, New Testament prophecies add nothing new to the content of the deposit of faith.
True prophecies, then, can never deviate from the message of
revelation. Their function is that of a concrete moral imperative
in the collective conscience of the Church.[115]

To the extent that prophecies involve visions of some sort, they
are subject to the same norms as for the authenticity of visions
outlined above.

NOTES

1. S, II, 96.   4. *Ibid.*, 250.
2. *Ibid.*, 96–97.   5. *Ibid.*, 250–253.
3. *Ibid.*, 97–98.   6. *Ibid.*, 253–254.

7. *Ibid.*, 254–255.
8. S, I, 377–378.
9. *Ibid.*, 382–387.
10. *Ibid.*, 388–391.
11. *Ibid.*, 393–396.
12. *Ibid.*, 400–401.
13. *Ibid.*, 402–403.
14. *Ibid.*, 410–412.
15. S, II, 255.
16. S, I, 255–256.
17. S, II, 256–258.
18. S, V, 498–500.
19. *Ibid.*, 502–507.
20. S, II, 259–260.
21. *Ibid.*, 260.
22. *Ibid.*, 261.
23. *Ibid.*, 261–262.
24. *Ibid.*, 262.
25. *Ibid.*, 262–263.
26. *Ibid.*, 263.
27. *Ibid.*, 263–264.
28. *Ibid.*, 264–265.
29. *Ibid.*, 265–267.
30. *Ibid.*, 269–271.
31. S, IV, 487–490.
32. *Ibid.*, 491–492.
33. *Ibid.*, 491–493, 499–501.
34. *Ibid.*, 504–508.
35. S, II, 272.
36. *Ibid.*, 99–103.
37. *Ibid.*, 103–105.
38. *Ibid.*, 105–106.
39. *Ibid.*, 106–109.
40. *Ibid.*, 110.
41. *Ibid.*, 111–112.
42. *Ibid*, 227–229.
43. *Ibid.*, 231–232.
44. *Ibid.*, 235.
45. S, II, 234–235; DK, 16–17.
46. S, II, 235–236; DK, 23–24.
47. SG, 88–97.
48. S, II, 236–237; DK, 17–18.
49. S, II, 237–239; DK, 24–26.
50. DK, 26–27.
51. S, II, 240–242.
52. S, II, 243; DK, 78–79.
53. DK, 86–92.
54. *Ibid.*, 102–106.
55. *Ibid.*, 106–108.
56. *Ibid.*, 109–110.
57. *Ibid.*, 110–113.
58. *Ibid.*, 113–115.
59. *Ibid.*, 115–116.
60. *Ibid.*, 117–119, 124–130.
61. *Ibid.*, 136–143.
62. *Ibid.*, 144–145.
63. S, II, 243.
64. SG, 102–103.
65. *Ibid.*, 103–105.
66. *Ibid.*, 106–115.
67. S, II, 244–245.
68. DK, 38–43.
69. *Ibid.*, 43–44.
70. *Ibid.*, 47–52.
71. *Ibid.*, 52–55.
72. *Ibid.*, 55–57.
73. *Ibid.*, 59–60.
74. *Ibid.*, 61–63.
75. *Ibid.*, 63–65.
76. *Ibid.*, 65–68.
77. *Ibid.*, 68–72.
78. *Ibid.*, 73.
79. S, V, 527–529.
80. *Ibid.*, 529–531.
81. *Ibid.*, 532–533.
82. *Ibid.*, 536–537.
83. *Ibid.*, 542–546.
84. *Ibid.*, 547–549.
85. *Ibid.*, 551–554.
86. *Ibid.*, 555–559.
87. *Ibid.*, 565–567.
88. *Ibid.*, 568–571.
89. *Ibid.*, 572–573.
90. *Ibid.*, 574.
91. *Ibid.*, 572–576.
92. VP, 13–17.
93. *Ibid.*, 21–28.
94. *Ibid.*, 31–36.

95. *Ibid.,* 38–42.
96. *Ibid.,* 43–44.
97. *Ibid.,* 44–47.
98. *Ibid.,* 48.
99. *Ibid.,* 49–54.
100. *Ibid.,* 54.
101. *Ibid.,* 55–59.
102. *Ibid.,* 59–74.
103. *Ibid.,* 76.
104. *Ibid.,* 74–78.
105. *Ibid.,* 78–79.

106. *Ibid.,* 80–82.
107. *Ibid.,* 82–83.
108. *Ibid.,* 89–92.
109. *Ibid.,* 92–95.
110. *Ibid.,* 97–99.
111. *Ibid.,* 99–100.
112. *Ibid.,* 100.
113. *Ibid.,* 101–102.
114. *Ibid.,* 103–106.
115. *Ibid.,* 106–107.

SUGGESTED READINGS

The Dynamic Element in the Church, W. J. O'Hara (tr.), (New York: Herder, 1964).

Visions and Prophecies, Charles Henkey and Richard Strachan (trs.), (New York: Herder, 1963).

Free Speech in the Church, George Lamb (tr.), (New York: Sheed and Ward, 1960).

"The Theological Concept of *Concupiscentia,*" *Theological Investigations,* Cornelius Ernst, O. P. (tr.), (Baltimore: Helicon, 1961), Vol. I, pp. 347 ff.

"Freedom in the Church," *Theological Investigations,* Karl Kruger (tr.), (Baltimore: Helicon, 1963), Vol. II, pp. 89–108.

"On the Question of a Formal Existential Ethics," *Theological Investigations,* Karl Kruger (tr.), (Baltimore: Helicon, 1963), Vol. II, pp. 217–235.

"The Dignity and Freedom of Man," *Theological Investigations,* Karl Kruger (tr.), (Baltimore: Helicon, 1963), Vol. II, pp. 235–264.

"The Order of Redemption within the Order of Creation," *The Christian Commitment,* Cecily Hastings (tr.), (New York: Sheed and Ward, 1963), pp. 38–74.

"The Significance in Redemptive History of the Individual Member of the Church," *The Christian Commitment,* Cecily Hastings (tr.), (New York: Sheed and Ward, 1963), pp. 75–113.

"The Individual in the Church," *Nature and Grace,* Dinah Wharton (tr.), (New York: Sheed and Ward, 1964), pp. 9–38.

"The Appeal to Conscience," *Nature and Grace,* Dinah Wharton (tr.), (New York: Sheed and Ward, 1964), pp. 39–63.

"A New Form of Heresy," *Nature and Grace,* Dinah Wharton (tr.), (New York: Sheed and Ward, 1964), pp. 64–82.

On Heresy, W. J. O'Hara (tr.), (New York: Herder, 1964).

X. The Mother of the Lord

Because the Church is the sacramental manifestation of freedom in the world, the history of the world is in a real sense the history of the saints. The theology of the saints, therefore, is ultimately bound up with the theology of the Church itself. To understand the one is in some measure to understand the other.

Devotion to the Saints

Although the basis of the Church's power to canonize saints is a complex theological problem, this much at least seems clear to begin with: if the Church is really justified in honoring the saints, then she should have absolute certitude concerning their salvific status. The question of canonization is, then, reducible to that of why the cult of the saints is an essential element of Christian piety.[1]

As the primal sacrament, the Church is duty-bound to acknowledge God's gift of love to men consciously and explicitly. Now, since God's gift of grace is not an abstract essence but an incarnational reality transforming the minds and hearts of living human beings, the Church is also duty-bound to acknowledge the concrete manifestations of God's grace in the lives of her members and to bless the giver for his gifts. The official expression of this conscious acknowledgment and benediction is the process of canonization.[2]

For the saints are a vital, existential part of the Church's total sacramental reality, a living sign to unbelievers of the liberating grace which is hers in Christ. Even more, they are an existential summons to belief: the triumph of graced freedom manifest in their lives is incomprehensible except to one who sees with the eyes of faith. Finally, the saints are an important part of the Church's very message: they manifest visibly in every age of the Church's existence that the grace of Christ is truly an efficacious grace which abides within the Church as a permanent source of freedom and of holiness.[3]

Moreover, just as there is an evolution of dogma within the Church's collective consciousness, so too, in an analogous fashion, there is in the Church an evolution of holiness. This evolution, because it is a truly charismatic process, does not simply follow deductively from universal norms of ethical conduct. The canonized saint is not, therefore, just another example of one and the same abstract idea of holiness. He is rather an incarnation of grace, a personal expression of the spirituality of a given age.[4]

The Church, then, does not canonize a saint simply because his holiness happened to be extraordinary. Canonization involves a reflexive realization on the part of the Church that this or that Christian embodied in a striking manner the spirituality characteristic of his time.[5]

But even though we can regard each canonized saint as a characteristic embodiment of the spirituality of an age, we should never make the error of thinking that the lives of the saints were anything else than a spiritual revolution. Because true holiness is charismatic, it is also creative. Those whom we honor today as models of sanctity were frequently shunned and misunderstood by their own contemporaries. Indeed, to suppose Christian holiness to be anything but revolutionary is to reduce the holiness of Christ and the inspiration of his spirit to a static sort of ascetical determinism.[6]

The saints, therefore, are an important aspect of the Church dynamic. It is through the creative spirituality of his saints that Christ enlightens and guides his Church concretely and existentially in her progress through history.[7]

On the other hand, the outstanding public witness of the canonized saints can never render superfluous the less spectacular witness to the Church's holiness given by ordinary Christians. Rather, it is through the lives of her canonized saints that the whole Church becomes reflexively conscious of the essential holiness that belongs to every member of the body of Christ and of the vocation of sanctity to which every Christian is called.[8]

Mary's Role in Salvation History

But if these reflections are true, if the history of the Church is indeed a history of the saints, then Mary, the mother of Jesus, by reason of her unique role in the history of salvation must also occupy a unique place among the saints of God.

Mary's role in salvation history may be summed up very briefly in the simple statement that she was the mother of Jesus Christ, the Son of God. Yet implied in this very statement is the entire theology of the incarnation plus the whole meaning of Christian man and of creation. For God created the world in order that he might communicate his love gratuitously to men in the incarnate Christ. As mother of the Savior, Mary is, then, God's chosen instrument for introducing his grace and love definitively into human history. In other words, because the whole of salvation history reaches its pinnacle in Christ who is our salvation, Mary's personal relationship to her divine son cannot be significant for herself alone. Mary's salvific meaning for the rest of the human community of which she is a member can only be measured by the salvific meaning of Christ himself, whose incarnate

reality she mediates to men. On the other hand, her relationship
to Christ and to the rest of mankind is not of purely public significance either. Because her assent of faith at the annunciation
was fruitful of redemption itself, Mary can only be in God's
salvific plan the most perfect flowering of his redemptive grace.
Hence, because she is mother of the Lord, the second Eve in
God's salvific plan, Mary is indeed blessed among women, queen
of saints, the one creature most worthy of our praise.[9]

Although the Church's teaching concerning Mary is based
upon Sacred Scripture and upon the primitive Church's fiducial
awareness of her unique role in salvation history, the Christian
community has reached a reflexive awareness of the full implications of that role only through a long process of dogmatic
development. Theological reflection must, therefore, bring to the
basic mariological message of Scripture a consciousness of the
salvific meaning and destiny of man revealed to us in Jesus Christ
and of the historical unity of all men in Christ through Mary.[10]

In the light of this theological reflection, then, the Church has
come to recognize that Mary is the most perfect embodiment of
Christianity, the most perfectly redeemed of all God's creatures.
But what precisely does this mean? Although Christianity is in
the first instance God's action upon man, still, to be fruitful of
redemption, the divine act of love must provoke in man himself
a free response of answering love for God and for one's fellow
men. Mary's perfect Christianity, her perfect redemption, implies,
then, a total acceptance of God's gift of love through a total
response of love for God and for all mankind. This response is
epitomized in Mary's *fiat.* Through her sacramental words of
consent to the angelic message, grace entered definitively into
God's creation in the person of the Word made flesh. It is her
"yes" to the divine offer that she should be the mother of God
which marks the central turning-point of all human history and
ushers in the eschatological age. Hence, even though we can
conclude that Mary is herself redeemed, not the redeemer, never-

theless, because in her own free response to grace she mediates the redeemer himself to all other men, she herself is privileged to be the most perfectly redeemed of all God's creatures.[11]

The Meaning of the Immaculate Conception

The fact that Mary's role in salvation history demands that her response to grace be total throws considerable light upon the meaning of the Immaculate Conception. The Church's teaching that Mary's conception is immaculate does not imply in any way that human conception is something defiled; it means quite simply that God's redemptive love has so encompassed Mary's life that from the first moment of her existence she was possessed by his grace.[12]

Far from deifying Mary, the Immaculate Conception, therefore, underscores her status as a creature. Indeed, it would be difficult to find any mystery in the life of Our Lady which demonstrates more clearly the primacy of God's saving action in her regard and of her own human need for redemption. For before any free act on her part, God freely calls Mary to a special destiny and promises her the efficacious means she will need in order to fulfill that destiny.[13]

On the other hand, the Immaculate Conception also manifests the privileged character of Mary's redemption. For just as the time-lag between our own conception and our redemption through baptism manifests both our need for redemption and the fact that our individual salvation is not so intimately connected with Christ's incarnation that it is predetermined in the divine will to become flesh, so, by contrast, the very fact that Mary's total redemption is inseparable from the divine will to become incarnate makes any time-lag between her conception and her justification quite meaningless.[14]

Moreover, at the same time as it teaches us the special significance of Mary's redemption, the Immaculate Conception also reveals the meaning of our own. For in preserving Mary from all taint of sin, God has demonstrated clearly that his grace is infinitely stronger than our guilt and that the divine salvific will encompasses the whole of a man's life-span with faithfulness and with love. In other words, although without Mary we might know that men can through baptism actually share in the divine life before performing human acts of their own, through the Immaculate Conception God has made it clear that there is never a single instant of man's existence when he is not actually destined to share in the life of God himself.[15]

Finally, the fact that Mary was called by God from the very first to a special role in the history of salvation is a clear revelation that God's salvific plan cannot be encompassed within abstract universal principles but extends also to the individual as such. Hence, even though by comparison with Mary's salvific role our own may seem of minor importance, still, from the very fact that Mary's personal salvific mission was foreordained by God in all its uniqueness from the instant he created Mary's soul, we may conclude that every man is bound like her to search out his personal salvific destiny as an individual among individuals. To do so is to imitate the mother of God herself, whose response to grace during her life was nothing else than her free charismatic answer in love to God's personal call spoken at the very first moment of her existence.[16]

We may conclude, therefore, that the Immaculate Conception is extremely meaningful for Christian piety. But an intelligent piety should be careful to evaluate the religious meaning of the Immaculate Conception with a certain equilibrium. It is dogmatically true that Mary, because she was conceived without original sin, was thereby free from that concupiscence which results from the sin of Adam. It is also true that no other creature of God enjoys the same privilege, and that while Mary's way to God is the way of perfection, our own is a more ambiguous way filled with darkness and with light. Nevertheless, the Immaculate Conception was not intended by God merely as a revelation of our human degradation. Mary is not just an unattainable human ideal created by God to put our sinfulness to shame. For we know by faith that God can draw greater good from our evil, that even our sin is part of the divine salvific plan, and that through Christ the fall of Adam has become in truth a *felix culpa*. Seen in this light, the Immaculate Conception is a unique event in history, not a model for our imitation. It is more of a marvel than an ideal, a wonder of divine grace, a promise from God that the same grace which was powerful to redeem the mother of God completely from all sin is also powerful to lead each of us securely in the way of our salvation.[17]

The lesson which the Immaculate Conception teaches Christian piety is, therefore, one of immense confidence and of constant humility. From it we learn to place boundless trust in a God who can in his saving Providence use the very wickedness of men to produce such a wonder of grace as Christ and his mother. For just as the marvel of redemption in Christ results in a sense from human sinfulness itself, so too the marvel of Mary's redemption is still another triumph of divine love over the malice of men. By the same token, the Immaculate Conception teaches us the lesson of humility by manifesting the primacy of God's saving grace over any efforts of our own to find salvation. Mary did not choose God, she was chosen by him and confirmed by him in her vocation from the very first moment of her existence.[18]

In honoring the Immaculate Conception, therefore, we pay fitting homage to Mary's total "yes" to God in the saving grace of Christ; and by affirming Mary's total redemption as the fitting corollary of that "yes," we also reaffirm the Church's eschatological longing for the ultimate restoration of all things in Christ. For a reflective piety, then, our hope for glory in spite of our sinfulness and our belief in Mary's Immaculate Conception are two inseparable realities.[19]

The Divine Maternity

But Mary's "yes" to grace implies much more than the Immaculate Conception. Contained in that "yes" is also Mary's consent to be the mother of God. There is an unfortunate tendency on the part of some Catholics to think of the divine maternity in purely biological terms. Maternity is primarily a personal relationship. This is one reason why Scripture emphasizes not the biological fact of Mary's motherhood but her faith in answering the divine offer of grace. Indeed, for the men of the New Testament, Mary's relationship to the new covenant is analogous to that of Abraham to the old. Both Mary and Abraham stand at the source of a new eruption of grace into history, and both mediate that grace to men through their response in faith to a divine call.[20]

But Mary's role in salvation history surpasses that of Abraham to the same degree that the grace of the New Testament surpasses that of the Old. The grace mediated by the faith of Abraham was neither definitive nor truly eschatological; God's call to Abraham was not his final saving word to men. The revelation of the Old Testament was not the full revelation of God's salvific intention in creating the world.[21]

But Christ is God's definitive word to men; he is our only source of eschatological grace; he is the ultimate revelation of the meaning of creation and of man's salvific destiny.[22]

The annunciation is, then, the central moment in that salvific dialogue between God and the free will of men which we call salvation history. For upon Mary's free assent in faith to the Father's offer that she be mother of his Son depends the definitive introduction of eschatological grace into the world. At this key moment in salvation history, Mary steps forth as the spokesman for the whole human race to declare herself the handmaid of the Lord and to pronounce her "yes" of faith. At that very moment, therefore, she becomes not only the mother of the Savior but spiritual mother of all mankind as well.[23]

The Controversy Over the Virgin Birth

In discussing the religious vow of chastity, we have already reflected a bit upon the eschatological meaning of Mary's virginity. We have seen that Mary's virginity is paradoxically a necessary consequence of her divine maternity, that it is an expression of her total possession by grace and of the transcendent origin of our salvation. We have also seen that Mary in her virginity is the biblical type of the Christian who vows a life of celibacy to God. Both manifest to the world in a visible, existential manner the eschatological hope of the Church for the glory that will be ours in Christ.[24]

There is no need here to repeat these considerations. More profitable perhaps would be to reflect a bit upon Rahner's contribution to the recent theological controversy concerning the meaning of the virgin birth.

At the origin of this controversy is A. Mitterer's theory concerning the meaning of maternity as applied to Our Lady. Unlike many traditional presentations, Mitterer's discussion of the virgin birth begins, not with a speculative *a priori* concerning the need for the Savior's miraculous delivery in order to preserve intact Mary's corporeal integrity, but with modern scientific concepts of maternity and virginity. He suggests that true motherhood includes all those events which traditional explanations exclude from the birth of Christ, namely, labor pains, the opening of the reproductive organs, and the injury of the hymen. On the basis of these medical reflections, Mitterer suggests that a normal delivery is an integral part of Mary's divine maternity and that Mary's virginity should not be so exaggerated as to deprive her of full motherhood with regard to the Christ child.[25]

In reacting to Mitterer's proposals, Rahner points out that modern theologians are more hesitant than they used to be in assigning a theological note to the theory of the miraculous virgin birth. At issue in this hesitation, he feels, is the basic theological question whether theologians really need to think about the virgin birth in all its physical details. But granted, for the sake of argument, that theologians actually should speak of it in detail, then how are they to describe it with biological precision? These questions are not answered very easily. We certainly find no clear evidence for a miraculous birth in the apostolic tradition. Similarly, although the Church has always referred to Mary as *semper virgo* (always a virgin), the precise biological meaning of this phrase remains obscure. It would be extremely difficult to demonstrate that the synods and papal documents which speak of the virgin birth ever intended to exclude Mitterer's position as untenable. Hence, we may conclude that an investigation of the relevant theological sources reveals that even if the virgin birth were a *de fide* teaching of the Church, the biological content of this teaching would still remain at the very least a disputed question.[26]

The problem of the virgin birth offers us, therefore, an interesting study in the development of dogma. The theory of a miraculous delivery is not clearly present in the apostolic tradition; it is first proposed in the third century for theologically questionable motives; and it has never been the primary object of an ecclesiastical definition.[27]

But even though the theory of the miraculous delivery has been proposed by some theologians as *de fide,* the mere fact that we can trace it back to the third century is by itself no indication that it is revealed. At the very least, its proponents have got to show that the miraculous delivery of the Christ child is implicit in Scripture. That it is certainly not explicit is clear from the texts of the gospels themselves. St. Luke speaks of Christ's miraculous conception but makes no mention of a miraculous delivery.[28]

Against this theory is the fact that since the Church has never really recognized the miraculous delivery of the Christ child as part of revealed truth, the proposals of the Fathers and of later theologians pro or con can be regarded as personal opinions until proved to be otherwise. Moreover, as we shall see, the important fact that both Jesus and Mary were subject to suffering during their lives could be used as a suasive argument against the need for a miraculous birth.[29]

Is there a way out of this theological impasse? Rahner suggests that any decision for or against a miraculous delivery must involve a prior decision as to whether the birth of Christ is to be regarded as a pure work of grace or whether it must also include a natural biological element as an integral part of its total reality. Thus, the theological problem of the virgin birth is reduced to a quest for any elements in salvation history which would support the thesis of a miraculous delivery. The mere fact that Mary is the mother of God does not by itself warrant such a conclusion. Since virginity can, as Mitterer suggests, refer to the act of conception rather than to the act of bearing, any statement in tradition concerning Mary's virginity is subject to at least two different interpretations.[30]

Does Mary's freedom from concupiscence allow us to conclude to the necessity of a miraculous birth free from all pain? Rahner proposes that the meaning of man's freedom from concupiscence is revealed more clearly in Christ than it is in the scriptural accounts of man's fall. He suggests that since Christ's freedom from concupiscence did not include freedom from suffering, it must have involved Christ's ability to integrate his sufferings and his death into a free personal act of total self-giving to God.[31]

Now, while it is true that the birth of the redeemer cannot

bear the stigma of original sin from which both Jesus and his mother were free, we cannot conclude from this fact alone that the birth of Christ was free from all physical suffering. To be sure, an adequate theological evaluation of the place of suffering in the birth of Christ is no easy matter. One would have to determine beforehand exactly what suffering is, its basic psychological structure, and the extent to which physical pain is an expression of human guilt.[32]

In the present state of theological reflection, however, one can certainly defend the position that suffering in the strict sense can be experienced only by a person with concupiscence. Because of the division within such a person between nature and person, he can experience suffering only as something imposed from without, not as something really affirmed in a personal act of total self-oblation to God.[33]

Now, while it is true that Mary's freedom from concupiscence together with the transformation of her life through grace made every moment of her personal experience existentially different from our own, we should be cautious about defining the concrete details of that existential difference. It is clear, for instance, that when the Fathers excluded pain from the birth of Christ, they intended to speak of pain precisely insofar as it was an effect of sin. They were trying to say that God's curse of Eve recorded in Genesis did not apply to the birth of Christ. They certainly did not wish to imply that Mary's life was free from all suffering whatsoever.[34]

Rahner concludes that it is theologically permissible, therefore, to maintain that Mary was the mother of Christ in the full human sense of the term not only before and after his birth but in the very act of delivery. In the present state of theology, her freedom from concupiscence as a result of her immaculate conception would seem to justify the theory that her suffering in the birth of Christ need not have been a consequence of original sin any more than was the suffering she experienced at the moment of his passion and death. Both sufferings were fully integrated in her free and total self-offering to God in grace.[35]

At the very least, Rahner argues, this interpretation of the virgin birth (which is in fundamental agreement with that of Mitterer) is compatible with the evidence we now have in Scripture, patristic tradition, and the documents of the Church.[36]

Mary's Sinlessness

Because Mary is the most perfectly redeemed of all God's creatures, she is, as we have already seen, free from original sin; but the Council of Trent also teaches that Mary was free from actual sin as well.[37]

Many may find this claim somewhat startling. It certainly would have startled Origen and some of the early Fathers of the Church, who explicitly questioned Mary's impeccability. The reason for their hesitation was their conviction that Mary was in need of redemption like every other member of the human race and that the need for redemption implied of its nature at least some degree of actual sinfulness.[38]

But this scruple is really groundless; for we have no theological reason to suppose that a person whom the grace of Christ preserves from all sin whatsoever is any the less redeemed than the worst of sinners. On the contrary, such a person is more completely redeemed than one who rejects Christ's grace in order to sin. The Church's recognition of Mary's sinlessness is, therefore, only another aspect of her awareness that Mary plays a privileged role in the Church's sacramental manifestation of grace to men. In the triumphant victory of grace in the sinless mother of God, the holy Church of Christ sees its most perfect existential embodiment as the Church of the last age, the eschatological Church of definitive grace which imparts to men new life without measure, pressed down, and running over.[39]

Still, we should not be surprised that some of the early Fathers of the Church had difficulties with Mary's sinlessness. Men find it difficult on the basis of their own guilty experience to reconcile absolute perfection and an ordinary human life such as Mary's was. It took a certain amount of time for us to understand that there is no real contradiction between what is completely commonplace and what is completely pleasing to God.[40]

But once achieved, this realization is a source of great hope and of great consolation. For Mary's absolutely sinless life lived in obscurity and suffering teaches us that we too can hope to be pleasing to God in the tedium of our daily existence. It should also greatly comfort us in our fumbling efforts to manifest the grace of Christ to our contemporaries that there has been one of our race who has been wholly pleasing to God and whose life has reflected without blemish or distortion the splendor of the divine life given to men in Christ.[41]

The Meaning of the Assumption

But Mary's glory was not restricted to this life. So complete has been her redemption in Christ that the Church has not hesitated to affirm that Mary after death has entered wholly, soul and body, into the glory of the just.[42]

There is perhaps no single dogma concerning the mother of the Lord which troubles contemporary Christians more. Many Catholics let their ecumenical preoccupations cause them to regret that Mary's assumption was ever defined at all. They squirm when they learn that the first explicit indications we have of belief in the assumption are found in an early Christian apocrypha. But it is not for men to contradict the Spirit of God under whose guidance and inspiration the dogma of the assumption has emerged from implicit to explicit belief in the collective consciousness of the Church.[43]

As a result of this uneasiness, one of the important tasks of any theology of Mary is to trace the dogma of the assumption to its implicit basis in the belief of the apostolic Church. Which of the articles of the Apostles' Creed, for example, point to the existence of such an implicit belief?[44]

One such article would certainly be "born of the virgin Mary." For the first Christians, as for us, the birth of Jesus was primarily an event of universal grace, the definitive entrance of salvation into human history. It was, therefore, also an eschatological event indissolubly linked with the passion, death, and glorification of Christ. Moreover, the early Church was explicitly conscious of the fact that this unique event took place through Mary and as the result of her assent in faith to the grace of divine maternity.[45]

In addition to the divine maternity, three other articles of the Apostles' Creed are relevant to an understanding of a dogmatic basis for Mary's assumption. They are the death of Christ, his glorification, and the general resurrection of all men at the Last Judgment. These three articles of belief are intimately connected with one another. For it is by his death and glorification that Christ has freed all men from sin and death and has destined them to share in his glory when he shall come again to judge the living and the dead. Moreover, we believe with the primitive Church that, as in the case of Christ himself, our glory will include our whole person, body and soul. Exactly what the details of our risen state will consist in, however, remains obscure in revelation. We know what we are, but we do not yet know what we shall be. All that we can affirm with certainty is that while retaining our personal identity, we shall be changed body and soul. But we should avoid interpreting this change with a naive sort of fundamentalism. We cannot, for instance, interpret Christ's ascension in the unsophisticated localized sense in which the early Christians probably did. The heaven to which Christ ascended is not a place in the sense in which we experience place. We moderns regard place as a function of time, not, like the ancients, as that in which something happens. The real meaning of Christ's glorification is not that Christ is now physically located in a heavenly empyrean instead of on earth but that the glorification of the redeemer involves the creation of a new kind of place which transcends any human experience of time and space which we may now have. In simpler terms, the glorified Christ is God's living promise of a heaven and an earth which will be new because they are the radical transformation in glory of the heaven and earth we now experience. Hence, for a Christian to speak of the glorification of a portion of this world of time and space is extremely meaningful. Like the risen Christ and his glorified mother, the blessed souls of the saints in heaven are the already existing eschatological preparation of the world that is to come.[46]

Now, if we join these reflections concerning Christ's glorification and our own with our previous reflections concerning Mary's divine maternity, it is not difficult to find in the Apostles' Creed itself an implicit basis for belief in Mary's assumption. For if Mary in virtue of her divine maternity is privileged to be the most completely redeemed of all God's creatures, and if the age of glory has already begun in Christ, then Mary, as one who is totally sanctified by the grace of Christ, can have no partial share in the glory of her son. The complete transformation of Mary's life in grace while she was on earth finds its ultimate meaning through her perfect participation after death in the glory of her son, soul and body.[47]

But we would do well to reflect that although Mary's assumption is a privilege, it is certainly not abnormal. It is a privilege in the sense that the divine maternity gives Mary a kind of right to complete glorification after death. It is also a privilege in the sense that there is less of a time-lag between Mary's death and her glorification than there is in the case of others. But complete glorification is nothing abnormal for man. It is the destiny of every man in the glorified Christ.[48]

The dogma of the assumption is, therefore, only an aspect of our own promise of future glory. It teaches us the dignity of our bodies in a world which either deifies or despises the flesh. It helps us to acknowledge that nothing destined for glory could ever be intended by God to separate us from him.[49]

Mary as Mediatrix

Mary's assumption is also connected with another of her titles, that of mediatrix of all graces. In the light of what we have already said, this title should pose no serious problem; for to maintain that Mary is the mediatrix of all graces is simply to affirm that her life is of special salvific meaning for all mankind. There is, of course, a special sense in which Jesus is our only mediator with the Father, for he alone is the incarnate Son of God. But given the impotence of human language to express the reality of grace, there is a real sense in which Mary too is our mediatrix.[50]

For all men depend upon one another in Christ to work out their salvation. And while no man can save himself, since Christ only saves, still, every man can through a life lived in grace truly mediate the grace of Christ to his fellow men.[51]

Moreover, not every man mediates grace to others with the same concrete effectiveness. One's success as a mediator in Christ depends to a great extent upon the degree to which one is himself possessed of the grace of Christ.[52]

Mary mediates graces to her fellow men in a degree proportioned to her role in the history of salvation. Not only is she the sinless virgin and mother of the Lord, but by her complete glorification she has passed totally to eternity and assumed in body and soul a new universal relationship to the created world analogous to that of the glorified Christ. It is because God thus sees in her the perfect triumph of his grace that he will give graces to men for her sake. Far from calling into question the fact that only the grace of Christ is powerful to redeem us, Mary's mediation only serves to emphasize it. For it is only in virtue of her own complete redemption through the grace of God that she can mediate graces with special efficaciousness to her fellow men.[53]

Mary, Queen of Apostles

It is not difficult on the basis of these reflections to understand why devotion to Mary is the sign not only of the true Christian but of the true apostle as well. For Mary is not only the type of the Church, she is also the type of the Christian apostolate. Not only do the incarnation and the redemptive death of Christ have a pre-history in Mary; through her total acceptance of God's redemptive grace and of her predestined role in the history of salvation, she has changed irreversibly the course of human history. Not only, therefore, does her life possess unique redemptive value through Christ and in the Church; her life, after Christ's, is the Christian apostolic act *par excellence*.[54]

To the hierarchical Church, Mary's apostolate of docility under grace teaches the important lesson that every true apostolate draws its strength from the inner consent of the heart and not from rigid adherence to juridical formulas. From her life of perfect faith and love, the clergy can learn that the best defense of an institutional Church lies in a living zeal for the salvation of men which makes any formal defense superfluous.[55]

Those subject to authority in the Church can also draw inspiration from the life of Mary. They can learn to regard their own apostolate not only as a prolongation in time of the incarnation of the divine Word, but also as an imitation of Mary's own apostolic *fiat*, which was fruitful of the redemptive incarnation itself. They can, too, learn docility from the Mother of God, who did not stand upon her dignity as God's mother but subjected herself in imitation of her son to all legitimate authority.[56]

Mary also teaches us the fundamental unity which must characterize any apostolic activity Christians may undertake. Not only is her life a type of the apostolic work of clergy and laity alike, but in her, contemplation and action, personal conviction and external activity, exist in a single dynamic synthesis. Her apostolate teaches us to beware of separating the spirit from the letter of the law and to seek instead the spirit as the living soul of the law of Christ.[57]

Finally, Mary teaches us that every true apostolate comes, like hers, from above and that true apostolic action sometimes consists in waiting patiently for the salvific moment chosen by Almighty God. She teaches us the importance and salvific meaning of an apostolate of faithful service in all the humdrum circumstances of human existence. Finally, she teaches us that any man who would join in the apostolate of the incarnate Christ must also be prepared to take his painful stand with her upon the tragic hill of Calvary.[58]

NOTES

1. S, III, 133–135.
2. S, V, 114–115.
3. *Ibid.*, 116–117.
4. S, III, 117–121.
5. *Ibid.*, 120–121.
6. *Ibid.*, 122–124.
7. *Ibid.*, 124–125.
8. *Ibid.*
9. MMH, 1–12.
10. MMH, 15–27; S, I, 224–226.
11. MMH, 30–38; S, I, 227–229.
12. MMH, 39–40, 44; S, III, 157.
13. MMH, 41–44.
14. S, I, 236.
15. S, III, 160; MMH, 44–47.
16. MMH, 48–50.
17. S, III, 160–164.
18. *Ibid.*, 64–65.
19. *Ibid.*, 166–167.
20. MMH, 52–55.
21. *Ibid.*, 55–57.
22. *Ibid.*
23. *Ibid.*, 58–60.
24. *Ibid.*, 64–72.
25. S, IV, 173–174.
26. *Ibid.*, 175–180.
27. *Ibid.*, 182.
28. *Ibid.*, 188–191.
29. *Ibid.*, 191–193.
30. *Ibid.*, 198–199.
31. *Ibid.*, 199–200.
32. *Ibid.*, 201–202.
33. *Ibid.*, 202–203.
34. *Ibid.*, 203–204.
35. MMH, 62–64.
36. S, IV, 205.

37. MMH, 73–74.
38. *Ibid.*, 73–75.
39. *Ibid.*, 75–78.
40. *Ibid.*, 79–81.
41. *Ibid.*, 82–84.
42. *Ibid.*, 88.
43. *Ibid.*, 85–87.
44. S, I, 239–240.
45. *Ibid.*, 239–242.
46. *Ibid.*, 245–249.
47. *Ibid.*, 249–250.

48. *Ibid.*, 250–251.
49. MMH, 91–94.
50. *Ibid.*, 96–99.
51. *Ibid.*, 99–100.
52. *Ibid.*, 103.
53. *Ibid.*, 103–105.
54. *Ibid.*, 106; SG, 128–132.
55. SG, 133–134.
56. *Ibid.*, 134–137.
57. *Ibid.*, 137–140.
58. *Ibid.*, 142–145.

SUGGESTED READINGS

Mary, Mother of the Lord, W. J. O'Hara (tr.), (New York: Herder, 1963).

"The Immaculate Conception," *Theological Investigations,* Cornelius Ernst, O.P. (tr.), (Baltimore: Helicon, 1961), Vol. I, pp. 201–214.

"The Interpretation of the Dogma of the Assumption," *Theological Investigations,* Cornelius Ernst, O.P. (tr.), (Baltimore: Helicon, 1961), Vol. I, pp. 215–228.

"Mary and the Apostolate," *The Christian Commitment,* Cecily Hastings (tr.), (New York: Sheed and Ward, 1963), pp. 114–135.

XI. The Christian Mystery

The meaning of mystery is an important problem for contemporary theology. In a society marred by the absence of God, God's very hiddenness makes the divine reality appear all the more remote from modern men. Nevertheless, twentieth-century man is more willing to speak of mystery than were his predecessors. As a result of his inner fragmentation and isolation, modern man has gradually developed a certain reverence for the nameless and the incomprehensible. On the one hand, subtle distinctions which seek to explain too much only confuse and alienate him, while, on the other hand, any effort to avoid needed theological explanations by a gratuitous appeal to some mysterious divine decree that things be thus and so only arouses his suspicion. For he cannot help noticing that all too often this gratuitous appeal results more from the twistings and turnings of theological dialectic than from the structure of religious experience.[1]

The Meaning of Mystery

Frequently when Catholic theologians speak of a mystery, they refer to that quality of a proposition of revealed truth which makes it partially incomprehensible to human understanding. Since there are many such statements in Christian belief, theologians are accustomed to speak as though there are in fact many Christian mysteries.[2]

Without necessarily being false, this particular approach to mystery manifests a certain speculative bias. When, for instance, one's definition of mystery looks primarily to the mind of man and at most only implicitly to his affectivity and freedom, one is spontaneously inclined to look upon revelation itself as primarily a matter of words and propositions rather than of events; whereas, in point of fact, both words and events are essential elements of God's self-disclosure to men.[3]

Characteristically, those who approach mystery primarily via the intellect seek to define it negatively, by the fact that the mysterious is not comprehensible within the limits of human intelligence alone. Although implied in this negativity is, of course, the positive superiority of revealed truth to truths of reason, still the precise nature of that superiority remains implicit and obscure as far as the traditional definition of mystery is concerned.[4]

Rahner suggests that the speculative limitations of this more or less traditional approach to mystery are the result of a partial view of human reason, which in turn has its roots in scholastic speculation of the eleventh century. Eleventh-century schoolmen regarded the obscurity of many of the statements of revelation as only a temporary state of affairs intended by God as a kind of trial, a dark prelude to the clarity of understanding which comes with the face-to-face vision of God. In that vision, they fondly hoped that all present conceptual difficulties concerning revelation would be resolved once and for all.[5]

All of this is perfectly acceptable as far as it goes. But what, asks Rahner, if it is conceptual clarity and insight, not mystery, which are in fact transient? What if the beatific vision involves the positive absence of conceptual knowledge? What if knowledge is of its nature ordered, not to clear and distinct ideas, but to the mysterious as such? What, in other words, if the face-to-face vision of God is not the clarification of our present dialectical difficulties but the immediate presence within the soul of what is essentially and irreducibly mysterious? If this is indeed the case, then we have a new way of thinking about the meaning of mystery which, while not necessarily contradicting the old scholastic notion, still provides theologians with a new and important emphasis. For in this new viewpoint, mystery ceases to be the mere absence of conceptual clarity and becomes instead an integral part of man's knowledge of God. The ultimate goal of the intellect is no longer a quasi-Platonic contemplation of clear and distinct ideas within the divine essence, but the immediate confrontation of mystery as such. It is, moreover, the very transcendence of spirit, its openness to the nameless and ungraspable, which is the *a priori* condition for the possibility of conceptual clarity in this life. In other words, even while spirit as intelligence tends to conceptual thought, intelligence is itself ordered to self-transcendence in ecstasy through the immediate confrontation of mystery. The mysterious is, therefore, that ultimate reality before which the human spirit must either reach out in an ecstatic leap of transcendence or else despair in a self-constructed, self-enclosed prison of partial concepts and half-truths.[6]

But this ecstatic leap is not just a leap of knowledge. In a Christian notion of man, love has in the last analysis precedence over knowledge. For it is through love that man must find salvation in Christ, and not through knowledge alone. The ecstatic affirmation of mystery can, therefore, never be a purely intellectual act. It is accomplished perfectly only in love, through the openness of the heart in freedom to the mysterious and the unnameable.[7]

If, however, man is a being ordered ultimately to mystery, then for a Christian, mystery must be a constitutive element of man's present relationship with God. In other words, within the very givenness of human transcendence, God is himself given implicitly and unthematically as the ineffable goal of the human spirit. Moreover, precisely because God is present to human transcendence as the nameless, the unlimitable, the incomprehensible, any conceptualization of God in words and categories must find its ultimate meaning in the light of our prior experience of God as the transcendent end of the human spirit.[8]

Moreover, by the fact that we experience God as the goal of ecstatic, spiritual transcendence in freedom and love, we also experience him as the holy. Divine holiness and mystery are, therefore, not only inseparable; but, to the extent that they are one in God, they are also both ineffable.[9]

These reflections can throw a certain amount of light upon the relationship of grace to the beatific vision. It is by grace that we are now ordered to the face-to-face vision of God in glory. If, therefore, God is essentially a holy mystery and would cease to be God were he not so, then grace must itself be an anticipation in time of the immediate presence of mystery as such in the mind and heart of man. In the beatific vision, our present experience of graced transcendence, of openness to a distant mystery which is now the ground for all our conceptual thinking, gives way to the immediate presence of mystery as such, which renders all conceptual thinking about God henceforth superfluous. In other words, the beatific vision will not suddenly make the Blessed Trinity perfectly clear and conceptually comprehensible. Rather the beatific vision puts an end to dialectical difficulties about God precisely because in face-to-face vision the Trinity ceases to be mediated conceptually and is itself immediately present to the human spirit in all of its mysterious fullness.[10]

The true Christian mystery is, then, one which remains incomprehensible even in its evidence. For paradoxically the mysterious and the evident are not mutually exclusive. On the contrary, as the precondition for all human knowing in this life, the mysterious is the only truly evident reality, the only thing which completely justifies its own existence. Similarly, the particular mysteries of Christian belief have no other purpose than to lead man to experience the evidence of the divine mystery in the immediate vision of the triune God. It follows, therefore, that the Christian mysteries are all essentially bound up with the central mystery of God himself.[11]

The Three Basic Christian Mysteries

Here, however, an important problem arises. For although all creatures are connected with the mystery of God, there are no strict mysteries within the created order. Now since plurality also seems to be bound essentially to the order of creation, can we then truly speak of a plurality of strict mysteries in Christian belief?[12]

If, of course, one should consider anything to be a Christian mystery which in some way manifests the infinite perfection of God, then the possible number of mysteries is obviously without limit. But if one understands mystery in the strictest possible sense, then the number of Christian mysteries can be reduced to three basic ones. These three fundamental mysteries are, moreover, closely interrelated, as we shall see in just a moment. According to Rahner the three basic mysteries of Christianity are the Trinity, the hypostatic union, and the beatific vision together with its anticipation in grace. Any other mystery in Christianity (like the eucharist, for example) can be reduced ultimately to some aspect of these three fundamental ones.[13]

These three mysteries are, moreover, intimately connected with one another through the central mystery of the Godhead. The Trinity is the mystery of God as he exists within himself; the incarnation, grace, and glory are the mystery of God in his loving self-communication to his creation. The mystery of the Trinity is, therefore, the most fundamental Christian mystery. Were God not mysterious in himself, his relationship to his creatures would not be mysterious either. On the other hand, the incarnation, grace, and glory all involve the quasi-formal presence of God in his creatures. They thus establish the basic structure of the supernatural order.[14]

Moreover, the two basic mysteries of God's immanence are, as we have already seen in previous chapters, simply aspects of one and the same mystery. It is the hypostatic union of God with human nature which in turn mediates and renders possible the union of man with God in grace and glory.[15]

Even more, there is also an intimate connection between the mystery of God's immanence and the trinitarian mystery of God as he exists in himself. For the mystery of God immanent in creation is nothing else than the revelation in time of the mystery of God's inner personal life.[16]

This basic identity between the ontological and the economic Trinity is anything but a form of Sabellianism. Sabellius tried to reduce the temporal manifestations of God in sacred history to modalities of one and the same divine person. The true economic Trinity is rather the temporal revelation of three distinct divine persons who all share one and the same divine nature.[17]

A Brief Retrospect

Thus, the God of Abraham, Isaac, and Jacob appears to us in the clear revelation of the New Testament as none other than the Father of our Lord and Savior Jesus Christ. He is the nearness of divine mystery in its absolute source and ungenerability, a Person in his own right, who freely enters into loving commerce with the men whom he has created. The sovereign master of history, he has freely chosen to order the course of human events according to a salvific plan conceived from all eternity and now revealed to us definitively in Christ. The mission of his divine Son into the world is, therefore, the culmination of his historical dialogue with mankind. For by calling us to the most intimate personal communion with himself in the incarnate Christ, the Father has revealed himself to be a God of love. Not that his love was not already manifest in the Old Testament. But in the temporal mission of the Word, the Father's love takes the form of a decisive and definitive act, a perfect and irrevocable communication of divine life to man, the inauguration of the last age of salvation.[18]

It is, therefore, the mission of the incarnate Word which first reveals to us in time the inner life of the Godhead. But this very revelation presupposes, as we have already seen, a unique relationship between the Word of God and the human nature which he assumes: human nature is what comes into existence when the eternal Word of the Father expresses himself in the nothingness which is not God. The human nature of Christ is, therefore, the real-symbolic expression of his unique divine personality, just as the eternal Word is himself the real-symbolic expression of the Father.[19]

The incarnate Word is, therefore, the perfect historical revelation both of the Father and of the ultimate salvific meaning of man himself. The life and redemptive death of the Son of God demonstrate dramatically for all time that the Father's eternal love for us is stronger than our malice and that in his incarnation it reaches out to us even as we are, in our very sinfulness and misery. At the same time, the redemptive death teaches us our only possible response to divine love in a world marred by the mystery of iniquity: in Christ crucified we learn that although human life since the fall of Adam has indeed become a kind of dying in darkness, still through the redemptive death of Christ, man can now look forward in hope to that final act of total loving self-surrender to God in the darkness of faith by which he passes over from the shadows of time to the brightness of eternal light. Moreover, in the risen Christ he looks forward victoriously to his own total transformation in glory which even now is being prepared for in this life by the graced presence of God within his heart.[20]

It is, moreover, in the human intellect of Christ that the mystery of God immanent in his creation finds its first full verbal articulation. It is a verbal articulation already prepared by the books of the Old Testament, the written expression to Israel's historical experience of divine grace. But in Christ's human intellect, the true meaning of the religious experience of God's chosen people is transformed and illuminated by the unique grace of the hypostatic union. As a result there is genuine historical continuity between Christ's reflexive human awareness of his own divine reality, its anticipation in the Old Testament, and the Church's subsequent articulation of the full meaning of the Christian message of salvation. This continuity is, moreover, made possible through the temporal mission of the Holy Spirit, whose presence in the Church both completes the historical revelation of the Trinity and constitutes the Church as a real sacramental projection in time of Christ himself. This sacramental reality of the Church which results from the mission of the Spirit has for Rahner a number of dimensions. It means in general that the Church is the visible, conscious manifestation of the presence of the eschatological grace of Christ in the world. This grace so transforms the Church's awareness of her own supernatural destiny in Christ that she is able to bear conscious witness to him whose sacrament she is and thus lead all men to acknowledge their own redemption in the incarnate Word. This she does through her Scriptures, which she recognizes to be the authentic expression of the normative belief of the apostolic Church; through her preaching, which awakens the response of faith in the living hearts of men; and through the evolution of her dogmatic teachings, which are not only continuous with Scripture but are the necessary product of her tireless effort to communicate the message of Christ to men of every age and cultural condition.[21]

The Church's kerygmatic proclamation of the mystery of God revealed to us in Christ through the abiding presence of his Spirit is, moreover, continuous with her sacramental words. Her definitive commitment to individual Christians in the decisive salvific situations of their lives constitutes so many concrete self-realizations of the Church as the visible manifestation of the abiding presence of grace in the world. For the sacraments of the Church are real symbols of the Church's own eschatological reality just as the Church through the mission of the Holy Spirit is itself the real-symbolic manifestation of the incarnate Christ.[22]

Moreover, it is the same grace of Christ which the Church proclaims kerygmatically in her teaching and efficaciously in her sacraments that Christians manifest existentially by lives lived in docility to the Church and to the charismatic inspirations of his Spirit. By this lived existential witness, Christians testify to the abiding holiness of Christ's Church, each according to the particular vocation which is his by reason of his place in the Church's concrete social structure. But whatever his particular mission in the Church, every Christian—be he pope, bishop, priest, deacon, religious, or layman—must vindicate by a life lived in faith, hope, and love the freedom which comes to men only through the liberating grace of Christ. In the lives of the canonized saints, this freedom of God's adopted sons is, of course, spectacularly evident; but in every Christian the dynamic power of God's abiding presence patiently heals the inner division of concupiscence within the heart of man and prepares his total transformation, body and soul, in glory. The whole sac-

ramental order thus established through the temporal mission
of Christ and of the Spirit is, therefore, identical with the mystery of God's immanence in creation. It is the unique revelation
in time and space of the inner life of the triune God.[23]

This reflection on the basic unity of the Christian mysteries
helps to manifest the importance and the relevance of Christian
belief to a society marred by the absence of God. Belief in
Christ is not only possible today, it is in the last analysis the
only completely meaningful way for modern man to live.[24]

Christianity does not offer the world just another system of
logical propositions. It proclaims instead the ineffable mystery
of a God who is eternal, infinite, and unnameable, and yet intimately present to men through the grace of the incarnation.
Faced with the primacy of mystery in human experience, contemporary man may try to construct his own logical world of
coherent intelligibilities; but if in so doing he closes himself to
Mystery itself, he dooms himself to a life of meaningless absurdity. In a vague sort of way, twentieth-century man senses that
this is true. Christian belief only helps him to bring this unthematic feeling to a full and reflexive awareness. Belief in God
and in his immanence is, then, possible in a society marred by
the absence of God precisely because it is the healing openness
of the human heart in freedom and in love to the unique divine
Mystery intimately present to men in Christ which alone gives
ultimate meaning to human existence.[25]

NOTES

1. S, IV, 51–53.
2. *Ibid.,* 53.
3. *Ibid.,* 54–55.
4. *Ibid.,* 56–57.
5. *Ibid.,* 57.
6. *Ibid.,* 57–61.
7. *Ibid.,* 61.
8. *Ibid.,* 68–71.
9. *Ibid.,* 72–75.
10. *Ibid.,* 75–78.
11. *Ibid.,* 78–80.
12. *Ibid.,* 85–86.
13. *Ibid.,* 86–87.
14. *Ibid.,* 89–92; cf. Chapter III.
15. *Ibid.,* 92–93; cf. Chapter III.
16. *Ibid.,* 95.

17. *Ibid.*
18. S, I, 115–140, *passim.*
19. S, IV, 97; cf. Chapter I.
20. S, I, 141–142; IV, 94–97; cf. Chapter II.
21. Cf. Chapters II–VI.
22. Cf. Chapter VI.
23. Cf. Chapters VIII–X.
24. S, V, 11–14.
25. *Ibid.*, 14–15, 24–30.

Index